Challenging Institutional Analysis and Development

The Bloomington School has become one of the most dynamic, well recognized and productive centers of the New Institutional Theory movement. Its ascendancy is considered to be the result of a unique and extremely successful combination of interdisciplinary theoretical approaches and hard-nosed empiricism. This book demonstrates that the well-known interdisciplinary and empirical agenda of the Bloomington Research Program is the result of a less-known but very bold proposition: an attempt to revitalize and extend into the new millennium a traditional mode of analysis illustrated by authors like Locke, Montesquieu, Hume, Adam Smith, Hamilton, Madison and Tocqueville. As such, the School tries to synthesize the traditional perspectives with the contemporary developments in social sciences and thus, to re-ignite the old approach in the new intellectual and political context of the twentieth century.

The book presents an outline and a systematic analysis of the vision behind the Bloomington Research Program in Institutional Analysis and Development, explaining its basic assumptions and its main themes as well as the foundational philosophy that frames its research questions and theoretical and methodological approaches.

This book will be of interest to students and scholars of social science, especially those in the fields of economics, political sciences, sociology and public administration.

Paul Dragos Aligica is a Senior Fellow at the Mercatus Center and a Faculty Fellow at the James Buchanan Center at George Mason University, USA.

Peter J. Boetkke is the BB&T Professor for the Study of Capitalism at the Mercatus Center, and a University Professor of Economics at George Mason University, USA.

Challenging Institutional Analysis and Development
The Bloomington School

**Paul Dragos Aligica and
Peter J. Boettke**

Routledge
Taylor & Francis Group

LONDON AND NEW YORK

First published 2009
by Routledge
2 Park Square Milton Park Abingdon Oxon OX14 4RN

Simultaneously published in the USA and Canada
by Routledge
711 Third Avenue, New York, NY, 10017, USA

*Routledge is an imprint of the Taylor & Francis Group,
an informa business.*

Typeset in Times New Roman by Swales & Willis Ltd, Exeter, Devon

British Library Cataloguing in Publication Data
A catalogue record for this book is available
from the British Library

Library of Congress Cataloging in Publication Data
Aligica, Paul Dragos
    Challenging institutional analysis and development: the Bloomington school/
    Paul Dragos Aligica and Peter J. Boettke.
    p. cm.
    Includes bibliographical references and index.
    1. Rational choice theory. 2. Institutional economics. 3. Social institutions.
    I. Boettke, Peter J. II. Title.
    HM495.A445 2009
    306.01—dc22
    2008052128

ISBN 10: 0–415–77820–4 (hbk)
ISBN 10: 0–415–77821–2 (pbk)
ISBN 10: 0–203–87628–8 (ebk)

ISBN 13: 978–0–415–77820–6 (hbk)
ISBN 13: 978–0–415–77821–3 (pbk)
ISBN 13: 978–0–203–87628–2 (ebk)

Contents

Acknowledgements

This book could only have developed with the generous help of many mentors, friends and colleagues. We would like to thank first and foremost Vincent and Elinor Ostrom. Lengthy discussions and feedback on different versions of the manuscript were decisive for this project. The overwhelming majority of the materials quoted in this book were copyrighted by the Workshop in Political Theory and Policy Analysis, Indiana University, Bloomington, and we would like to thank for the generous permission to reproduce them.

Bob Bish, Mike McGinnis, Filipo Sabetti, Richard Wagner, Sujai Shivakumar, Olga Nicoara, Tenille Martin have been particularly helpful in providing feedback and comments on the entire manuscript, various parts of it or on key aspects of our arguments and efforts. We would like to express our gratitude to them as well as to Roberta Herzberg, Barbara Allen and Amos Sawyer. Among those whose feedback was critical for our work, Johan van der Walt deserves a special thank you note for his outstanding contribution.

Our greatest debt is to our colleagues at the Mercatus Center at George Mason University. We are deeply indebted to Brian Hooks and Claire Morgan and their hard work to create a hospitable and constructive setting not only for our research but also for the research program, of which our book is a part.

Introduction

In his article "Virginia, Rochester, and Bloomington: Twenty-five Years of Public Choice and Political Science," published in the journal *Public Choice* in 1988, William C Mitchell wrote:

> Aside from the family analogy, it seems that three schools of thought have appeared in Public Choice and that they are sufficiently different to warrant distinctive labels. Mine are taken from their geographical locations: Virginia (Charlottesville; Blacksburg; Fairfax), Rochester, and Bloomington. At each of these institutions one or two dominant figures led and continue to lead in the effort to construct theories of collective choice: Riker at Rochester, Buchanan and Tullock at various Virginia universities, and the Ostroms at Indiana.
>
> (Mitchell 1988, 101)

In the years after Mitchell's article was published, Bloomington has not only consolidated its position as one of the preeminent centers of the Public Choice and New Institutional Theory movement but also has become one of the most dynamic and productive centers of scholarly work in social sciences in general, touching a wide range of disciplines, from political science to economic history and from economics to anthropology. Moreover, besides being the home of a remarkable, unique and successful combination of interdisciplinary approaches and hard-nosed empiricism, the so-called Bloomington Institutional Analysis and Development (IAD) program has also become a model for a very efficiently run research organization, the heart of an international network of scholars and, even more important, the bearer of a really challenging intellectual vision. However, despite its wide recognition, the truly distinctive and unique nature of this program and its agenda is missed by many, both allies and critics.

There are several major reasons for that misunderstanding: first, both the *foundational research* done at Bloomington on coordination, cooperation and rationality and the *applied research* focused on institutional processes, with a special accent on governance systems, are incorrectly associated and conflated with the mainstream, rational-choice inspired research that focuses on similar or related themes. Second, the fact that many perceive the IAD agenda in a very narrow way: that is, basically only in relationship to the common-pool resources studies, which are indeed very salient but are in fact only one of the many dimensions of the program. The reality is that the study of "commons" emerged from a broader and deeper intellectual perspective that frames at a foundational level the work of the Bloomington scholars. As such it is only one of the ways in which that perspective becomes operational in the research practice. Third, even when astute readers were able to trace and put together from pieces some elements of this general vision, they stepped back puzzled, because by its very nature it is profoundly challenging and subversive to many of the scientific or policy orthodoxies of the day. And finally, and probably the most important, is the fact that no systematic attempt has been made until now to put methodically together all the main pieces, and to explicitly articulate for the public the foundational core of the program and the key elements of the intellectual vision behind it.

This book is an attempt to address precisely this last point. Its main objective is to explore, map, reconstruct and outline the essential conceptual and theoretical building blocks as well as the broader philosophy that shape, inspire and define the Bloomington IAD program. Thus, the true dimensions of the system within which are embedded the more salient and publicly visible pieces of the research produced by the Indiana scholars – such as the "commons research" – will become clearer, and both their deeper significance and the importance of the program they are part of will be better understood and appreciated. However, at the same time, the book will go beyond a mere conceptual reconstruction of the assumptions and foundations of a school of thought. Implicit in our effort is the hope that using as a vehicle the views advanced by the Bloomington scholars, one could get a fresh outlook on the nature and the future of the institutional theory and political economy – a discussion relevant for an entire range of fields from economics and political sciences to public policy and public administration. Given the preeminent place Vincent and Elinor Ostrom have in the intellectual history and intellectual landscape of the School, their work will occupy a central position in the economy of our book. And given the emphasis the book puts on the foundations of this research program, the work of Vincent Ostrom, who in the intellectual division of labor dedicated an important part of his efforts to foundational issues, will be given special attention.

The first part sets the stage for the rest of the book by presenting the origins of the School in its intellectual history context. It does that by defining the story of the Bloomington research program as an attempt to answer a specific challenge: a search for a proper language, including a vocabulary and a grammar, able to map and explore the institutional, social and normative complexity of collective action situations and polycentric systems of human governance. Thus, the book will start by introducing and discussing a set of theoretical concepts that predefine analytically, and in some cases temporally, the Bloomington research agenda. These concepts (co-production, public goods, industry, public entrepreneurship, polycentricity, etc.), presented in the context of the logic of their origination, cluster around the notion of "public economy" and they offer a very good entry point in Bloomington's intellectual universe. Most of these notions function at the borderline between the mainstream approach and the more complex and intellectually richer Bloomington-specific perspective. Therefore, they will be used as transitions and vehicles for moving the reader from the more familiar to the less familiar, from the quasi-orthodox to the unorthodox, and from the better known to the less known aspects of the School, aspects that will be explored in the other sections of the book.

The Bloomington program is better known today for the empirical work on the governance and provision of public goods with specific application to public economies in urban areas of the United States as well as to the management of diverse common-pool resources in many parts of the world. However, in parallel to that, an entire line of explorations in foundational issues in social and institutional theory has evolved and materialized in specific investigations into the nature of social order, the tension between freedom and organization, the nature and functions of social rules, the role of ideas and belief systems in institutional order and change, and the methodological implications of all of the above. The second part of the book will explore the ideas developed by Vincent Ostrom in this respect, ideas that amount to a unique attempt to build a social philosophy of institutional order and change.

The third part of the book is trying to project the IAD School on the canvas of the larger context of modern intellectual history and current scholarly debates. At the core of the Bloomington project lies an interesting paradox. On the one hand, time and again it makes recourse to Alexis de Tocqueville's assertion that "a new science of politics is needed for a new world." Yet on the other hand, the school is trying to revitalize and carry on an old mode of analysis in Western political thinking that starts with Hobbes and continues up to the Public Choice movement of the twentieth century. This paradox could be reconciled if one sees the Bloomington School as an attempt to synthesize time-honored ideas with the contemporary developments in social sciences (economics, political science and sociology). In other words, to re-ignite the old tradition that could be described with reference to another of Tocqueville's ideas, the notion of "a science and art of association," in the new intellectual and political context of the twentieth century. By focusing on its intellectual family and its intellectual neighborhood as well as on the way it is positioned regarding several key debates in contemporary social sciences, the last part of the book does two things. It not only offers an additional perspective on the Bloomington School but at the same time serves as a medium for a commentary on the nature of policy analysis, the disciplinary boundaries between economics, political science and sociology and the relationship between theory and practice in contemporary social sciences.

Finally, the book ends with a postscript consisting of two dialogues with Vincent and Elinor Ostrom. These interviews offer the reader a brief but comprehensive overview of the main themes, investigations and findings of the Bloomington School. Although in the book we have tried to stay as close as possible to the letter and spirit of the Bloomington texts, and to give voice to the authors of the referenced materials whenever possible through direct quotations, we thought that these twin interviews are important in more than one way, and deserve to be included in the volume. Those readers that are not very familiar with the tenets of the School, or those that want to refresh their memories, may start by reading first the postscript and then return to the in-depth treatment of those themes as elaborated in three main parts of the book.

To sum up, our book is an attempt to explore, reconstruct and outline the elements of the basic vision of the Bloomington research program in institutional analysis and development – the assumptions, themes and basic philosophy that frame the research activity and theory building done by the scholars associated with this School. As such, it is not meant to be a comprehensive monograph of all the work done by these scholars with all its facets, directions, publications and findings. Rather, our hope is that this book will be seen as a step in the direction leading to that comprehensive study, and that it will be considered a constructive contribution to that effort.

Part I

From metropolitan reform to a theory of governance systems

The origins and main themes of the
Bloomington research program

The Bloomington School of Institutional Analysis has its origins in the long
debates surrounding the nature and objectives of the public administration reform
in American metropolitan areas, debates that culminated in the academic arena in
the 1960s and 1970s. The Bloomington agenda grew by challenging the key theses
of the Metropolitan Reform Movement and by constructing step by step an alternative paradigm. At the center of the debate were very practical problems: whether
in each major urban area there should be only one local government, whether the
complete abolition of the separation of powers in local government is desirable, and
whether the administration should be organized as a single integrated system upon
the hierarchical principle, tapering upward and culminating in a single chief
executive officer. Challenging the "metropolitan reformers" whose answer was
"yes" to all of the above, the Bloomington scholars advanced the thesis that
centralization of governance units cannot be the universal problem solver because
"there can be no universal problem-solver capable of addressing diverse problems
as applying to societies as wholes." For them "human societies require diverse
patterns of association to cope with problems of varying scales under variable time
and place exigencies," and trying to reduce that diversity to one model was both an
analytical and practical mistake. While engaged in the battle, they have reached
another conclusion: the discussions were shaped by theories and a vocabulary
deeply inimical to ideas of self-governance and decentralization, a limited and limiting vocabulary that was dominating the mindsets of most participants. Therefore,
an entire effort to reconstruct the conceptual framework was needed in order to
counter what they perceived the mainstream's sterile and even dangerous
approach. Hence the slow growth and step-by-step development of a distinctive
research program. This part of the book presents the emergence of the Bloomington
School on the background of the Metropolitan Governance Reform debate and outlines the key concepts and arguments at the heart of the research program advanced
by it since then.

Part I

From metropolitan return to a theory of governance systems

The origins and main themes of the Binghampton research program

1 Political economy, polycentricity and the metropolitan reform debate

The intellectual history of the Institutional Analysis and Development program starts in the 1960s in the midst of a heated debate on the nature and objectives of the public administration reform in American metropolitan areas. From the very beginning it was as much a political theory debate as it was a public policy one. By the time Vincent Ostrom and a small group of scholars later to be associated to the prehistory of the Bloomington program started to explore the condition of public governance in metropolitan areas, both practitioners and the mainstream social scientists had long decided that the administration of those areas was in trouble (E. Ostrom [1972] in McGinnis 1999b, 140–141). Their diagnostic was based on a seemingly plausible account of the origins of the problem. A metropolitan region was viewed as one large community, functionally integrated by economic and social relationships. However, its functional unity was artificially divided administratively by *ad hoc* governmental units. A metropolitan region had no unitary administrative identity and it did not even exist from a legal standpoint (Hawley and Zimmer 1970, 2; Institute for Local Self Government 1970; Friesema 1966, 69). Instead, there were many federal and state governmental agencies, counties, cities, and special districts, each with its separate jurisdiction, overlapping and subverting each other, making efficient administration impossible. These disparate units of government, acting autarchic, were unable to perform the functions they were meant to perform. Even worse, without an overarching coordination center, each unit of local government acted in its own interest, without regard for the public interest of the metropolitan community. In other words, the diagnostic was straightforward. At the origin of the metropolitan administrative troubles there was one single cause: "the existence of a large number of independent public jurisdictions within a single metropolitan area" (E. Ostrom [1972] in McGinnis 1999b, 140–141; Institute for Local Self Government 1970).

Out of this diagnostic grew an entire literature converging around the idea that the "problem of metropolitan government" was that "the multiplicity of political units," made governance in metropolitan areas "a pathological phenomenon." There were "too many governments and not enough government" and as a result, a "duplication of functions" and confusing "overlapping jurisdictions." The existing governance structures were described as a "crazy-quilt pattern," and an "organized chaos." U.S. city government was "piecemeal and without a general plan," done "by local groups to meet transient needs" while "the web of local boundaries spreads unevenly and most chaotically over the land" (Anderson and Weidner 1950, 169). This view was tellingly captured in a Committee for Economic Development report released in 1970. The report quoted by E. Ostrom noted that:

> The present arrangement of overlapping local units is not serving the people well. Citizens in metropolitan areas are confronted by a confusing maze of many – possibly a dozen – jurisdictions, each with its own bureaucratic labyrinth. This baffling array of local units had made it difficult for citizens – the disadvantaged particularly – to gain access to public services and to acquire a voice in decision making.
>
> ([1972] in McGinnis 1999b, 140)

By that time not only had a fifty-year old literature been accumulated, but also fifty years of effort were squandered in a reform the objective of which was to build a different type of metropolitan governmental structure. The participants in this effort were far from having a common understanding of the many facets of *the* metropolitan problem. Neither did they have a common set of prescriptions for it. However, they agreed on a basic definition of the problem (i.e. too many, overlapping, dysfunctional governmental units), they shared a "relatively consistent, although implicit, underlying theoretical structure," and there was substantial consistency in their recommendations for change to talk about a single tradition (E. Ostrom [1972] in McGinnis 1999b, 140–141). Quite unsurprisingly their core prescription was reorganization into larger units. Creating a governance or administrative system with a single dominant center was seen as the optimal way of providing the public services and administering the various functions of government.

Underlying the discussion about metropolitan reform was also another theme of significant importance. Many of the reformers were animated by a very specific concern with social equality and strived for an even distribution of the costs of urban services. In fact, many viewed the very existence of the situation as pathological and a result of arbitrary boundaries that were drawn to protect rich suburban residents from paying for the costs of services provided by the city center. But since the spillovers of the services provided by the center city benefited everybody, reformers argued that all residents of the area should bear an equal share of these costs (Lineberry 1970).

From the very beginning three salient observations about the reformers and their ideas were in place. First, as the small group of scholars that started to question the validity of the mainstream approach noted, any realistic assessment of the bottom line highlighted that the mainstream effort was a failure. Despite the reformers' books, articles, reports and initiatives, no substantive progress in terms of consolidation or centralization was made. Second, the reformers' main ideas "were not initially stated as hypotheses; their validity was assumed, for they were part of the over-all ideology of the movement to save the cities" (Greer 1961, 193). Finally, and most crucially for a theoretically and historically grounded critique, the reformers were oblivious of the fact that the theme of "chaos" – *ad hoc* development and lack of coordination – was not at all new but in fact a major and constant theme in America's history (E. Ostrom [1972] in McGinnis 1999b; V. Ostrom *et al.*, 1961).

It was for Vincent Ostrom to fully articulate this last argument. While dissecting the metropolitan reformers' ideas he noted that "the illusion of chaos or the appearance of disorder is a phenomenon that has characterized U.S. public life for a very long time" (V. Ostrom [1972] in McGinnis 1999b, 119). One way of reaching this historical understanding was to go back to Tocqueville's work on the nature of democracy in America. At the beginning of the nineteenth century Tocqueville noted that neither "the appearance of disorder which prevails on the surface leads one at first to imagine that society is in a state of anarchy; nor does one perceive one's mistake till one has gone deeper into the subject" (Tocqueville 1945 [1835], 1: 89). Analyzing that puzzle, Tocqueville came to contrast "the government that administer the affairs of each locality" with one where "the citizens do it for themselves." In comparing the two he concluded that, "the collective strength of the citizens will always conduce more efficaciously to the public welfare than the authority of the government" (Tocqueville 1945 [1835], 1: 89). He went on to further observe that excepting the United States,

> In no country in the world do the citizens make such exertions for the common wealth. I know of no people who have established schools so numerous and efficacious, places of public worship better suited to the wants of the inhabitants, or roads kept in better repair. Uniformity or permanence or design, the minute arrangement of detail, and the perfection in administrative system must not be sought for in the United States; what we find there is the presence of a power which, if it is somewhat wild, is at least robust, and an existence checkered with accidents, indeed, but full of animation and effort.
>
> (Tocqueville 1945 [1835], 1: 91–92)

Tocqueville's distinction had a plain comparative and evaluative dimension. By contrasting "the government that can administer the affairs of each locality" to the one where "the citizens do it for themselves" he pointed to basic differences between the centralized system of France and the decentralized system of the United States; between a system of diverse foci of authority relying upon "methods of election and adjudication to resolve conflicts among public authorities" and a single hierarchy of command. Revisiting Tocqueville and his nineteenth-century observations and using them as a framework for understanding the American system, one can discover that what might seem as a deviation from the norm, an accident or a pathological state, may be in fact a structural feature of this system. What may seem to be chaos and accident might be in fact the misunderstood symptom of a systemic order at work. The invisible but powerful "social machinery" identified by Tocqueville might in fact operate in the metropolitan areas and the lack of uniformity and design might not be pathological in the end.

This historical perspective offers a background that better elucidates the failure of the mainstream approach and the irony of the situation. On the one hand, the scholarly and promotional fervor of the reformers fighting, in fact, not with an anomaly but with something that was a local expression of a structural feature of an entire socio-political system based on individuals and their freedom of association. On the other hand, a constant practical failure which, given the circumstances, shouldn't have been a surprise but still was surprising and obfuscating to the reformers. Thousands of books, reports and articles were written. Specific proposals for metropolitan "reform" by consolidation or centralization, to name but a few, were "placed before the voters in city after city." Yet, when presented to the residents, such proposals "have usually been met with a rousing defeat at the polls" (Press 1963, 113; E. Ostrom [1972] in McGinnis 1999b). "The number of local units in metropolitan areas has in fact increased" (Advisory Commission on Intergovernmental Relations 1966, 22). However, the failure did not lead to a realistic reassessment. Rather, the blame went on voters for their irrationality, lack of information and inconsistency (Hawley and Zimmer 1970, 140) or for being "influenced more by arguments promising to keep the tax rate low, and the government close to the people and free of corruption, than by arguments stressing the correction of service inadequacies and the economical and efficient provisions of services" (Zimmerman 1970, 531).

Indeed there was yet another possible explanation for these failures: metropolitan reform proposals were based on theoretical assumptions and created expectations that were not grounded in the reality and the lessons of the existing experience. As Vincent Ostrom noted, the theory underlying the major reform proposals was a collection of implicit presuppositions for the most part unsupported by specific research aimed to determine their epistemic status. The basic working hypotheses of the metropolitan reform proposals "have rarely been clearly formulated and subjected to empirical research by those who recommend drastic change" (E. Ostrom [1972] in McGinnis 1999b, 140–142). Because of that, the reformers had no way to recognize that they might have set their zeal against the powerful "social machinery" of the American system, and put into motion by the collective strength of its citizens:

> The changes recommended are presumed to lead to the postulated consequences without need for empirical investigation of the relationships involved. Without empirical examination of the postulated relationships implicit in the reform tradition, it is possible that different consequences than those predicted flow from adopting the recommendations made by metropolitan reform advocates. If this is the case, voters may have had a better intuitive understanding of the relationship among structural variables in metropolitan areas than the social scientists who have consistently made, and are still making, the same recommendations. Empirical research investigating the warrantability of the postulated relationships may be long overdue.
>
> (E. Ostrom [1972] in McGinnis 1999b, 119–120)

But precisely because the empirical effort was so important, its conceptualization was significant too. The way the framework for evaluation was designed was essential for the success of the assessment process. Conceptualization was vital because without a clear conceptual map of the domain, one was prone to make similar mistakes to the reformers: to take accidents as essence and essence as accidents. What was needed was a framework with the ability to capture the diversity, complexity and dynamics of the various institutional arrangements defining a metropolitan area. An alternative theory was required and with it an alternative conception of urban problems.

That was the beginning of the intellectual assault on the mainstream of political science and public administration, mounted by the group out of which very soon emerged what was later to be called the Bloomington School of Institutional Analysis and Development (IAD). The story of this assault that started with the empirical research program aimed at solving the riddle of metropolitan governance reform is one of the most interesting episodes in the recent history of social sciences. Out of the very process of constructing an alternative vision and an alternative approach to metropolitan governance, emerged an entirely new program. With inventiveness and determination, what started as a debate over municipal reform becomes a profound exploration into the new yet deep-rooted theory of social order.

Political economy and the analysis of non-market decision settings

In redefining and reinventing the terms of the discussion the first important step was to introduce in the "municipal reform debate" a new conceptual framework and a fresh logic: what was called "the political economy approach." From a history of political science perspective, that was one of the first efforts to insert modern economics and economic models of reasoning in political science and public administration. From a conceptual perspective, the first major implication was that the new framework was allowing for a more complex and nuanced approach. What a standard public administration perspective perceived as *the* urban problem (a jurisdictional and command and control issue) was seen in the new light as an entire system of compounded problems. Consequently the objective was to identify and investigate specific urban problems rather than *the* urban problem (E. Ostrom [1972] in McGinnis 1999b; 1983). Thus from the very beginning the conclusions of the political economy approach were set to diverge from the traditional "reform" prescriptions. The difference could be clearly seen in the works of economists like Stigler, who by that time were exploring the application of economic logic to non-market settings and were a source of inspiration for the new approach to public administration that questioned centralization and the technocratic, top down perspective:

> If we give each governmental activity to the smallest governmental unit which can efficiently perform it, there will be a vast resurgence and revitalization of local government in America. A vast reservoir of ability and imagination can be found in the increasing leisure time of the population, and both public

functions and private citizens would benefit from the increased participation of citizens in political life. An eminent powerful structure of local government is a basic ingredient of a society which seeks to give to the individual the fullest possible freedom and responsibility.

(Stigler 1962, 146)

The policy implications of the traditional reformist approach and the political economy approach couldn't be more dissimilar. The chasm between them is so stark that one could say that they are a textbook case of two competing paradigms. In order to compare and test the two rival paradigms, the first task was to fully articulate them. Explaining the fundamental differences in the concepts, methods and assumptions of the two schools of thought become critical. That meant that before making any further step the conceptual framework of the political economy approach to metropolitan areas needed an elaboration (E. Ostrom [1972] in McGinnis 1999b; Ostrom and Ostrom, 1971; 1977).

In this respect, the group of scholars challenging the mainstream concluded that the political economy of urban areas should be no different in its basic assumptions from the market-oriented political economy. The individual is the basic unit of analysis; producing and distributing through the workings of private market arrangements is a natural process; some goods and services, once provided, generate extensive spillovers beyond those individuals who are directly involved in a transaction; and those problems should be seriously considered as external economies or external diseconomies. These basic assumptions that were used to understand complex private industries and competitive structures were equally functional in the case of public structures.

The political economy perception of urban areas governance issues was thus shaped by the familiarity with precisely the analysis of private industries involving numerous enterprises, large and small, producing and distributing vast quantities of goods on more or less efficient and competitive markets. Consequently, and from the very beginning, the problem posed by the large number of public enterprises operating in a metropolitan area was not a totally unfamiliar territory. Scale and scope issues could be easily transferable from one domain to another.

For instance, Stigler's comment that he is accustomed to find that "the activity in an industry with a complex technology is usually efficiently conducted by a firm smaller by almost any measure than the government of a town of 25,000" introduces the notion of optimum scale of performance in a way that is easily translated in the metropolitan problem area. To the question of whether there is "some special characteristic of governmental functions that makes large units necessary to efficiency" one cannot avoid the answer that efficiency depends on the nature and type of service that a governmental agency is meant to produce and not on some special characteristics of governmental functions associated to the scale of the activity. Thus, the mere application of standard economic logic raises serious doubts about the validity of the metropolitan reformers' notion that efficiency was a function of centralization.

In other words, the introduction into the metropolitan reform debate of the political economy logic challenges from the start one of the basic theoretical tenets of the "reformers." Quoting political economist after political economist, Vincent Ostrom and his associates hammered the vital fact that the optimum scale of production is not the same for all urban public goods and services and that some services may be produced "more efficiently on a large scale while other services may be produced more efficiently on a small scale (E. Ostrom [1972] in McGinnis 1999b; Oakerson 1999; V. Ostrom *et al.* 1988). The corollaries were clear and by compelling and simply following Stigler's logic one could establish, if not an explanation, at least a robust conjecture leading to an explanation of the metropolitan areas "crazy-quilt pattern":

> Every enterprise must use goods and services, or produce goods and services, which must be produced or sold on a much wider scale than the enterprise itself can undertake. Even a huge department store is not large enough to make its own delivery trucks, or to print the newspapers in which it advertises. Just as cooperation in these matters is brought about by the price system, so cooperation among governmental units has been developed.
>
> (Stigler 1962, 167)

That is to say, the existence of multiple agencies interacting and overlapping, far from being a pathological situation, may be in fact a natural and healthy one. This overlapping and duplication is the result of the fact that different services require a different scale for efficient provision and that the principles of division of labor, cooperation and exchange function in that sector, too:

> Duplication of functions is assumed to be wasteful and inefficient. Presumably efficiency can be increased by eliminating "duplication of services" and "overlapping jurisdictions." Yet we know that efficiency can be realized in a market economy only if multiple firms serve the same market. Overlapping service areas and duplicate facilities are necessary conditions for the maintenance of competition in a market economy. Can we expect similar forces to operate in a public economy? If we can, relationships among the governmental units, public agencies, and private businesses functioning in a public economy can be coordinated through patterns of interorganizational arrangements. Interorganizational arrangements, in that case, would manifest market-like characteristics and display both efficiency-inducing and error-correcting behavior. Coordination in the public sector need not, in those circumstances, rely exclusively upon bureaucratic command structures controlled by chief executives. Instead, the structure of interorganizational arrangements may create important economic opportunities and evoke self-regulating tendencies.
>
> (Ostrom and Ostrom 1965, 3)

But that entails special problems. There are two basic challenges. The first is when a jurisdiction is larger than the group receiving benefits. In this case some individuals may pay for services that they do not receive. The second is when a political jurisdiction is smaller than the group receiving benefits. In this case some individuals may receive benefits without paying their dues. The solution in the second case is to establish a unit fitted to the most efficient scale of production. But that means not only that the relationship "between the size of governmental units and the number of governmental units within an area on the distribution of costs within the area is a far more complex relationship for the political economist than for the metropolitan reformer" but also that the political economy logic has no bias against larger units and centralization nor a pro-status quo stance (E. Ostrom [1972] in McGinnis 1999b, 144–148; 1983). On the contrary, it deems itself as a coherent but adaptable approach, following a clear and unbiased logic.

The insights brought by applying the standard political economy perspective were remarkable and instructive, yet they were not considered sufficient. The political economy conceptual framework needed special adjustments in order to be adapted to a phenomenon that was in the end different from the standard market-based phenomena. Indeed, some of the concepts and insights derived from the private economy could find a direct application, others needed further adjustments. For instance, the observation that most private enterprises purchase many of the goods and services that they need from other enterprises led to the notion that production (physical rendering) of urban government services should be considered separately from the provision of such services (i.e. the decision to provide, and possibly the billing and/or other financing). Developing that insight leads to a refinement of the framework: issues of scale and efficiency, concerned mainly with production, could be considered separately from questions of the provision or the distribution of such services (Ostrom and Ostrom 1965; E. Ostrom *et al.* 1994).

On the other hand, there were cases when further adjustments were needed. For instance, another basic assumption that challenged the introduction of the political economy perspective into the metropolitan reform debate was related to the very notion of competition. The political economy approach did not assume a priori that competition among public agencies is necessarily inefficient (V. Ostrom *et al.* 1961; Bish 1971; Wagner and Weber 1975). The simple existence of multiple producers within the same geographic region changes the dynamics of the citizen–public official relationship. However, competition in such cases may not take the same forms as market competition:

> The presence of more than a single producer of urban public goods within a metropolitan area may enable citizens to make more effective choices about the mix of services they prefer to receive than reliance upon voting mechanisms and a single producer. Multiple governments existing within a metropolitan area enable citizens to "vote with their feet." The presence of multiple producers within one metropolitan area may also reduce the cost for citizens of comparing the levels of output provided by different jurisdictions. Public officials who are representing one constituency in a bargaining process with other public officials over cooperative arrangements (such as contracting for services to be performed) may be able to bargain more effectively if alternative public producers are present in the area. However, it is also possible that multiple producers of some urban public goods may nullify each other's actions

and lead to a reduction in the net output of urban public goods. The political economist will consider the effect of competition among public agencies as an empirical question. The effect may be positive or negative depending upon the type of urban public good being considered.

(E. Ostrom [1972] in McGinnis 1999b, 148)

To sum up, what was called "the political economy approach" questioned the assumption deeply ingrained in the traditional view that large bureaucracies were more efficient in solving problems and in providing public goods and services than the systems based on competition or bargaining. The Ostroms and their associates also provided the beginnings of an analytical tool that could explain why that was the case, while at the same time offering a basis for a systematic empirical assessment of the structure and functioning of the institutional arrangements involved in that sector. The next challenge was to develop an empirical evaluation program.

The empirical agenda

To move the argument further and to avoid sterile debates, it was not enough to note the differences between the two approaches to metropolitan governance (metropolitan reform vs. political economy) and to suggest that one is better. A mere comparative assessment of the most salient elements of the two theories was inconclusive:

With basic differences in theoretical perspectives, scholars will adopt quite different orientations to their subject matter, will use different concepts and languages, and will pursue their inquiries in quite different ways. These differences will not be resolved by discussion and deliberation alone. Instead, ... we can attempt to undertake critical tests where divergent theories imply contradictory conclusions. The theory that has the weaker explanatory capability presumably would give way in the course of time to the theory with the stronger explanatory capability.

(E. Ostrom [1972] in McGinnis 1999b, 148)

Precisely because of the different vocabularies used by the two, the first step in their comparative assessment was to make explicit the theses which otherwise were implicit, and to formulate them in propositional form. Hence a number of propositions implicit in the work of the metropolitan reformers and the political economy counter-reaction were derived and formulated in testable forms for the first time. For the first time the parameters of an empirically grounded debate were set up. Over-viewing the most important of them dispels the rhetorical cloud created around the issue and gives a genuine insight into the real substance of the contention. Once stripped from their ideological and theoretical mantle and formulated in empirical form, the claims implicit in the metropolitan reform literature became very plain:

1 Urban public goods and services are relatively homogeneous and similarly affect all neighborhoods within a metropolitan area.
2 Urban voters share relatively similar preferences for urban goods and services.
3 Voters can effectively articulate their preferences for urban goods and services through one electoral mechanism.
4 Elected officials can effectively translate citizen preferences into policy objectives assigned to public bureaus and determine tax rates for producing the revenue needed to achieve these objectives.
5 Heads of public bureaus have effective command over street-level bureaucrats, who produce the highest level of public goods and services given the budget they receive.
6 Street-level bureaucrats deliver goods and services to passive clients.
7 Increasing the size of urban governmental units will be associated with higher output per capita, more efficient provision of services, more equal distribution of costs to beneficiaries, increased responsibility of local officials and increased participation by citizens.
8 Increasing the size of urban governmental units will be associated with more professionalization of the public service and a greater reliance upon hierarchy as an organizing principle.
9 Reducing the number of public agencies within a metropolitan area will be associated with more output per capita, more efficient provision of services, more equal distribution of costs to beneficiaries, more responsibility of local officials, and more participation by citizens.
10 Reducing the number of public agencies within a metropolitan area will increase the reliance upon hierarchy as an organizing principle and will decrease the number of locally elected public officials within the metropolitan area.
11 Increasing the professionalization of public employees will be associated with a higher level of output per capita, more efficient provision of services, and increased responsibility of local officials.
12 Increasing the reliance upon hierarchy as an organizing principle within a metropolitan area will be associated with higher output per capita, more efficient provision of services, more equal distribution of costs to beneficiaries, and increased responsibility of local officials.
13 Increasing the number of locally elected officials within a metropolitan area will be associated with less responsibility on the part of public officials and less participation by citizens.

(E. Ostrom 1972, 476–477)

The next step was to derive in a similar way a group of alternative propositions from the political economy approach. The objective was to match the two parallel sets of propositions and to make the inter comparisons as substantive as possible. Focusing on relatively equivalent issue areas, the political economy approach was traced back to the set of similar claims:

1 Urban public goods and services differ substantially in regard to their production functions and their scale of effects.
2 Individuals with relatively similar preferences for public goods and services tend to cluster in neighborhoods. Preferences will tend to be more homogeneous within neighborhoods than across an entire metropolitan area.
3 Citizens who live in multiple jurisdictions learn more about the performance of any one jurisdiction by seeing or hearing about how problems are handled in other jurisdictions.
4 Multiple jurisdictions with different scopes and scales of organization allow citizens to make better effective choices when selecting packages of services most important to them, to better articulate their preferences and concerns, and, if necessary, to move to other jurisdictions.
5 The presence of large numbers of potential producers of urban goods and services in a metropolitan area allows elected officials to make more effective selections when choosing producers.
6 Producers who must compete for contracts are more likely to search for innovative technologies, to operate at close to optimal scales of production, and to encourage effective team production, as well as co-production, so as to enhance their own performance.
7 Whether increasing the size of urban governmental units will be associated with a higher output per capita, more efficient provision of services, more equal distribution of costs to beneficiaries depends upon the type of public good or service being considered.
8 Increasing the size of urban governmental units will be associated with decreased responsibility of local officials and decreased participation by citizens.
9 Increasing the size of urban governmental units will be associated with a greater utilization of hierarchy as an organizing principle.
10 Whether reducing the number of public agencies within a metropolitan area will be associated with more output per capita, more efficient provision of service, and more equal distribution of costs to beneficiaries depends upon the type of public good or service being considered.
11 Reducing the number of public agencies within a metropolitan area will be associated with less responsibility of public officials.
12 Reducing the number of public agencies within a metropolitan area will increase the reliance upon hierarchy as an organizing principle within the metropolitan area.
13 Whether increasing the reliance upon hierarchy as an organizing principle within a metropolitan area will be associated with higher output per capita and more efficient provision of services depends upon the type of public good or service being considered.
14 Increasing the reliance upon hierarchy as an organizing principle within a metropolitan area will be associated with decreased participation by citizens and decreased responsibility of local officials.

(E. Ostrom 1972, 478–479)

Moving further the agenda also required the careful and consistent definition of all concepts included in operationalizing those propositions. Otherwise any meaningful comparison between the two sets could have been undermined by the fact that frequently a term when used in one paradigm had different meanings when used in the other. For example, the term "efficiency" was used as a dependent variable by both. However, it was usually conceptualized differently (E. Ostrom [1972] in McGinnis 1999b, 151). Similar problems existed with such concepts as "output," "equal distribution of costs," "responsibility of local leaders" and "citizen participation." Not only did the definitions vary, but the indicators utilized for operationalizing them had serious validity problems. Consequently, one important effort the Bloomington scholars made as part of this investigation of metropolitan governance was to further elaborate this measurement and evaluation dimension in two areas: (a) conceptually, to clearly articulate the concepts and evaluation criteria involved; (b) operationally, to devise new methods and approaches based on field work and hands on experience in order to capture the reality of those concepts in real settings.

Out of that effort grew a solid empirical research agenda, an entire new domain out of which was later to emerge the outstanding work on commons and common-pool resources and the applied institutional analysis tools for which the Bloomington School is well known today. However, the inquiry into the two models of metropolitan governance analysis and their implicit policy recommendations revealed that the differences between the two were not merely theoretical and methodological (political economy vs. traditional public administration theory; individualism vs. holism). A deeper and more foundational difference of vision was revealed. A paradigmatic pair of correlate concepts seemed to define those visions and understanding the nature and implications of the differences between the two seemed crucial for the fate of the debate. The two concepts were: "polycentrism" and "monocentrism." Thus together with the empirical agenda focused on the diversity and performance of various institutional arrangements in non-market settings (of which the metropolitan governance system was one example) the foundational explorations in the nature of polycentricity and monocentricity and their institutional manifestation become the other trademark of the Bloomington institutional analysis and development research program (Wagner 2005; Herzberg 2005).

Polycentrism and monocentrism

One of the main problems encountered by the argument advanced initially in Ostrom, Tiebout and Warren (1961) and later developed by them and their associates on many fronts was that it was misidentified as a "market model." This allowed many to dismiss the entire approach as being based on "an inappropriate analogy." Others complained later that V. Ostrom used the reference to "market model" as "an occasion for free association about atomistic individualism and other attributes of classical economic theory" (V. Ostrom 1972). However, in their pioneering article, Ostrom, Tiebout and Warren were doing much more than merely developing a simple market model, derived from classical economic theory, and applying it to a non-market setting (i.e. an academic exercise that was later to become very popular). Their goals were much bolder:

> We never intended to develop a strict market model for the supply of public goods and services to individual buyers. Nor did we intend to present an economic analogy based upon classical economic theory. On the other hand, we thought an indication that quasi-market mechanisms were operable in a public service economy would imply important new dimensions for a theory of public administration.
>
> (V. Ostrom 1972)

Developing that dimension was not just a "normal science" task – replicating or applying an existing model or concept to an additional domain. Instead, it was an effort to change the paradigm. A new domain was to be defined and that required an entire new framework. In order to do that, V. Ostrom and his associates had to look beyond the horizon of standard public administration theory or standard neoclassical economics. Thus, they introduced the correlated concepts of monocentricity and polycentricity.

> By conceptualizing metropolitan areas as polycentric political systems, we were suggesting that a system of ordered relationships underlies the fragmentation of authority and overlapping jurisdictions that had frequently been identified as "chaotic" and as the principal source of institutional failure in the government of metropolitan areas. We identified a polycentric political system as having many centers of decision making that were formally independent of each other. A "system" was viewed as a set of ordered relationships that persists through time.
>
> (V. Ostrom 1972)

Once defined in this way, the new framework gets different dimensions that go beyond the standard parameters of the neoclassical economics approach. Of special importance in this respect is the fact that the conceptual spaces defined by the two notions are interlinked. Studying polycentricity is also a study of monocentricity. The relation is not only logical – the two being correlated concepts – but also empirical: "The possibility that a polycentric political system can exist does not preclude the possibility that a monocentric political system can exist." Each possibility "depends upon conceptualizing the essential defining characteristics for each system and indicating the logically necessary conditions that must be met for the maintenance of a system having those defining characteristics." Furthermore, "a predominantly monocentric political system need not preclude the possibility that elements of polycentricity may exist in the organization of such a system." Conversely, "the existence of a predominantly poly-centric political system need not preclude elements of monocentricity from existing in such a system" (V. Ostrom 1972).

Seen from the new perspective, the initial debate gains fresh dimensions too. Translated into the new vocabulary of polycentricity, the issue was whether there was any prima facie ground for expecting less efficient performance from polycentric arrangements than from a centralized system. More precisely, metropolitan reformers considered that many local jurisdictions should be consolidated or merged into monocentric units of governance because overlapping jurisdictions created a duplication of services or functions. A duplication of services, one of the main features of polycentric systems, was thus assumed to be wasteful and generated disorder. But to that the proponents of the new approach argued that it should have been, at best, a conjecture and not an assumption:

> The study of government in metropolitan areas conceived as a polycentric political system, should precede any judgment that it is pathological. Both the structure and the behavior of the system need analysis, precisely on the empirical lines outlined by them, before making any assessment of its performance and advancing measures of reorganization and reform. However, if the general conditions revealed by the political economy analysis hold, one may expect that the performance of any particular polycentric system depends on the measure in which the actual arrangements on the ground corresponded to the theoretically specified conditions for efficient performance such as: the correspondence of different units of government to the scales of effects for diverse public goods; the development of cooperative arrangements among governmental units to undertake joint activities of mutual benefit; and the availability of other decision-making arrangements for processing and resolving conflicts among units of government.
>
> (V. Ostrom 1972)

It was clear that reformers and the mainstream political scientists were going in different directions as they saw the fragmentation of authority and overlapping jurisdictions as generating something described as "chaotic." But the very application of the term "chaotic" to a phenomenon raised a very important theoretical problem as it implied the absence of an explanatory theory to account for that state of affairs and an inability to determine the measure in which the reality corresponds to theoretical conditions. Elucidating the problem of polycentricity and chaos (defined as lack of order or perceived lack of order) is thus central in the effort of defining the tasks and advancing the agenda. There are two aspects in this respect: (a) there is no theory because there is no order to be reflected by it; (b) the order exists but there is no awareness of it because of the conceptual inability to discover order out of the apparent chaos. If that is the case, the real stake was to identify and chart the patterns of order looming underneath the apparent chaos intrinsically associated to the experience of polycentricity:

> For a polycentric political system to exist and persist through time, a structure of ordered relationships would have to prevail, perhaps, under an illusion of chaos. If such a structure of ordered relationships exists one might assume that

specifiable structural conditions will evoke predictable patterns of conduct. Only if predictable patterns of ordered relationships could be established would it be possible to evaluate the performance of a polycentric system and anticipate its future performance as against some other structure of ordered relationships. The development of an explanatory theory must precede the evaluation of alternative patterns of organization in relation to normative criteria.

(V. Ostrom 1972)

But if that was the case, at stake was noting less than a theory of hidden order, a theory of the "invisible hand" directing the "social mechanism" evoked by Tocqueville. Faced with this revelation, Ostrom, Tiebout and Warren realized the limits of their initial approach and the magnitude of the intellectual challenge ahead (V. Ostrom 1972). All of a sudden they realized that they were in search of nothing less than a general theory applicable to many instances of social order. Polycentricity was in fact applicable to a large range of social phenomena. If polycentric systems of government in metropolitan areas are just one case of polycentrism, if metropolitan areas were just one instance of polycentric order, then that specific case could be used as a vehicle for building a working definition or a general description of the phenomenon in point. Polycentricity raises fundamental challenges to political theory that have broader ramifications that go beyond the issue of the governance of metropolitan areas. That is to say that a discussion of polycentrism in political-administrative systems was one out of many possible first steps in discussing polycentrism in general and constructing step by step the understanding of polycentrism. It was to be decided later if polycentrism was just a political concept or if and in what measure it could be used outside the realm of politics.

One of the key features in defining a polycentric – or for that matter, a monocentric – order is the issue of the monopoly over the legitimate exercise of coercive capabilities. A monocentric political system is one where the prerogatives for determining and enforcing the rules are "vested in a single decision structure that has an ultimate monopoly over the legitimate exercise of coercive capabilities." On the other hand, a polycentric political system is one where "many officials and decision structures are assigned limited and relatively autonomous prerogatives to determine, enforce and alter legal relationships" (V. Ostrom [1972] in McGinnis 1999b, 55–60). In a polycentric political system no one has an ultimate monopoly over the legitimate use of force and the "rulers" are constrained and limited under a "rule of law." Thus, ultimately, polycentric systems are rule of law systems. That is the reason why in defining a polycentric system the notion of "rule" is as important as the notions of "legitimacy," "power" or multiplicity of "decision centers" are.

And if that is the case then the study of rules is central for any understanding of the phenomenon. Yet, the initial approach, framed as it was by the political economy concepts, did not reveal enough of this. It was only when the Bloomington scholars started to move from the specific issue of metropolitan governance to the general issue of polycentric systems that they fully realized the central role of rule systems. There were several sources that supported that deeper and more refined understanding.

The first was the work of M. Polanyi. While looking for a way to define and conceptualize the complex reality of municipal governance systems, Polanyi's work was the source not only of a substantive description of polycentric order but also of the very concept of polycentricity. In his *The Logic of Liberty* (1951), Polanyi distinguished between two different methods of organization or two kinds of order. One is a deliberate or directed order that is coordinated by an ultimate authority exercising control through a unified command structure. The other one is identified as a spontaneous or polycentric order. A polycentric order is one where the elements of a complex system are allowed to make mutual adjustments to each other "within a general system of rules where each element acts with independence of other elements." Within a set of rules, "individual decision makers will be free to pursue their own interests subject to the constraints inherent in the enforcement of those decision rules" (V. Ostrom 1972; Polanyi 1951).

Polanyi's emphasis upon a general system of rules as a working framework for ordering relationships in a polycentric system stuck Ostrom, Tiebout and Warren as the real functional principle behind polycentricity. The multiplicity of decision centers (as a feature of polycentricity) was a meaningful way of defining polycentricity only under the rule of law:

> The task of formulating a general system of rules applicable to the conduct of governmental units in metropolitan areas and of maintaining institutional facilities appropriate to enforce such rules of law are a problem that we failed to treat. Whether the governance of metropolitan areas can be organized as a polycentric system will depend upon whether various aspects of rule making and rule enforcing can be performed in polycentric structures.
>
> (V. Ostrom 1972)

Implicit was a second insight that was instrumental in clarifying the key function of rules in defining polycentricity. An analysis of the class of phenomena displaying a multiplicity of decision centers shows that there are many forms of organization that might seem analogous to a polycentric order. However, not all of them had the attributes associated to polycentricity. The necessary condition was the existence of an encompassing system of rules. A breakdown of order and rules may lead to situations where multiple decision centers coexist. In the case of metropolitan areas that might be the result of political corruption where various forms of bosses divide "territories" and "jurisdictions." Therefore, it was of outmost importance to specify that only rules could create a system of government organized in a polycentric manner.

Finally, while starting to understand the meaning and conditions of polycentricity, Ostrom and his associates realized that the study of polycentricity and even more precisely the problem of whether the government of a political system can be organized in a polycentric manner had a considerable history. It was no historical accident that Alexis de Tocqueville made his observations about the invisible mechanisms of social order while studying the democracy in America. The design of polycentric order is one possible way of identifying the challenge faced by the founding fathers of the American constitution. More specifically, while Alexander Hamilton and James Madison in *The Federalist* did not use the term polycentricity, "their conception of the principles of federalism and separation of powers within a system of limited constitutions meets the defining conditions for polycentricity" (V. Ostrom 1972; 1990b; 1973a; 1971). The federal system assumes a fragmentation of authority in many centers of decision making and with it a separation of powers. Designing the American constitution could thus be viewed as an experiment in polycentricity while federalism could be seen as one way to capture the meaning and to operationalize one aspect of this type of order.

The normative or political dimensions of polycentric forms of organization in political relationships are momentous. Polycentricity seems to be a necessary condition for achieving political objectives such as "liberty," "freedom" and "justice." The dispersion of decision-making capabilities associated to polycentricity "allows for substantial discretion or freedom to individuals and for effective and regular constraint upon the actions of governmental officials" and as such is an essential characteristic of democratic societies. Also, a polycentric arrangement has a built in system of self-correction:

> While all institutions are subject to takeover by opportunistic individuals and to the potential for perverse dynamics, a political system that has multiple centers of power at differing scales provides more opportunity for citizens and their officials to innovate and to intervene so as to correct maldistributions of authority and outcomes. Thus, polycentric systems are more likely than monocentric systems to provide incentives leading to self-organized, self-corrective institutional change.
>
> (E. Ostrom 1998)

The very nature and existence of democratic societies depends on the presence of sizeable elements of polycentricity in their governance systems. Yet it is important to note that at the same time polycentric systems depend on individuals creating them and acting within their frameworks and whether or not a significant number of individuals share or aspire to those values is critical for the operation of the system.

To sum up, the discussion on polycentricity is not just a discussion about multiple decision making centers and monopolies of power but also a discussion about rules, constitutions, fundamental political values and institutional adaptability in maintaining them. Moreover, an important aspect of polycentricity is missed if the role of the individuals in such systems is not properly considered. While the emphasis put on rules, constitutions and checks and balances systems points to the systemic dimension, the issue of political values and culture reminds of the fact that the individual is central (V. Ostrom 1972). In a theory of polycentric order, individuals are the basic unit of analysis. Individuals are understood as decision makers who can calculate potential benefits and costs subject to elements of risk and uncertainty and who drive through their preferences and actions of the dynamics of the entire system. Even more important, in a polycentric arrangement the maintenance of polycentricity depends on the selection of political leadership. The entire system relies on individuals able to organize the formation of political coalitions in the light of principles supportive to the maintenance of the polycentric order.

Any discussion of polycentricity has sooner or later to deal with the issue of spontaneity or spontaneous order. Polanyi's use of the term spontaneous as synonymous with polycentric implied that the attribute of spontaneity is in a deeper sense an additional defining characteristic of polycentricity (or at least theoretically related to it). In his attempt to put forward a coherent concept of polycentricity, Vincent Ostrom embarked on an effort to elaborate Polanyi's point: spontaneity means that "patterns of organization within a polycentric system will be self-generating or self-organizing" in the sense that "individuals acting at all levels will have the incentives to create or institute appropriate patterns of ordered relationships." That is to say that in a polycentric system the "spontaneity" is a function of self-organizing tendencies occurring, under specific conditions, at several different levels.

The first condition is the freedom of entry and exit in a particular system. If the establishment of new decision centers under the existing rules is blocked, then one could not expect a polycentric order to emerge. The freedom of entry ensures the spontaneous development of the system. Markets are a good example in this respect. On a simple market, if individuals are free to enter or exit as either buyers or sellers, the result is a spontaneous evolution of market processes well documented in the economics literature. In more complex markets, the viability depends not on mere individual's entry but on whether individuals create organizations (firms) and whether such organizations are free to enter and operate the market. Firm entry and not individual entry is then the determining factor. This example is important for the case of public administration and public services. Individuals acting alone are unable to produce the needed quantity and quality of public goods and services. Therefore it is necessary to organize special firms and to finance them from potential beneficiaries: "The principle of spontaneity, in this case, can be met only if individuals will be led to undertake the task of public entrepreneurship in the creation of appropriately structured public enterprises to supply public goods and services" (V. Ostrom 1972).

The second condition is related to the enforcement of general rules of conduct that provide the legal framework for a polycentric order: "If individuals or units operating in a polycentric order have incentives to take actions to enforce general rules of conduct, then polycentricity will become an increasingly viable form of organization" (V. Ostrom 1972). Finally, the third condition that spontaneity should be manifested is the reformulation and revision of the basic rules that define the framework of a specific polycentric order. The idea is that individuals should be free not only to play the game or have the incentives to self-enforce the rules of the game but also to change those rules in an orderly way. In this respect there are two prerequisites. One is procedural: there should be rules on changing rules. The other is cognitive: an understanding of the relationship between particular rules and the consequences of those rules under given conditions. "If conditions were to change and a particular set of rules failed to evoke an appropriate set of responses, rules could then be altered to evoke appropriate responses" (V. Ostrom 1972). This has an important implication for the very way the relationship between spontaneous order and design is understood. Understanding and learning from experience are in fact the vectors of an ongoing process of knowledge integration in the institutional system and the prerequisites of subsequent adaptations to the changing environment. Institutional design, the understanding of rules and consequences and the conditions that determine their interplay, is part and parcel of spontaneous order and not inimical to it. Among the designs that plan to abolish and replace polycentricity with central command and control hierarchies only one type of design is inimical to it. Design and spontaneous order are not irreconcilable. The link between the two is given by the notion of knowledge and its correlate concepts such as learning (V. Ostrom [1972] in McGinnis 1999b, 60).

The domains of polycentricity and the monocentric–polycentric dynamics

The structure of a polycentric system is a function of the presence of polycentricity in the governance of each basic type of social activity. The basic social functions or institutional arenas of a society could be organized in various degrees under a polycentric order: polycentricity in the structure of governmental arrangements, polycentricity in economic affairs, polycentricity in political processes and the formation of political coalitions, polycentricity in judicial affairs, polycentricity in constitutional rule (V. Ostrom 1972). The relationship between these domains is extremely important. Both theory and evidence show that in order to be fully functional, polycentricity in economics requires a certain degree of polycentricity in judicial decision making, and polycentricity in judicial decision making requires a certain degree of polycentricity in the political system. This interlinkage points out to the systemic and dynamic character of polycentricity. There is an inherent tendency of polycentric order in one domain to entail polycentricity in another.

The example of the market as the quintessential polycentric system is very illustrative. From Smith to Polanyi the study of markets revealed their structural polycentric features. The market is doubtless the most studied, although probably not always the best understood, form of polycentricity. Its relationship to the judicial system offers a simple but telling example of polycentric interlinkages. Since Adam Smith, market systems have been described as systems of spontaneous order. Market participants are not subject to specific commands by some superior authority. Instead they generate order by mutual adjustment. The mutual adjustment of the market system functions "as though it were governed by an invisible or hidden hand." While each individual seeks to gain his own advantage, the market adjusts to variations in supply and demand so that each participant in the market tends to behave in a way that is consistent with the welfare of the larger community. However, in the study of markets the overemphasis on the logic of the hidden hand has led to the neglect of the fact that the mutual adjustment process does not take place in a void but in a rule-defined context. Rules are the basic conditions and parameters that generate an orderly adjustment. In his effort to counter this incomplete interpretation of the market process, M. Polanyi emphasized again and again that participants are free to pursue their individual advantage subject to general rules of law that are impersonal. He insisted that "no marketing system can function without a legal framework which guarantees adequate proprietary powers and enforces contracts" (Polanyi 1951, 185). That is to say that property rights are the foundational prerequisite for markets and while they are sustained by markets, they are created, maintained and enforced outside them, in the legal and judiciary system (V. Ostrom 1972).

Thus markets, as polycentric systems, depend in their structure and functioning on legal relationships and the enforcement of property rights and contractual obligations. If that is the case, then a question of maximum interest is whether polycentricity in judicial decision making is an optimal condition for an economic polycentric system. Although the question may not be settled, there is sufficient evidence not only that "courts of law and the larger legal community who participate in the settlement of conflicts under common rules of law could be organized as a polycentric order" (V. Ostrom 1972) but also that there is a correlation between performing market systems and the presence of legal and judicial systems displaying attributes of polycentricity. Also, the evidence shows that the existence of such judicial processes is associated with political and enforcement systems that have important polycentric features.

To sum up: examples and cases of polycentric order (in economy, law, and politics) show that a polycentric order means more than just a matter of different centers of decision making operating in competition with each other in a specific domain or area. Polycentricity is a complex system of powers, incentives, rules, values and individual factors combined in a complex system of relationships at different levels. Even more important, one may detect a very interesting dynamics at work. Market polycentrism seems to entail judicial polycentrism, judicial polycentrism to entail political polycentrism, and political polycentrism to entail constitutional polycentrism. If one accepts the hypothesis of the existence of such a systemic logic, one may visualize the entire social system shaped by underlying currents originating in pulsating polycentric domains. Any island of polycentric order entails and presses for polycentrism in other areas, creating a tension towards change in its direction.

However, at the same time, one can imagine monocentricity operating under similar dynamics. The result of the ongoing tension between the two principles is an unstable coexistence. One area or domain opened to polycentricity strives for polycentricity in another area, one area or domain under monocentricity strives for monocentricity in other domains. This vision finds a powerful illustration in the history of socialist systems: once the logic of monocentricity was introduced in one domain, it required the extension of its rule in all other areas. There was almost no way to stop the growing monocentricity into creating a totalitarian state other than the fact that after a certain time a tipping point was reached and the system came to stasis imploding under its own monocentric weight. Once the control of economy was introduced in the Soviet system, the political control and a structural or constitutional change towards consolidation of powers at the center was required. (The

Hayekian problem of the "road to serfdom" deals precisely with this phenomenon.) On the other hand, the experience of reforms tells the other side of the story: once a breakthrough is created for market, pressure for openings in political areas ensues; once political liberalization takes place, pressure for economic liberalization increases. The traditional tension between state and the market is a peculiar case and as such defines in a telling way the field of forces at work in the friction between the two principles of polycentrism and monocentricity. However, this vision is incomplete as markets and states are just one set of specific ways of describing the phenomena at work. The study of these forces and their tensions requires an analytical framework that is not the prisoner of the market vs. state dichotomy.

One of the most important aspects of the discussion about the two visions is how different the analytical approaches they imply and generate are. The monocentric vision assumes the existence of a center of power and authority and naturally the goal of the analysis is to identify and analyze this center and its operations. The entire approach is based on the notion that "there is always a centre of power . . . within any system of government." Because most of the times the "formal repository of authority" is different from "the effective center of power" one of the first tasks is "to penetrate behind the façade of authority to find the essential machinery of power." That task is framed by questions such as: "Where in this system is that centre?"; "In whose hands is [this] self-sufficient authority lodged?" and "Through what agency does that authority speak and act?" (Wilson [1885] 1956, 30). The issue of the ways of location and application of power is shaping the research and the conceptual vocabulary of the monocentric approach. The entire exercise becomes power-centered in ways that may become extreme and limiting. Choices, decisions, rules, preferences, ideas, values become secondary. They are just inputs or outputs in the power process or even worse a veil that is clouding the view on power and its workings. These analytical implications of the monocentric approach constituted the reason of one of the major concerns of the Bloomington scholars. Their fear was that even when not explicitly dealing with the issue of power, this vision has deeply penetrated and shaped the language of political analysis. Most of political science was infused or defined by the hidden assumptions of its approach and by its language. Hence a concern not only for the limits and the dangers of the mainstream approach but also for the fact that once the monocentric presumption was abandoned, one was confronted with difficulties arising from an entirely new horizon of complexities that evade the mainstream vocabulary.

An approach based on a polycentric vision could not rely on the convenient pre-definition of the research agenda in terms of power and of using "government" or "state" as the key unit of analysis. An alternative should be constructed. In it the government as a basic unit becomes secondary and the individual takes the front of analysis (V. Ostrom 1982a, 1–2; 1982b; 1991b; 1993b). Putting the individual at the center of the picture meant a lot normatively but technically it did not mean a simplification at all, on the contrary. Individuals develop intricate interdependent relationships with other individuals. They also operate in complex situations or environmental conditions where they have to cope with different events. Individuals are also living in an organized society that creates both capabilities and constraints regarding an individual's "choice of strategy in the pursuit of opportunities inherent in different structures of events or environmental conditions." Individuals make choices and have to adjust to the choice of others. Competition, cooperation or coordination problems arise. The agenda is larger and more complicated. To simplify things, a methodology and a theoretical language that focuses on the consequences that follows from the combination of individuals, structures of events, and decision rules needs to be adopted. In other words, looking at the individual is a way to look at sequences of decisions, events, causal sequences, and consequences in complex environments and situations instead of looking at the location, operation and administration of power.

The conceptual framework and the vocabulary of a theory of polycentricity are not centered around abstract systemic features such as "the state" but on very concrete human actions. In other words, it is a theory of human action within the natural and institutional environment. This theory of human action is at the same time a theory of social organization drawing upon

> a substantial structure of inferential reasoning about the consequences that will follow when individuals pursue strategies consistent with their interests in light of different types of decision structures in order to realize opportunities inherent in differently structured sets of events.
>
> (V. Ostrom [1972] in McGinnis 1999b 52–75, 119–139)

Although centered on individual and human action, this mode of analysis can be extended to collectivities seen as aggregations of individuals, to patterns of governance in metropolitan areas, to international affairs, or to any other situation where one can conceptualize "circumstances where individuals are confronted with a choice of strategy where each course of action becomes a potential move in a series of simultaneous games" (V. Ostrom 1972; 1991b; 1993b).

But, if one is consistent with the interrelated logic of the sibling concepts of polycentricity and monocentricity, one is forced to see the dynamics of monocentricity as driven by individuals, too. One cannot avoid the conclusion that the dynamics of monocentrism is amenable to similar analytical treatment. This means that the language of polycentricity, as a paradigm or as a set of theoretical lenses, is not applicable just to polycentric systems. Both monocentrism and polycentricity and the entire dynamics of the field of tensions and friction between them could be approached using it. If that is the case then it should not be surprising to find that constructing or building the proper vocabulary is in fact the main task of an approach to social order from the perspective of polycentricity scholarship. As V. Ostrom put it:

> Penetrating an illusion of chaos and discerning regularities that appear to be created by an "invisible hand" imply that the tasks of scholarship . . . will be presented with serious difficulties. Relevant events may occur without the appropriate proper names being attached to them. Presumably events implicated by definitions used in scholarship may deviate from conventions

that apply to the use of proper names. Patterns and regularities which occur under an illusion of chaos may involve an order of complexity that is counterintuitive.

(V. Ostrom 1972)

Even more significant, the fact that the concept of polycentricity is polar and correlated to that of monocentricity and the fact that the monocentric vision dominated political sciences for such an extended time, had left their mark. It was not only that those proper concepts needed to map, to describe and analyze polycentric systems were lacking, but even worse, the existent language in political science was deeply contaminated by the monocentric vision. Perceiving polycentricity through the lenses shaped by a monocentric vision and describing it using the vocabulary growing out of that vision was doomed to be deeply distorting and misleading, which meant that the existent conceptual frameworks and their associated vocabulary needed to be tested, refocused and reconfigured in ways that would make their limits and preconceptions explicit. This also meant that new frameworks and concepts were to be created while engaging with the immense challenge of complexity and diversity posed by polycentricity. This was a worthy challenge and the rest of the story of the Bloomington research program in institutional analysis may be seen in a sense as an attempt to answer that challenge: a search for a proper language, including a vocabulary and a grammar, able to map and explore the institutional, praxeological and normative complexity of polycentric systems of human governance.

2   Crossing the great divide
The nature of public economies

The lessons from the metropolitan areas governance investigations cut deep into the intellectual core of political sciences, challenging both major traditions that divided it. On the one hand, there is the tradition defined by Adam Smith's theory of social order. Adam Smith and his intellectual descendents focused on the pattern of order and the positive consequences emerging out of the independent actions of individuals pursuing their own interests and trying to maximize their own welfare within a given system of rules. This was the "spontaneous order" school within which the study of the markets – the competition among producers and consumers of pure private goods leading to a better allocation of resources – occupied a pre-eminent place. On the other hand, there was the tradition rooted in Thomas Hobbes's theory of social order. As per this perspective, individual actors pursuing their own interests and trying to maximize their welfare led inevitably to chaos and conflict. From there the necessity of a single center of power imposing order is derived. Social order is thus the creation of the socially and politically unique "Leviathan," a monopoly over the authority to make law and the legitimate use of coercion, and not the outcome of the actions of self-organized and independent individuals. Most modern theories of "the State" have their origins in Hobbes's vision of Leviathan.

For various reasons, the theorists in both traditions managed to keep not only the theories of market and state alienated from each other but also the basic visions of the two separated. As the Workshop scholars noted, when confronted with the question "how far the logic of market organization can be applied to the organization of productive activities beyond strictly private goods" the answer was given by introducing concepts such as market failure and by prescribing a centralized authority to provide for collective goods. In other words, Smith's concept of market order was considered applicable for all private goods and Hobbes's conception of the single center of power and decision for all collective goods. Yet, as Elinor Ostrom noted in her 1997 Seidman Award in Political Economy acceptance speech:

> Since many of the goods and services desired in a modern economy are not pure private goods, this leads to the prescription that the State – in the singular – should provide and produce all the goods and services where markets fail. Showing that one institutional arrangement leads to sub-optimal performance

is not equivalent, however, to showing that another institutional arrangement will perform better.

(E. Ostrom 1998)

By the time she was making that argument the evidence that government monopolies "also fail in providing and producing local public goods and common-pool resources efficiently and equitably" was overwhelming. Thus, the conclusion was that some of the domains of modern political-economic life could not be understood or organized relying merely on the concepts of markets or states. Consequently needed was "a richer set of policy formulations" than just *the* Market or *the* State.

The presence of order in the world is largely dependent upon the theories used to understand the world. We are not limited, however, to only the conceptions of order derived from the work of Smith and Hobbes. A polycentric theory offers an alternative that can be used to analyze and prescribe a variety of institutional arrangements to match the extensive variety of collective goods in the world.

(E. Ostrom 1998)

The study of metropolitan governance confronted the Bloomington School's scholars not only with an alternative vision of governance but also with an alternative approach to political science from the one offered by the mainstream scholarship of the time. To articulate it, one concept inspired by Michael Polanyi's work, polycentricity, was a good starting point. However, that was not sufficient. What were needed were an entire vocabulary and an entire grammar to elaborate it. Also, an entirely new set of approaches and methods was required. To address this challenge, the Bloomington scholars devised an inventive strategy. From their preliminary work on metropolitan systems they knew that the alternative approach or "the science of polycentrism," which they were in the process of devising, needed a solid methodological individualist basis centered on human action and deliberation. They also realized that the most efficient way to begin the reconstruction was to use as a vehicle the academic discipline and scholarly discourse that was closest in spirit and method: neoclassical economics. Out of that observation emerged one of the most enduring features of the Bloomington research program, the dialogue with neoclassical economics. It meant first identifying relevant concepts and models from standard neoclassical economics and then readjusting, reshaping and recalibrating them. Once that was done, they were placed next to newly carved concepts in a new configuration that gave them a novel and enhanced meaning and a deeper relevance.

McGinnis's (1999a; 1999b; 2000) outstandingly edited volumes collect some of the most significant work done by the Workshop in this respect and thus do a great job in illustrating how, over the years, concepts related to rationality, decision making, trust, entrepreneurship, goods, production, cooperation, enforcement or efficiency have been cast, re-cast and restored to a new life by the Bloomington scholars, while Shivakumar's (2005) thorough outline of the main patterns of the broad vision emerging offers a systematic perspective on the same subject matter. Thus, one could see how an alternative to the conceptions of order derived from Smith and Hobbes was craved in the process and a new domain of the complex institutional reality of social life explored. Surveying several such key concepts as they are clustered around the notion of "public economy" is the best way to glimpse this effort. Their relevance is due not only to the fact that they offer an excellent illustration of the Bloomington program at work in this specific domain but also, and more importantly, because these concepts reveal in one way or another something important about the foundations of this program.

Co-production: consumer producers and the problem of the separation of production from consumption

From the very beginning the empirical work on metropolitan area public services and administration encountered a very interesting situation. Analysis revealed a whole series of cases wherein the collaboration between those who supplied a service and those who used it was the factor determining the effective delivery of the service. For instance, it became apparent that the health of a community depended not only on the professional quality of the personnel but also on the informed efforts of individual citizens. In a similar way, the quality of an "educational product" was "critically affected by the productive efforts of students as users of educational services." The quality and the supply of fire protection services depended on the efforts of citizens to prevent fires while the security of communities depended on the joint efforts of citizens as well of the professional policemen. In other words, it became clear that in many instances the users of services also function as co-producers. Without the informed and motivated efforts of service users, "the service may deteriorate into an indifferent product with insignificant value" (Ostrom and Ostrom [1977] in McGinnis 1999b, 93). As other scholars noted, that was a special situation defined by the fact that the production was not separated from consumption. Instead (the client or consumer) was part of the production process, consumer's input being essential "if there was to be any production at all." Therefore, "the resources, motivations, and skills brought to bear by the client or consumer are much more intimately connected with the *level* of achieved output than in the case of goods production." In this case "the output is always a jointly produced output" (Garn *et al.* 1976, 14–15). Co-production means more than the existence of at least two producers; it means the existence of two types of producers, a regular and a consumer producer, who "mix their efforts."

> Individuals and groups in a society who produce for exchange are, in our terms, *regular producers* of those goods and services they supply. These same individuals occupy consumer roles with respect to other goods and services. However, individual consumers or groups of consumers, *acting outside of their regular production roles,* may contribute to the production of some goods and services they consume. In such cases they act as *consumer producers.* In many

instances, consumer production is an essential complement to the efforts of regular producers; without the productive activities of consumers nothing of value will result. This appears to be characteristic of much public service production.

(Parks *et al.* 1985, 1001–1002)

The role of co-production came in many respects as a revelation. Indeed despite the role that co-production had in public service delivery, almost the entire metropolitan reform literature and the efforts inspired by it missed its significance. Instead of trying to understand its role and implications, the focus was put on bureaucratic structures or public firms. The consumer inputs were considered secondary and were given only an insignificant, auxiliary role. But for the institutional analysis scholars the productive roles of consumers as *co-producers* of the services they receive become a major area of investigation (Kiser and Percy 1980; E. Ostrom 1996; Ostrom and Ostrom 1977; Percy 1984; Whitaker 1980).

Their first observation was that once clearly defined, co-production problems could be identified in many sub-domains of the service industries in both the private and public sectors. The metropolitan areas were salient because they just offered a high concentration of very extreme and obvious cases. But those cases set light on a widespread phenomenon. It was the standard assumption of the separation of production from consumption that blinded everybody from identifying the source of what was called the "service paradox."

When professional personnel presume to know what is good for people rather than providing people with opportunities to express their own preferences, we should not be surprised to find that increasing professionalization of public services is accompanied by a serious erosion in the quality of those services. High expenditures for public services supplied exclusively by highly trained cadres of professional personnel may be a factor contributing to a service paradox. The better services are, as defined by professional criteria, the less satisfied citizens are with those services. An efficient public service delivery system will depend upon service personnel working under conditions where they have incentives to assist citizens in functioning as essential co-producers.

(Ostrom and Ostrom [1977] in McGinnis 1999b, 93–94)

Usually the attention in public services management and evaluation was on the production side. However, intelligent and efficient strategies of consumption are as important as intelligent and efficient strategies of production. Co-production requires that "both production and consumption go hand in hand to yield optimal results." The organization of a public economy that "gives consideration to economies of consumption as well as of production and provides for the co-ordination of the two is most likely to attain the best results" (Ostrom and Ostrom [1977] in McGinnis 1999b, 94). But in order to be able to do that, more was needed to be known about the nature and conditions of productive processes.

Three factors determining the presence or absence of co-production processes were identified: technological, economic and institutional. Technology "determines whether there are production functions for a service where both regular and consumer producer activities contribute to the output." The economic factors determine "whether it is efficient to mix regular and consumer producer activities to produce the service." Finally, in some cases co-production is technically feasible and economically efficient. The institutional factors are the ones that determine when the "mixing" will take place (Parks *et al*. 1985, 1002). One may imagine situations when the mixing is both technologically feasible and economically efficient but discouraged by the institutional structures, or on the contrary when the mixing is inefficient but gets encouraged:

> Institutional arrangements bar or limit the use of particular inputs, fail to provide sufficient incentives for the employment of particular inputs, or mandate the employment of particular inputs. On the other hand, institutional arrangements may call forth co-productive behavior where it is economically undesirable. Mandated employment of particular inputs or production processes are examples.

> (Parks *et al*. 1985, 1001–1002)

Consequently, institutional arrangements are crucial for determining the emergence of efficient co-productive arrangements. Various institutional arrangement structures could be employed. The market is one of them. In some cases, market arrangements could produce at efficient levels. In other cases, alternative institutional arrangements are needed. These alternatives could be very complex and may vary in function of the nature of goods, specific context, technological parameters and economic factors. Both market and non-market structures could be involved in co-production. Both have strengths and weaknesses. Therefore understanding the mechanisms by which institutional arrangements foster or inhibit co-production is the bedrock in designing efficient service production systems. Co-production becomes, thus, a key concept in institutional analysis. Focusing on it one could get a deeper understanding of the very nature and functioning of basic institutional structures and processes.

It is noteworthy that the notion of market and market theory were central to the argument. Given the fact that traditionally the discussion was framed in a polar way, markets vs. states or markets vs. government, the clarification of the role and capabilities of the market in the extreme case of co-production had an increased significance. In fact, clarifying the conditions of a functional market mechanism was a step in the direction of clarifying the conditions of other possible arrangements.

Market arrangements have some specific strengths: in some cases pricing mechanisms may be employed to induce an efficient mix of activities or to avoid mixing where it would be inefficient. Some regulation may be required but details of service arrangements can be left to the bargaining process that takes place between producers and consumers. As long as consumers are able to choose the price and the service mix they prefer the system works toward efficiency. Nevertheless, market arrangements encounter difficulties when it comes to organizing the supply of services requiring interdependent production relationships. One of the basic problems is the unfeasibility of creating a distribution of costs and benefits among producers in a way that gives incentives to produce the service in case. A free-riding situation ensues in which: "each individual consumer has an interest in seeing that the correct amount of consumer producer activity is forthcoming, yet has a personal preference that others supply the activity" (Parks *et al.* 1985, 1007).

In search of a solution, the institutional analysis scholars looked at economics and the economic approach to hierarchical, non-market arrangements as a means of solving interdependence problems. Following Alchian and Demsetz (1972), they looked at how firms work to cope with such problems. In other words, they looked at a substitution of market relationships with hierarchical structures as a means to create incentives that generate "additional output from use of the interdependent production relationship, while protecting each from exploitation by the others." Within firms, because monitoring is feasible, free riding is discouraged and the output is greater than what it might have been through individual, uncoordinated actions. The question was in what measure the firm-based solution as described by Alchian and Demsetz was applicable to a public service providing situation? Could such a solution be employed to link and monitor the efforts of regular producers and consumer producers in a public service setting?

Trying to answer this question V. Ostrom, Tiebout and Warren (1961) offered a model of the local government acting as *service provider,* by, on the one side, organizing service financing through collective consumption units and, on the other side, purchasing services from alternative public or private suppliers. The distinction and its implications are straightforward. Provision refers to "taxing and spending decisions, determining appropriate types of service and levels of supply, and arranging for and monitoring production." Production denotes "the transformation of inputs into outputs." The corollary is that a governance unit may be organized to provide a public service but it need not necessarily be the producer of the service. Once a provision unit is organized, it has several production options: create its own production unit, contract for the service with an external producer or create a joint venture with other provision units in order to have the service produced. The implication is that the organization of provision and the organization of production have different principles of operation and could be institutionalized in different separated ways.

In the model, providers have a double monitoring function: they monitor the behavior of the regular producers they contracted with on the production side while at the same time they monitor the behavior of the consumer producer. In that way they link inputs in an interdependent relationship and may be seen as a functional equivalent of the Alchian and Demsetz monitor. However, difficulties with non-market arrangements still remain. In the firm, noted the institutional analysis scholars, the monitor has two attributes that make its role functional. First, the monitor has the credible power to punish and replace any of the input contributors in case of free riding. Second, in the firm replacements are ready available (Alchian and Demsetz 1972). But in the case of public services both elements are missing:

Consumer producers who shirk cannot be easily replaced. . . . large local bureaucracies may use their political power to prevent replacement through civil service and union agreements. . . . A private monitor has ample incentive to monitor vigorously, as his direct reward is derived from surplus generated by interdependent production relationships. This is not the case with most collective arrangements, where surpluses cannot be readily appropriated. Since their compensation is divorced from the efficiency of input mixing, public providers find it comfortable to avoid unpleasant or costly monitoring activities.

(Parks *et al.* 1985, 1010)

For all these reasons, and others similar to them, collective organization of public service delivery is usually unable to match the efficacy of private firms in organizing interdependent production.

However, despite the lack of a precision comparable to the one displayed by market mechanisms, the search for solutions in the public arena is not blind. A notion like co-production could be used as a diagnostic tool and with it an entire battery of concepts and theories could be developed for institutional design and assessment. Merely using the notion of "co-production" opens up an entirely fresh perspective and with it a more complex view of the economic system is beginning to take shape. The particular nature of each good and service plus the technological and economic conditions of its production and consumption require a complex institutional system in which public and private, markets and hierarchies combine to generate an institutional architecture with diverse patterns of organization and diversely organized systems of governance.

The concept of public economy

The notion of co-production had a significant contribution in developing the conceptual universe of the polycentricity paradigm. It offered a very clear and constructive way of approaching some intricate mechanisms of the institutional arrangements and patterns of governance of a polycentric order. But even more important, it put in a new perspective the institutional structures of that type of order. A complex system was revealed in which not only markets and hierarchies but also more hybrid and peculiar arrangements were combined to generate a special institutional architecture. The concept of co-production was a powerful instrument in revealing all this. Using it was like discovering a new species by employing new, powerful theoretical lenses. For lack of a better solution, the Bloomington scholars decided to denote that institutional architecture through the concept of "public economy." Until then, the private sector and the public sector were viewed as two mutually exclusive parts of the economy. The private sector was associated to market transactions and competition while the public sector was associated to governmental administration, and with a bureaucratic system.

What the institutional analysis scholars identified was the possibility of an alternative conceptualization of the organization of public sector activities to the one that had at the center "a bureaucratic system of public administration in which all relationships are coordinated through a command structure culminating in a single center of authority" (Ostrom and Ostrom [1977] in McGinnis 1999b, 99). In fact, that alternative was inconceivable in the mainstream view because from its perspective in such a public system no place existed for private enterprise by definition. The public and private sectors were seen as mutually exclusive. But building on their metropolitan governance experience and on the insights given by notions such as co-production, they discovered the possibility to conceive a situation when the units of government were "collective consumption units" whose first order of business is to articulate and aggregate demands for those goods that are subject to joint consumption where exclusion is difficult to attain. In that specific situation:

> Relationships are coordinated among collective consumption and production units by contractual agreements, cooperative arrangements, competitive rivalry, and mechanisms of conflict resolution. No single center of authority is responsible for coordinating all relationships in a public economy. Market-like mechanisms can develop competitive pressures that tend to generate higher efficiency than can be gained by enterprises organized as exclusive monopolies and managed by elaborate hierarchies of officials.
>
> (Ostrom and Ostrom [1977] in McGinnis 1999b, 99)

The notion of public economy was meant to accomplish two goals: to save the concept of public from the false notion that "public" meant "the State" and "centralized systems of governance" and second – to make clear the difference from the market economy. In other words, to show that it is possible to have systems that are neither markets nor states, which preserve the autonomy and the freedom of choice of the individual – a theme that later will become central to the message of the program:

> Local public economies are not markets. Nor are they hierarchical in structure. Individuals are not able to engage in a wide diversity of independent *quid pro quo* relationships with any vendor they choose. Decisions are made for collectivities of individuals who are then held responsible to provide tax revenue and user charges to pay for the provision of public goods and services. Like markets, however, there are regular relationships among entities in a local public economy.
>
> (Ostrom and Ostrom [1965] in McGinnis 1999b, 107–108)

One way of defining public economies was to see them as composed of *collective consumption units* and to build the definition around that solution. Those "consumption units" are in fact associations of individuals who organize themselves in order to have a good system with special features, provided individuals use organizational means to produce and regulate the access to, and create and enforce the use of, collective goods (V. Ostrom *et al.* 1961). One of the most concise explanations of those reasons behind this form of organization was given by Elinor Ostrom:

> There is no need to organize collective consumption units in a private economy, because individuals and households already serve as the active decision

makers related to demand articulation and consumption. Whenever exclusion is problematic – as with public goods and common-pool resources – creating a collective consumption unit larger than a household is essential to overcome problems of free riding and strategic preference revelation, to determine how costs will be shared among those who benefit, to arrange for production, and to regulate patterns of access, use, and appropriation.

(E. Ostrom 1998)

This means that in order to understand a public economy all one has to do is to follow a functional logic. The social function is to solve problems of provision. In order to do that, collective consumption units are established. However the way production is organized is an entirely *different* question. The *producers* in a public economy "may or may not be the same organizing unit as the collective consumption unit that organizes the provision side." There are many examples of technical and organizational forms used in establishing collective consumption units – consumer cooperatives, municipal corporations, public service districts, etc. Many possible combinations of consumption, production and delivery of services are possible. In the case of municipalities, for instances, there are cases when they organize their own school systems, road departments, and police departments. In other cases they contract with others including other levels of government to have produced such services for their community. In other words, the producers in a public economy could be either for-profit or not-for-profit firms that produce collective goods for collective consumption units paying for goods or services. Examples of consumption units abound. They are small and large, multipurpose or just focused on one good or service. There are consumption units organized on a governmental basis: small suburban municipalities, or the national government, and there are non-governmental associations as collective consumption units: neighborhood organizations, condominiums, churches, voluntary associations. Yet, once identified, the functional principle behind them (non-private goods supply), the very diverse forms could be understood as part of a broader pattern, and the logic of the institutional process involved could be relatively easily revealed.

As the Ostroms have shown: collective consumption units have at least six different options for institutional arrangements meant to supply local public goods: (1) establishing and operating its "own" production unit, (2) contracting with a private firm, (3) contracting with another governmental unit, (4) obtaining some services from its own production unit and other services from other governmental or private producers, (5) establishing standards of service that must be met by authorized producers and allowing each consumer to select a private vendor and to procure services from an authorized supplier, and (6) issuing vouchers and permitting consumers to purchase service from any authorized supplier. What applies at the local level also applies at regional, national or international levels. That bewildering diversity is one reason why

public economies are not as well understood by economists or political scientists as either market economies or hierarchies. Scholars working within the traditional disciplines of political science and public administration have long been perplexed, for example, by the sheer complexity of the delivery arrangements existing in American metropolitan areas. A frequent view of metropolitan institutions has been that they are chaotic and incomprehensible. Given that scholars studying metropolitan service delivery arrangements could find no order in them, the reaction has been to recommend that metropolitan institutions should be radically consolidated and streamlined.

(E. Ostrom 1998)

But an invisible order existed, and while consolidation might be a viable option in some cases, one important principle shaping that order is at work irrespective of the nature of the case: competition. When the variety of arrangements for the supply and delivery of a public service is open to many options, the wider the range of these options, the greater the degree of competitive pressure that will exist in that particular public service industry. The greater the competitive pressure the better the performance, be it defined as costs minimizing or as responsiveness to demands and needs.

Competitive pressures are the key factors in maintaining the viability of a democratic system of public administration. The traditional principles of public administration imply monopoly organization applied to the entire public sector. Private enterprises as producers of public goods and services can significantly improve the efficiency of the public sector so long as competitive pressures can be openly and publicly maintained. The characteristics of public services and the important role for diverse organizations, including private enterprises, in the delivery of such services dictate the nature and structure of a public economy. The public economy need not be an exclusive government monopoly.

(Ostrom and Ostrom [1977] in McGinnis 1999b, 99)

To sum up "a sector" different from those traditionally conceptualized by using the mainstream political science and economics theoretical lenses was revealed. Public economies are different from state economies but also are different from market economies. A private entrepreneur has very few incentives to engage in the delivery of a public service by relying on traditional market mechanisms because the chances of failure are overwhelming.

The entrepreneurs must instead understand the logic of a public economy and learn to pursue opportunities within those constraints. *"The private delivery of public services is a different ball game from the private delivery of private goods and services."* To understand the new domain whose contours emerged from behind the old concepts of market and state required a renewed theoretical effort. In this respect one of the obvious observations emerging from the discussion of public economy was that at their most fundamental level they are based on the nature of goods or services (Ostrom and Ostrom [1977] in McGinnis 1999b, 76; Ostrom and Ostrom 1977). Hence, the theory of goods should be a basic building block of a theory of public economics.

The public goods institutionalism

Compared to other schools of institutional theory, of the variety of institutionalism developed by the Bloomington scholars, the nature of the goods and services is seen as the main driver of institutional arrangements. Therefore, it is also considered the main analytical entry point. The key in understanding local economies is to see their institutional arrangements as driven by a functional structure defined by the nature of goods or services their institutions are supposed to satisfy. Crucial in this respect is the conjecture that strictly private market arrangements are unable to deliver when confronted with public goods and common-pool resources. Yet, centralized and monopolistic arrangements fail to deliver in many of these cases either. Thus, in clarifying the logic of a public economy, the Bloomington scholars were forced to consider the nature of public goods as different from private goods and to engage in a profound study of goods in general as key factors shaping the structure and performance of an economic system.

Because the nature of goods was revealed as the vital determinant of the various institutional structures meant to produce these goods, a typology of goods was a first step in understanding institutional diversity. The main elements of that typology were "exclusion" and "jointness of use or consumption." But exclusion and jointness of consumption are characteristics that vary in degree. There are some extreme or pure cases distinguishing *purely* private from *purely* public goods but most situations are in the gray area between them. For instance, partial subtractibility occurs whenever the use of a good by one user subtracts *in part* from the use by other users. But, irrespective of the gray areas and nuances, when applied, these criteria generate a clear dichotomy between public and private goods. On the one hand, there are the private goods: relatively easy to have their quantity and quality measured, easy to exclude those who do not pay, can be consumed by only a single person, their payment is closely co-related to demand and consumption, and allocation decisions are made primarily by market processes. On the other, are the public goods: relatively difficult to have their quantity and quality measured, difficult to exclude someone who didn't pay, consumed jointly and simultaneously by many people, payment for goods is not closely related to demand or consumption, and finally, as a result of all of the above, allocation decisions are made primarily by political processes. As one may expect, these differences have significant implications for their production and delivery.

It is very important to note that as in the case of co-production, in most cases the nature of the goods is not an ontological given and that technological and institutional arrangements have an effect on the degree of choice and accordingly on the way the nature of goods is perceived and their production organized (Ostrom and Ostrom [1965] in McGinnis 1999b, 80). In other words, there is a complex interplay between goods, technology and institutions. Technology and institutions could create or destroy forms of exclusions thus changing the nature of goods. In turn, this will require a change in institutions in order to adjust to the new reality. This dynamic opens up one possible way of understanding institutional change in a public economy. But before focusing on institutional change, the first step is to try to understand the institutional structure of a public economy.

Public or collective goods have a well-known structural problem. By their nature if a public good is supplied, everyone is free to take advantage of the good since one cannot be excluded from it. The result is that efforts to supply it and the benefits of consuming it are not correlated. The good is undersupplied due to the very nature of incentives. Therefore, it is considered that in order to supply public goods and services, sanctions (or even coercion) should be used. In other words, mobilizing coercive action is mandatory for the operation of an economy of public and collective goods. In this respect "government" could be seen as just a name for the institutional arrangement meant to provide public goods (Ostrom and Ostrom [1977] in McGinnis 1999b, 80). However, if "mobilizing collective action implies the use of coercion" that creates a potential for abuse. In turn, it requires checks and balances and a new layer of institutions. To sum up, public economies, organized around goods that have characteristics such as nonexclusion, jointness of consumption, lack of unitization and direct measurability, have to cope with substantial problems. The solutions to those problems are institutional but each new institutional solution creates new problems. The complexity of the institutional system of a public economy seems not to be an exception or an accident and one should not expect a one fix-all solution:

> Recognizing that the world is composed of many different goods and services that have these characteristics, and that such goods come in many different forms, we are confronted with the task of thinking through what patterns of organization might be used to accommodate these difficulties and yield reasonably satisfactory results. Just as we can expect market weakness and failure to occur as a consequence of certain characteristics inherent in a good or service, we can also expect problems of institutional weakness and failure in governmental operations as a consequence of the characteristics of certain goods and services.
>
> (Ostrom and Ostrom [1977] in McGinnis 1999b, 82)

Because of their diversity and complexity, and because they deviate from the shared ideal types of organization, public economies are easier to conceptualize the "neither markets nor states" than to be described through a specific listing of institutional features. Markets have important self-regulating or self-governing characteristics but all market systems depend on non-market decision-making arrangements. Establishing and maintaining property rights, enforcing contracts, and providing infrastructure require mobilization and coordination of activities outside the sphere of the market. In a similar way the functioning of a governmental structure depends on the signals given by the market. In describing the organization of a public economy, one gets a better understanding of the mix of market and non-market architecture that is in fact behind not only "public economies" but also behind "states" and "markets."

The concept of industry and the public economy

By articulating the concept of public economy, a concept built around the notion of public goods and co-production, an important step further was made in the direction of the articulation of the polycentricity vision. Now a finer and more precise understanding of the mechanisms defining the complexity of the polycentric order was in the making and a framework for understanding the role and functions of the various governance units in metropolitan areas was created. However, that was just a first step forward. The mere identification and the description of those units were not enough. To advance the agenda, the systemic character of intergovernmental relations needed to be explored. Hence, a search "for the nature of the order that exists in the complex of relationships among governmental units" that avoids "the assumption that all of these relationships are unique or random." This required evading the assumption that "a system of government composed of numerous, independent, specialized units of government is necessarily fragmented and ineffective" and, instead, trying to understand "how the system works" (Ostrom and Ostrom [1965] in McGinnis 1999b, 107).

In order to shift attention to the system of functional relationships between governance units, a concept that could capture this aspect of the systemic dimension of the polycentric order was needed. Again, an insight from economics offered a starting point. That insight was given by the concept of "industry" defined as "a set of interrelated enterprises that uses a common body of knowledge and methods in the production of similar goods and services" (Ostrom and Ostrom [1965] in McGinnis 1999b, 107). This simple but very powerful notion is fully consistent with the goods-centered analysis as it takes as a starting point the production process and even more precisely the type of products produced. It was noted that the type of product determined the organizational structures and production methods. Consequently one can use the similarities in production methods as they are shaped by a particular product line as a heuristic to identify as a particular "industry" the set of enterprises that create, distribute and utilize such products.

The conception of an industry is crude, but even a crude concept may be a useful tool for exploring the systemic character of a complex structure of events lying somewhere between individual units of government and a general system of government. Those in the same industry share a common body of information and knowledge about the nature of the products, their production, and their uses. Intelligent decisions, whether by a producer, a distributor, or a consumer in the same industry, require access to a similar body of knowledge. The similarities in production methods, technology and information lead to considerable similarities among firms in the same industry and to the development of a characteristic structure of interrelationships among the firms in an industry. The industry concept is one way of considering an intermediate level of organization where many separate enterprises have developed interdependent patterns of organization based upon complementarities of functions in producing and using a similar type of product or service (Ostrom and Ostrom [1965] in McGinnis 1999b, 108).

Both the usefulness and the limitations of this concept can be illustrated by reference to industries in the private sector of the economy. To make that point, Elinor and Vincent Ostrom ([1965] in McGinnis 1999b, 108) chose the oil industry, the electric power industry and the automobile industry as examples. In each case there is a different configuration of different production technologies and organizational structures and each is based on different corpuses of knowledge. In the electric power industry, the distribution system makes more difficult the development of an arrangement enabling consumers to choose their source of electricity from alternative distributors. Consequently that industry tends to be composed of producers occupying monopoly positions in their respective service areas. That specific problem is avoided in the automobile industry, but the high capital costs substantially restrict the number of producers able to enter it. Similar structural patterns could be detected in all other industries. This has important analytical implications. The application of the concept of an industry "creates an approach for analyzing the interrelationships that exist among separate agencies using similar methods to deal with closely related events in order to provide a similar type of public service" (Ostrom and Ostrom [1965] in McGinnis 1999b, 109).

Yet, the very elementary exercise of discussing the broad patterns intrinsic in specific production-centered lines of economic organization reveals one of the limitations of the concept of industry: its failure to specify the exact boundaries to any specific industry. Boundaries change with minor shifts in product definition or technological changes. However the Bloomington scholars insisted that an important analytical setback as it may be, this lack of precision should not be a serious impediment to the use of the concept. This concept is robust enough to capture "the regularities that occur in the behavior of the many organizations that perform closely interrelated activities in the production of similar goods or services." That in itself is sufficient to move the analysis forward. If the "essential structural elements to account for the conduct of an industry as a whole," are captured, then "meaningful generalizations can be made about an industry as a social system composed of many interacting organizations" (Ostrom and Ostrom [1965] in McGinnis 1999b, 109).

The power of the notion of industry fully reveals itself when applied to the public sector. One of the first outcomes is the ability to identify the multitude of different agencies and units of government involved in the provision of similar public services and how their interrelationships are structured in this respect. Thus, used as a framework, the concept of industry reveals that there are two different dimensions and dynamics in a public economy: one of unity and another one of diversity. First a unitary system of interrelationships is revealed. One expects public organizations to cluster in function of the type of production. Common characteristics distinguish any one industry from other industries. However, at the same time, when the clusters are identified, differences within an industry become more salient. The internal organization varies in function of specific contextual factors related to the production or delivery process.

These simple insights were a double blow to the traditional and mainstream approaches. The traditional approach considered that all public organizations were either governments or governmental agencies and treated them in an undifferentiated way, expecting that all of them have similar functioning, and relatively similar organizational structures irrespective of the nature of service or product they delivered. But, the reality is that there are and should be structural variations and inter-industrial diversity. The public sector industries are as diverse in terms of organization, functioning and technology, as one may expect industries in the private sector to be. The water industry, for example, one of the topics of Vincent and Elinor Ostrom's detailed case studies, is a mix of highly independent federal, state and local governmental agencies, private utility companies, cooperative associations, and individual proprietorships, all of them relating to "a similar form of phenomenon," which is the subject of "a common body of knowledge and can be controlled by the use of similar facilities and production methods." The provision of police services at local, state, and federal agencies who use "closely related production methods to attempt to control similar sets of events in relation to similar objectives or intended outcomes" or the U.S. educational system could be also conceptualized as industries. Expecting that one model of production and organization (administrative and bureaucratic) could do justice to the variety of goods and services produced in the public sector is a major mistake. The U.S. system was in fact characterized by a "highly differentiated complex of public industries, each of which has its own characteristic production methods and is organized to take account of its own particular production problems" (Ostrom and Ostrom [1965] in McGinnis 1999b, 109).

The mere introduction of the concept of industry opened up new avenues in terms of a systematic analysis of the production and organizational methods performed by the agencies operating in specific domains. Nevertheless, establishing the relationship between the type of product produced in the public sector, technology and production methods, and their structural implications for the organization of this sector is incomplete as long as an additional dimension is not taken into account: the diversity of interests in an "industry." Different products, different scales of organization, different technologies come with their own stakeholders and their community of interests. The interests of consumers of goods are different from producers' interests. The interests of the stakeholders affected by the externalities of the process are different from the interests of those directly involved in the process of production or consumption. Differences of interests generate different organizational forms and levels. It should not be surprising that the diversity of interests in the public service industries is even larger than in private industries. In the California water industry, the example thoroughly studied by Vincent Ostrom and later by Elinor Ostrom, the interests of a community of farmers, the interests of the residents of the floodplain, the interests of the fishermen, and the interests of the shippers are part and parcel of the forces that shape that industry. Different water industries' arrangements emerge when all of these interests are weighed in. From a structure dominated by one or more large-scale water production agencies, to a structure composed of several intermediate producers and wholesalers, or of a large number of local distribution agencies that also produce a portion of their own water supply from local sources, the combinations defy the notion of a unique, best practice mode of organization. Similar structural variations are found in other public industries including the public education industry and the police industry with its municipal, county, state and federal police forces.

In brief, the diversity of goods and services, technologies, production processes, and the diversity of interests involved in a public industry generate a daunting structural and functional diversity. If that is the case, the concept advanced by the reformers, i.e. of the single self-sufficient public firm organizing and producing all of the public goods and services for its resident population, is no viable way of understanding the structure and conduct of a public economy. In fact, it is quite unrealistic and misleading. And if the conceptualization of the problem was wrong it meant that the standard policy approach might also be wrong and should be reconsidered. Given the very diverse and dynamic nature of the industry system that defines a public economy one may imagine that in such circumstances some agencies function as producers and other agencies operate as buyers. Together they ensure the provision of such municipal services such as police services, library services, planning services and public works services. That system may result into the development of a "quasi-market arrangement" involving competition among producers and competition among buyers. A vibrant contract system may emerge making the force of competition "a positive force toward efficient performance" (see Ostrom *et al.* 1961; Warren 1964)

The absence of an efficient market arrangement for the private provision of goods and services does not necessarily mean that public provision of goods and services under non-market conditions will assure efficient solutions. More efficient and more responsible performance in the public sector may be attainable if selective consideration is given to the formulation of user service charges to reflect deliberate public pricing policies, to the development of general criteria for public expenditure and public investment decisions, and to the development of quasi-market and pseudo-market arrangements to regulate the conduct of public agencies functioning in particular public service industries (Ostrom and Ostrom [1965] in McGinnis 1999b, 116; 1971; 1977).

Real life examples of such successful experiments with deliberate pseudo-price and pseudo-market arrangements abound: fishing and hunting licenses, the pricing of private fire insurance policies factoring in public fire protection services, polluters charges (Ostrom and Ostrom [1965] in McGinnis 1999b, 115). The contrast between these methods and the free provision or minimum-cost pricing of scarce public resources is stark. One of the most important aspects is the reduction of the incentive to introduce political factors into the process. For instance, in the case of free provision of water supplies the evidence suggests that it increases the political stakes, places a premium on political maneuvering, and results in overinvestment in large-scale water transfer schemes:

> To the extent that mechanisms can be designed to regulate the economic relationships among independent public enterprises functioning within any particular public industry, the burdens for regulation through the political process can be reduced proportionately. Public enterprises will always have to depend upon the political process to make adjustments in the self-regulating mechanisms within a public industry and to exercise a substantial burden in supplementing the regulatory force provided by mutual accommodations within a public industry. Without the availability of self-regulating mechanisms within particular public industries, there can be little confidence that a viable and efficient public economy can be maintained.
>
> (Ostrom and Ostrom [1965] in McGinnis 1999b, 115)

The importance of the political decision in public economies draws attention at two important observations. The first is methodological. To understand the operation of a public enterprise system composed of diverse public industries requires knowledge of both political and economic processes. In other words, to understand the structure, conduct and performance of different public industries, an interdisciplinary approach is needed. The second is a challenge and it relates to the functional aspect of the process: What are the mechanisms which, in the absence of market processes and in spite of the dangers raised by the political process, work to put together a public industry or even more specifically, a public economy unit? How does a community get mobilized to build a viable system? What is the force that puts together the pieces needed to generate a move towards more efficient outcomes?

Public entrepreneurship and the role of initiative in a public economy

The structural features of fragmented, polycentric systems do not preclude efficiency and good performance; on the contrary, they seem to be necessary conditions for them. Yet, those outcomes do not emerge mechanically, with no agency directly involved. The potential for good performance in existence in the structure needs to be transmuted into action and results. Identifying what are the agencies through which complex public economies systems generate preferred consequences is thus critical for understanding the dynamics of a public economy. How do we account for the seemingly counterintuitive results in the complex metropolitan areas? How do fragmented systems of local government induce efficiency? (Oakerson and Parks [1988] in McGinnis 1999b, 308). Several arguments, relying on the concepts of Exit and Voice, could be made and were indeed made in an attempt to answer this puzzle.

The "Tiebout model" is such an argument. The model is based on the assumption that citizens "vote with their feet," i.e. they simply leave a jurisdiction when dissatisfied with the management or services in place (Tiebout 1956; Hirschman 1970). A metropolitan area is seen as ultimately a special market. A citizen practically shops for jurisdictions that offer the bundle of local public goods and services that are closest to the ideal one, as imagined by the citizen. Consequently, the location decisions of citizens put a pressure on local government officials. The more the jurisdictions, the more the competition, the greater the efficiency. There are, however, limits on the measure citizens' exit alone can operate in this respect. First, exit means to relocate; the homeowner must sell the home. The cost of moving may be very high and relocating very disruptive.

Second, on a normal market, with normal goods, the decisions of consumers to buy or not to buy have direct and instant effects on private producers and sellers. If a business does not respond to market signals, the business will not make profit. "Market discipline" will force the business to adjust or perish. But entry and, particularly, exit do not have direct effects on public officials. The loss of tax revenue and the signal given by the decline of real estate market come as longer-run phenomena. There is no immediate effect on local officials. The negative consequences are dispersed. Failures of the local governance systems generate a process of community decline that leads to lower property values. Thus, not so much the local officials but the community is the one taking the brunt of market discipline (Oakerson and Parks [1988] in McGinnis 1999b, 308–310).

To sum up, exit is insufficient as a mechanism of keeping the public officials attuned to citizens' preferences. The tax revenue decline is a long run phenomenon and anyway not directly affecting the officials. The signals coming to them from the real estate market are weak and their ultimate effect is diffused among the citizens. However, that doesn't mean that the entry and exit decisions are irrelevant for local governance. A self-sorting process operates as individual households locate and relocate. This self-sorting process, however, is not fully functional in forcing local officials to adapt to citizens' preferences. "Voice," as an alternative to exit, becomes the important complement of the sorting process (Hirschman 1970). Voice not only signals the dissatisfaction with the existing situation but also articulates it:

> The power of voice is linked more directly to the ballot box than to exit. The local citizen who comes to a city council meeting and loudly complains about a municipal service is surely more effective than the citizen who writes to the mayor threatening to move out of town. If local officials feel unconstrained by the ballot box, where the potential effect is quite immediate, they are unlikely to feel constrained by the more remote and uncertain consequences associated with a potential for citizen exit.
>
> (Oakerson and Parks [1988] in McGinnis 1999b, 310)

Both voice and exit operate in a complementary way in structuring the functioning of a public economy. Consequently, increasing the opportunities for citizen entry and exit and creating a basis for citizen voice are two key conditions for a functional public economy. If that is the case, then the processes that "link jurisdictional fragmentation to efficiency and effectiveness in service delivery may be considerably more complex than the operations of a market mechanism, as seen by the standard approaches" (Oakerson and Parks [1988] in McGinnis 1999b, 310). Yet, citizen voice and exit offer only a partial picture of the forces shaping the dynamics of a public economy. Both operate mainly as forces of *control* on the local officials. However, the exercise of *initiative* by the citizens and those very local officials is the one that moves the system forward.

> Organizational innovations, especially those that involve multiple jurisdictions, emerge from discussions and negotiation – processes that enable individuals to discern common interests among diverse communities. Innovation is therefore costly, especially in terms of time and effort. Some individuals must be willing to incur those costs if a complex metropolitan area is to function effectively. This is the work of individuals we call "public entrepreneurs" namely, persons who propose ideas and carry the burden of ensuring discussion, compromise, and creative settlement.
>
> (Oakerson and Parks [1988] in McGinnis 1999b, 320)

To function properly, a public economy needs an institutional environment that encourages entrepreneurship. The more a system is creating spaces for initiative and decision, the more likely the system will display public entrepreneurship. In other words, it is necessary to have an institutional structure constraining and channeling the entrepreneurial initiative in a constructive direction. But the mere manifestation of public entrepreneurship as a response to citizen voice is not enough.

> Public entrepreneurs, like private entrepreneurs, seek to build enterprises that can survive and grow. To do so, a private entrepreneur must relate both to a product market where consumers make the critical decisions and to a factor market where a combination of individual factor owners and firms makes the critical decisions. A public entrepreneur is in a similar position. To succeed, he or she must relate both to a set of primary local jurisdictions in which citizens make the critical decisions and to a multijurisdictional environment in which other public agents make the critical decisions. Private entrepreneurship without the constraint of the marketplace is dysfunctional; it leads to monopoly power and the sacrifice of consumer interests. Public entrepreneurship without the effective constraint of citizen voice may be similarly dysfunctional.
>   (Oakerson and Parks [1988] in McGinnis 1999b, 320)

Public entrepreneurship introduces a dynamic element into the picture of a public economy. Public entrepreneurs' endeavor leads ultimately not only to more and better services at lower costs but also at new and better forms of organization, better suited to each context and situation. They induce and organize change. Entrepreneurship means that an ongoing process of institutional adaptation is in place. The result is not "a single, most efficient pattern of organization but to a continual search for more efficient ways to perform" (Oakerson and Parks [1988] in McGinnis 1999b, 320). This process also offers an explanation of the puzzling diversity and complexity of polycentric arrangement. Public entrepreneurship generates a variety of "emergent properties" in metropolitan systems by simply staying attuned and following (and in some cases shaping) the choices of citizens. Citizens have different preferences and when the system is designed to accommodate that, one should not be surprised that that will lead to different jurisdictional choices and different functional arrangements. What was characterized as an organizational "patchwork" inasmuch as "different communities arrange for the delivery of similar services in different ways" is nothing else than the overall result of citizens' choices channeled through public entrepreneurship initiatives (V. Ostrom 1971).

   The concept of public entrepreneurship is a crucial piece in the puzzle of a public economy (Kuhnert 2001). That is why theories that neglect entrepreneurship and attribute the efficiency of complex metropolitan areas principally to competition among local governments for residents have a limited explanatory power. Competition is a necessary condition but in the absence of entrepreneurship, citizen voice alone could not function as a mechanism for "translating jurisdictional fragmentation and overlap into relatively efficient outcomes." Only when together, competition, voice and entrepreneurship create a situation in which citizens are the main drivers. Citizens can,

> on their own initiative, create, modify, or abolish local governments; hold the purse strings of local government by exercising a veto over tax rate increases in local referenda; approve or disapprove expansions in the boundaries of local units; and, through their elected local officials, enter into mutually productive relationships with citizens in neighboring and overlapping jurisdictions.
>
> (Oakerson and Parks [1988] in McGinnis 1999b, 326)

This is a self-reinforcing situation. When citizens are the main drivers and the appropriate channels of governance are created, public entrepreneurs "are given both incentive and opportunity in this context to configure and reconfigure productive organizational and inter-organizational arrangements." Public entrepreneurship responds to citizens' voice and the way citizens' voice capacitates public entrepreneurship can explain the "efficiency-inducing properties of complex metropolitan areas and may be essential to the preservation of local democratic governance in an age of complexity" (Oakerson and Parks [1988] in McGinnis 1999b, 326).

Lessons and implications: underlying themes of the institutional analysis and development program

When seen in conjunction, the concepts of co-production, public economy, industry and public entrepreneurship generate the basic elements of a robust conceptual framework for institutional analysis and development. A good part of the history of the Bloomington research program is the history of the development, elaboration and application of this framework. The study of public economies has evolved into many different but related directions, engendering a complex agenda with theoretical, empirical and epistemological facets kept together by a common vision. There are nevertheless several powerful themes that emerged out of the empirical studies of metropolitan governance, the explorations into public economies, and the investigations of co-production and public entrepreneurship that become basic defining features of the Bloomington program. In no other place were these themes more convincingly and forcefully articulated than in Elinor Ostrom's, acceptance award speech of the Seidman Award for the work done in the area of public economies.

The first theme is a warning about the "danger of self-evident truths." As Elinor Ostrom noted, self-evident truths are frequently invoked in policy and political sciences. The idea is that "common sense dictates our understanding of the problem and the solution." Yet, the fact that something is widely believed, does not make it correct. The example of the metropolitan reform movement is a case in point. Centralized governments were considered better than small governmental units in providing public goods and services. Based on that belief and lacking systematic empirical evidence, for much of the twentieth century, a movement towards centralization and consolidating local governments plagued the advanced industrial democracies. By most standards, those reforms have failed. The self-evident truth of centralization proved not to be operational. A similar example was given by the self-evident truth of the "tragedy of the commons." Individuals were assumed to be trapped in their self-interested situational logic shaped by perverse incentives leading to overuse and depletion. Based on this self-evident truth national governments were thus called to create new institutions and to nationalize these resources. The result was exacerbated overuse and real destruction. These examples illustrate the general dangers of self-evident truth as principles shaping public policies.

At the same time these examples illustrate more than an epistemic principle in public policy analysis and design. They illustrate a powerful social order principle. The examples exemplify the dangers of misunderstanding the nature and role of polycentrism and monocentricity in the constitution of social order. It was believed that decentralized or polycentric systems are by their very nature generating disorder and inefficiency. Efficiency is related to centralization; order is an attribute of monocentricity. This common-sense assumption, however, led to proposals to improve the operation of political systems that had the opposite effect. By consistently taking the power to make decisions about the ways to innovate, adapt and coordinate efforts away from those who are directly affected, policymakers have designed institutions that are less able to respond to the problems they were meant to address.

Thus, a related but different theme emerging naturally from the metropolitan reform debate was that there is no "one best system" for all local public economies. Both the extensive empirical and theoretical research demonstrated that the notion of one type of governance arrangement fit for each metropolitan area, the idea of one "best way," is naïve and primitive. As Elinor Ostrom put it, by operating under the monocentric assumption, the political science and public administration scholars "have done a huge disservice by directing informed and interested citizens and public officials to identify and enact a single best design that would have to cope with the wide variety of problems faced in different localities." Instead of the monocentric assumption, a polycentric theory could encourage them to "design effective local institutions well-matched to local circumstances" (E. Ostrom 1972, 480–481).

By explicitly pointing out the relationship between an idea or a paradigm and its implementation, and from there the connection to the consequences emerging out of it, another powerful theme underlying the Bloomington School is revealed: the role of ideas and the link between institutional theory and a theory of beliefs. Ideas change the world, and that change could be for better or for worse. Ideas matter, and criteria for choosing ideas, and the criteria for assessing their institutional impact, matter too. What political scientists do, more or less aware of their theoretical and normative assumption, matters because ideas change the world.

Using a monocentric theory that predicts a single, large-scale, hierarchical organization is the most effective and efficient form of government, proponents have tried (and sometimes succeeded) to change the world to make it comprehensible to them. Citizens living in urban areas whose governmental structures have been "modernized' to make them comprehensible to scholars and public officials have had to pay a high price for the inadequacy of earlier approaches to the study of public economies.

(E. Ostrom 1998)

Finally, another underlying theme of the Bloomington research program is the ongoing challenge addressed to the standard academic approaches and the "poverty of formulations" that stems "from the separation of political economy into two disciplines that have evolved along separate paths." This is a program inspired by the ambition "to cross the great divide between economics and political science (as well as the other social sciences) in the conduct of comparative institutional analysis" (V. Ostrom 1993b; E. Ostrom 2000). Recognizing the advantages of academic specialization, the Bloomington scholars rejected the "sweeping prescriptions based on stylized notions of the institutional arrangements studied by other disciplines" as "negative fallouts of overspecialization." That required an additional dimension of the project – not only to define and chart institutional reality, not only to participate in a policy debate but to address in a foundational way the deepest epistemic and methodological problem in social sciences. This is why any understanding of the Institutional Analysis and Development School is incomplete if the centrality of this dimension is missed.

The Bloomington research program is better known today for the empirical work on the production and provision of public goods and common-pool resources with specific applications to public economies in urban areas of the United States, as well as to the government and management of diverse common-pool resources in many parts of the world. However, in parallel to that, an entire line of explorations in foundational issues in social and institutional theory has evolved and materialized in specific investigations into the nature of social order, the tension between freedom and organization, the nature and functions of social rules, the role of ideas and belief systems in institutional order and change, the methodological implications of all of the above, or in normative and political philosophy studies on the meaning of democracy and the meaning of the American political experiment. The rest of this book will address precisely these issues.

Part II

The "human condition" and the foundations of social order

Elements of a social philosophy of institutionalism

The empirical and analytical contributions of the Bloomington School to the advancement of the new institutionalism agenda and to the theories of collective action are well known as they have become increasingly salient in several academic disciplines during the last decades. This part of the book will not address directly that effort, already well documented elsewhere. Instead, it will explore a less known and discussed dimension of the program, the foundational vision, or the broader framework in which those contributions were rooted. This will be called the "social philosophy of institutional order and change," and the following chapter will explore it as well as some of its theoretical and methodological implications. With this end in mind, the following chapters will identify and illuminate the main building blocks of this social philosophy and will discuss the logic connecting them. The discussion will continue by tracing its implications for institutional theory with special attention given to the problem of ideas both as social forces and as focal points of social theorization. This means that at this juncture, our attention will be turned mostly on Vincent Ostrom's contribution. In the intellectual division of labor of the Bloomington School, a large part of his work has been dedicated precisely to the articulation of the social philosophy foundations and of the broader vision encapsulating and fueling the research agenda developed together with his colleagues. Exploring his work in this area leads us to the roots, as well as to the "grand design" of the Bloomington program.

3 Knowledge and institutions

Developing a social philosophy of institutional order and change

Given its interest in public economies, social organization and polycentrism, the study of collective action has become a central topic of the Bloomington research program. As Elinor Ostrom (1997, 1–2) pointed out, the key to a theory of collective action was to be found in the application of that theory to a "social dilemma," situations that occur "whenever individuals in interdependent situations face choices in which the maximization of short-term self-interest yields outcomes leaving all participants worse off than feasible alternatives." The problem was that the standard rational choice models – understanding humans as self-interested, short-term maximizers – were unsuccessful in explaining or predicting behavior in social dilemmas. The theoretical prediction for one-shot interactions was that no one will cooperate. If extended to indefinitely (or infinitely) repeated social dilemmas, standard rational choice models predicted "a multitude of equilibria ranging from the very best to the very worst of available outcomes without any hypothesized process for how individuals might achieve more productive outcomes and avert disasters." Yet, on the other hand, substantial empirical evidence demonstrated that "cooperation levels for most one-shot or finitely repeated social dilemmas far exceed the predicted levels." Moreover, those levels were "systematically affected by variables that play no theoretical role in affecting outcomes." Finally, the policy implications of those models were questionable too. Field research showed that individuals "systematically engage in collective action to provide local public goods or manage common-pool resources without an external authority to offer inducements or impose sanctions." In other words, the limits of standard theory were evident (E. Ostrom 1990; 1996; 1997; Dolsak and Ostrom 2003).

This meant that the foundation of a theory of collective action and social organization could not be built on the approach that generated flawed predictions. Yet, at the same time, there was a keen awareness that to build a viable and realistic theory of collective action meant more than extracting a set of generalizations from concrete cases; hence a very interesting evolution. On the one hand, an analytic and operational framework was advanced trying to capture for concrete research purposes both the formal and empirical stringencies of collective actions and social dilemma situations and to navigate through the challenges posed by them. On the other hand, emulating the tradition of the grand scale approach of Adam Smith's and Thomas Hobbes's efforts of building their theory on a broad perspective on human condition, an entire vision of human action in its social milieu was conjured. The work of Elinor Ostrom illustrated mainly the first direction. The work of Vincent Ostrom illustrated mainly the second one.

Vincent Ostrom advanced as a foundation for the research program, a social theory that instead of being rooted in an abstract or formal model had its "stylized facts" rooted in a broader vision of man and nature (Sproule-Jones *et al.*, 2008). In fact, one could say that such a work is social philosophy in the traditional sense of the word. If that is the case, that means that the Bloomington variety of institutional theory is grounded in a distinctive and relatively well articulated social philosophy that sets it apart from other forms of new institutional theory. It is hard to overestimate the importance of the conceptual background created by it. What ultimately keeps together the IAD approach and gives it a unique identity is an intriguing vision and a grand analytical narrative of human condition and its historical and social circumstances. In a sense, this return to a "worldview" to anchor a research program could be seen as a step backward – to a time when social theory was not so much a function of a technical epistemology and a pervading methodology but it was embedded in a specific "philosophical" vision – as opposed to, for instance, the axioms of positivism. Yet, a closer look at the ways Vincent Ostrom makes his case, reveals a refreshing perspective of an unusual persuasiveness.

Choice and human condition: a social philosophy vision of institutional order

If Vincent Ostrom is right, the starting point and the key of the study of social order does not rest in a formal definition of rationality as many of the fellow new institutionalists suggest, but in an anthropological and historical understanding of "the human condition and what it is about that condition that disposes human beings to search out arrangements with one another that depend upon organization" (V. Ostrom 1982a, 5). In the picture emerging out of the series of stylized facts reflecting that understanding, the crucial element is choice. Yet, the view on choice differs from the one advanced by the standard rational choice paradigm. Its basis is not formal or axiomatic but philosophical. The argument is shaped by a bold ontological assertion that choice is the basic and defining element for both humans and the social order they create. Choice – loosely defined as being able to consider alternative possibilities and to select a course of action from among a range of such possibilities – is not only a fundamental part of human behavior, but also the source of social order and social change. From an evolutionary standpoint, choice could be seen as a particular form of selection: alternative possibilities are assessed and compared. The more diverse and better defined the possibilities, the better founded the choice will be. The better the choice, the better the adaptation. And because choice is a basic form of adaptive behavior, social organization could be seen as the expression of choice as a form of adaptive behavior.

Yet, the cycle of adaptation doesn't stop there: organization solves problems but also creates new problems. Humans have to adjust to them through learning and new choices. The very solutions create at their turn new problems and challenges.

And thus the cycle is continued. Precisely because it is the outcome of choice and it is engendering new choices, social organization is always fluid and vulnerable to ongoing challenges. Vulnerability, uncertainty, ignorance, learning and adaptability are thus key concepts: "An appreciation of the tenuous nature of order in human society is the most important lesson to be learned about the human condition" (V. Ostrom 1982a, 3; 1973b; 1982b). At a very basic and oversimplified level, these are the parameters of the social philosophy on the background of which the Indiana institutional theory should be read. Elaborating them reveals the fine links that connect a theory of choice to a theory of institutions via a theory of learning, knowledge and ideas.

The first step is to elaborate the link that embeds the issue of choice in an analytical narrative of human adaptation and evolution. From this perspective, choice is seen as part of an entire line of adaptation modes, starting with genetic adaptation and ending with cultural adaptation. Learning is one of the mechanisms that pushed adaptation to a new level (V. Ostrom 1982a, 6). Organisms that are capable of learning are able to adapt to a variety of environmental circumstances within the course of their individual life spans. Learning is thus both fine tuning and an amplification of the adaptive potential. Crucial for the learning process is the generation and selection of ideas (mental images of different moves, actions, possibilities). Indeed, such a process need not be a purely human and mental process, as search behaviors like trial-and-error methods can be used to generate ideas. However, the generation and selection of ideas, as key elements of learning, is exponentially amplified in human beings. That amplification is directly associated with language. What sets apart human beings from the rest of the species is the use of language. Language radically amplifies human capabilities to shape ideas, to accumulate knowledge and transmit it (V. Ostrom 1982a, 7–11).

With language, the fact of choice is profoundly affected too. With language, the power of choice increases in an unprecedented and unique way in evolutionary history. With it, thought processes and the realm of ideas go beyond the bounds of immediately observable events. This leads to more sophisticated modes of adaptation that greatly expand the repertoire of possibilities available to human beings. But the increase of options (imagined or real) makes the act of choice daunting. In the absence of rules and heuristic devices that could diminish the diversity of possibilities, economize and focus cognitive effort, reason-based choice becomes impossible. Rules and routines become crucial. Thus the progression towards language and rules sets up a pattern: increase in adaptability leads to an increase of the varieties of behavior based on ideas and imagination, the increase of the varieties of behavior leads to an increase of the possibilities of action and interaction. With increased possibilities, come increased problems and challenges. To coordinate, cooperate and work through the looming chaos and structural uncertainty, rules and their institutionalization are needed. This very simple equation or chain of reactions lies, in Vincent Ostrom's view, at the foundation of our understanding of human institutions and of political organization.

Before further elaborating this view, one should stop and notice the large measure in which it is an ideas-centered account. Ideas – or correlated concepts such as learning or knowledge – frame and permeate choices. Ideas set into motion actions, ideas give solutions but they also generate new problems and challenges. Ultimately, an account of human societies is fundamentally an account of the social avatars of ideas and knowledge, manifested through choices. Understanding the nature of institutions is rooted in understanding of the role of ideas and knowledge in the human condition. Ideas are present at different levels: ideas on possibilities, ideas on rules, ideas on institutions. Everything pivots around them because everything pivots on choice. Or, the other way round, it pivots on choice because it pivots on ideas.

Out of these observations emerges a methodological insight. The formula of the pattern of institutional adaptability is also the formula of the pattern of institutional analysis: institutional analysis should follow the challenge–response dyad. Ultimately, institutions are responses or solutions to generic challenges or "threats." Understanding the nature of the "threats" operating at different levels offers the clues for understanding the institutional arrangements emerging as a response to them. Ideas, learning and knowledge are involved on both sides of the process: ideas act as threats and ideas act as responses. Following that dialectic reveals essential insights on the nature and functions of institutions. In his work, Vincent Ostrom (1973b; 1982a) outlines four such keys: the "threat of potential chaos," the "threat of tyranny," the "threat of uncertainty" and the "threat of ignorance and error."

The threat of potential chaos

The constitutive role of ideas, free will, learning and imagination in the human condition does come with the price of generating an ongoing "threat of potential chaos." The capacity to imagine scenarios and possibilities increases the problems of maintaining order in inter-human relationships. Increasing the potential variety in human behavior, the multitude of combinations, combinations of combinations and patterns of interactions, threatens the maintenance of a predictable order (V. Ostrom 1982a, 18). "If all of the potential variety in human behavior were to be expressed in a random way, rather than in highly selective ways, human beings would face a state of affairs approximating chaos." The paradoxical corollary is that choices require constraints:

> Mechanisms for ordering or constraining choices must simultaneously occur if human development is to advance beyond a most primitive level. The development of order out of chaos requires that each human being establish a basis for anticipating how others will behave so that each person can act with an expectation that other persons will act with constraint. Otherwise, individuals will act in ways that may enhance their own well-being at a potential cost to the well-being of others.
>
> (V. Ostrom 1982a, 19)

The basis for anticipating others' behavior is what one calls a "social rule." Rules are the mechanism constraining and ordering choice and, thus, "a necessary condition, but not a sufficient condition, for establishing ordered social relationships." If people act with reference to a common set of decision rules, their actions will take place in an "orderly and predictable manner." Outside predetermined limits and constraints, human behavior is unpredictable. Thus, a new paradox: society emerges out of this foundational unpredictability of human nature and human ideas. Rules are the magic that transform and stabilize that potential chaos. Out of the range of potential diversity, individuals are being constrained from exploiting all possibilities and are being limited in their choice to a smaller range of possibilities. Consequently, human behavior can be surprisingly predictable in the presence of relevant decision rules:

> Reliance upon decision rules as a means for creating order from potential chaos indicates why we can refer to human beings as political animals. Our extraordinary ability to learn and to transmit learning implies that a random use of ideas would create potential chaos. Decision rules become a basis for ordering choice and for creating order in human relationships. We would anticipate that rule-ordered arrangements go hand in hand with the growth of human knowledge and the development of human civilization. The growth of human knowledge must be accompanied by the creation of social relationship based upon concepts, words, and rules. Institutions are social artifacts created through human reason and choice and built upon a language pertinent to rule-ordered relationships.
>
> (V. Ostrom 1982a, 21)

In "Artisanship and Artifact" ([1980] in McGinnis 1999a, 377–394) Vincent Ostrom further elaborates the relationship between ideas, rules and social organization by emphasizing the role of information-streamlining that organizations have. While doing that, he is explicitly addressing the issue of uncertainty and the future, the two twin themes that sooner or later lie beneath any theory of social order centered on ideas and knowledge. Finally, and at the same time, he introduces a theme that stays beneath the entire discussion – the problem of error and human fallibility in tying together the major threads; he offers a concise new angle on the issue:

> Reliance upon institutions as ways of elucidating and processing information is especially important when we understand the implications that derive from human capabilities for learning. The capacity to anticipate the future course of events is critically dependent upon knowledge. The future as perceived by human beings is always a creation of the mind: an artifact of human intelligibility. The future course of human development is always influenced by the generation of new knowledge. New knowledge opens possibilities that could not have been comprehended without access to that new knowledge. So long as new knowledge continues to accrue, long-term planning is an impossibility. New knowledge contributes to the erosion of technologies based upon prior knowledge. The further plans are projected into the future, the less confidence we can have in their reliability. Any creature that has unique capabilities for learning and generating new knowledge inevitably faces an uncertain future. Learning and the generation of new knowledge are themselves marks of

fallibility. Infallible creatures would have no need to learn and generate new knowledge. Fallible creatures need to accommodate their plans to changing levels of information and knowledge.

(V. Ostrom [1980] in McGinnis 1999a, 382)

It is interesting to note how in Vincent Ostrom's argument, the mainstream notion of "imperfect knowledge" is transmuted into the notion of "fallibility." Constraint is introduced by rules, but that constraint does not exhaust the potentials for choice. Decision rules create only a partial form of ordering. Between conduct that is permitted and conduct that is not permitted, a wide range of options are still available in most circumstances to individuals. Human societies can then be considered as relatively open systems of order, and error and failure are part and parcel of it. However, that openness and the degree of tolerance to error and failure varies from society to society. What is permitted in one society affects learning, knowledge generation and in the end its adaptive potential. The specific constraints and restrictions introduced by rules define not only the nature of that society but also its functioning, performance and further evolution. Societies whose rules enable the individuals to identify and focus on the most adaptive possibilities have better chances of surviving and growing. If that is the case, changing and adjusting rules in function of the new knowledge, resulting from the learning process, is crucial. Learning is embodied in the rules. Through the maintenance of continuous of systems of rules over generations, human beings "accumulate the bodies of learning that are entailed in systems of rules" (V. Ostrom 1982a, 22).

To sum up, the overview of the "threat of potential chaos" theme illustrates the measure in which the vision behind the Bloomington School is built around a series of concepts such as adaptability, choice, learning, knowledge, ideas and rules. Together they map the dynamics of an evolutionary process. They are the "primitives or the axioms of social organization." However, postulating the emergence of rules (either as behavioral parameters or constrains, or as guidelines resulting from adaptive or evolutionary processes) is just one part of the story. The specific and deepest foundations of institutional order could be understood only if the specific problems or "threats," from which they emerge as responses, are examined separately. Thus, to understand the nature of institutions and institutional change, one has to go beyond the abstract "rules of the game" definition or the "adaptation-selection" framework and delve into the most basic functional reasons that generate their emergence. Mapping these threats and responses gives a richer vision of social organization and a better basis for understanding collective action. Besides the "threat of chaos" that looms behind all forms of social organization, three other such "patterns" are discussed by Vincent Ostrom: the "threat of tyranny," the "threat of uncertainty" and the "threat of ignorance and error."

Rules, enforcement and "the threat of tyranny"

As Vincent Ostrom noted following Hobbes, by "themselves decision rules are but words." As such, they need enforcement. Social order depends on human agents who have the task to formulate, determine and enforce rules. But that creates drastic asymmetries between those agents and the rest. This is an unavoidable consequence. Collective action and social order always implies "organized inequalities in the management of interdependent rule-ordered behavior." Rules, thus, by their very nature, generate two social types: the rulers and the ruled. Therefore, it is fair to conclude that the most fundamental source of inequalities in human societies is the inevitable use of rules to order social relationships (V. Ostrom 1982a, 22–23; 1984).

The problem of rules is amplified by the fact that social order depends on the use of sanctions. That means that social order "not only requires an assigning of authority to those who govern but also requires giving them the right to use coercion." For Vincent Ostrom, coercion is more than just a technical term. As social beings, humans are forced to "accept coercion as use of instruments of evil to permit orderly social relationships." As in the case of other key concepts he employs, he is projecting this notion on a broader philosophical and semantic context. The ubiquity of coercion means that order and organization in human societies "depend upon a Faustian bargain where the use of instruments of evil, i.e. sanctions, including those of organized force, become necessary conditions for deriving the advantages of social organization" (V. Ostrom 1982a, 2). That is undoubtedly introducing a tragic element in human condition. What Vincent Ostrom calls a "Faustian bargain" is inevitably ensuing from the "tensions which arise from efforts to give force and effect to words and ideas in structuring human relationships."

> This condition makes a Faustian bargain of human societies; and no one can escape from the burden of using such instruments of evil to do good. [...] We are all intricately bound in a Faustian bargain which we as human beings cannot avoid. At most, we can attempt to understand the fundamental tensions that are inherent in such a bargain and conduct ourselves accordingly. We are all potential tyrants unless we learn to act justly.
>
> (V. Ostrom 1982a, 35)

The implication is that social order and its institutional dynamics are perceived as shaped by and operating under the shadow of the ongoing tension between the threat of chaos and the threat of tyranny. Having the authority to control rules, "rulers" can shape things so that some members of society are systematically advantaged against others. Because they have control over the instruments of coercion, "rulers can abuse it in the employment of those tools and act as tyrants" (V. Ostrom 1982a, 2). Force and political constraint can be used both as "instruments of tyranny as well as instruments to support productive and mutually advantageous relationships." In other words, "political relationships are sensitive relationships; and, like fire, need to be treated with care" (V. Ostrom 1982a, 24). By extension the same is true about rules. Instruments are to be distinguished from the agents using them and from the norms that are guiding their employment.

> The use of instruments may come to dominate social relationships so that rules become oppressive rather than liberating. The greatest evils inflicted upon

humanity have been the work of those who are so confident of their effort to do good that they do not hesitate to use the instruments of evil available to them on behalf of their righteous cause. But the problem is a general one and not limited either to self-serving or cause-serving individuals: all organizations rely upon instruments of evil to do good.

(V. Ostrom 1982a, 23)

If that is the case, the question "whether people can develop appropriate precautions in the use of such instruments of evil and constrain them from dominating organized activities" becomes critical. Could the problem of elemental asymmetry in the relationship between the "rulers" and the "ruled" be dealt in any way? Does, by its very nature, social order require that someone rules over society and cannot be held accountable to other members of society? It seems that government defined as "decision-making institutional arrangements specialized to formulating rules, determining conflicts, enforcing decisions, and altering decision rules" necessarily involves monopolizing the legitimate use of force in society (V. Ostrom 1982a, 22). The challenge is this: Is it possible to conceptualize the relationship between rulers and ruled so that rulers themselves are subject to a rule of law? Could such a solution be implemented and made sustainable in the long run?

And thus we find ourselves in the traditional territory of constitutional and political theory. The route reaching it was slightly different from the standard one but, in the end, the territory looks familiar. Conceptualizing and implementing such a solution would reintroduce, at another level, symmetry in political relationships where "those who govern are subject to rules of law and those who are ruled also exercise basic prerogatives of rulership." In other words, the challenge is to design a "meta-level rule of law" where rulers themselves are subject to enforceable rules. The very effort of specifying such a solution is a means to appreciate the deep tensions that are involved in establishing a system of governance where both the "threat of chaos" and the "threat of tyranny" are circumvented. The political process and its institutionalization, insists Vincent Ostrom, become crucial. To secure a viable social order one needs a process that not only introduces the rule of law but also encapsulates conflict and enables persons to contemplate the consequences of their political actions before making decisions. In short, a political process meant to encourage deliberation, to reduce the prospect of gross error, and to enhance the calculation of more general, long-term interests (V. Ostrom 1982a, 24).

All of the above suggest the notion of a three-step process. To create social order out of chaos rules are needed. But implicit in it is the fact that inequality and constraints are unavoidable. That creates a deep strain in society; the specter of tyranny and injustice always looms large. A step further towards a "humane, mutually advantageous and productive social order" is to create a special set of rules, institutions and processes to deal precisely with the challenge of injustice and tyranny and to anticipate and counter those challenges. A shorthand term for that is "the rule of law" system. Yet, in order to have that sustained, one needs to encapsulate it in a climate dominated by deliberation and critical reason. The goal is to temper the rulers and the application of force by checking and balancing them not only with the force of rules but also with reason and deliberation.

A corollary of this discussion deserves a special note. Although the basic threats and challenges to social organization are universal, the institutional architecture of social order is very diverse. For instance, the institutional arrangements emerging to cope with the threat of tyranny may take many forms. These institutional forms may exist in some societies and not in others. Not all societies or types of social organization have grown such that the institutions are able to deal with the threat of tyranny, or if they have, that doesn't necessarily mean that they are of a similar nature and extension. However, one expects them to exist in some form or degree in all societies. A successful society avoids the two extremes of chaos and tyranny by creating a robust meta-level system of rules backed by a culture and formal and informal institutions aimed at controlling the "rulers" and the way they are administering the rules. That being said, discussing the institutional dynamics as a tension between the threat of chaos and the threat of tyranny, one should not forget a fundamental assumption on which the discussion is predicated: the fact that the stability of the institutional order is always challenged by the very process of learning and by the accumulation of new knowledge in society. The forces that lead to the identification of institutional solutions – learning, knowledge and ideas – are the very forces that threat to destabilize the order they are creating.

Knowledge, "the threat of uncertainty," rules and institutions

In dealing with the dialectic of ideas and institutions one should keep in mind that as human capabilities for learning and communication increase, the growth of new knowledge increases the range of possible or imaginable possibilities. That has the effect of disrupting existing or established relationships as well as the expectations about the future based on them. New knowledge gives rise to new possibilities. New possibilities, "if acted upon, manifest themselves as new events, relationships, or occurrences which could not have been anticipated by those who failed to take account of those new possibilities in anticipating the future course of events." In other words, new knowledge, and action based on an expanding body of knowledge, means an ongoing creation of new uncertainties about the future. This is in fact a Popperian argument: learning and generating new knowledge "necessarily imply that human beings cannot anticipate the future course of human development" (V. Ostrom 1990a; 1991b; 1991c; Popper 1964). The fact that the increase of knowledge generates increased social uncertainty couldn't be counted as anything else other than as a paradoxical reality:

> The human potential for learning yields a fertile imagination where any given level of achievement is always being challenged by the conceptualization of some new possibility. The use of present means to attain some future apparent good is a perpetual and restless desire that ceases only with death. Human beings can always be expected to test limits. This is of the basic nature of learning. Yet human beings as the species having the greatest capabilities for

> learning ideas confront fundamental tensions. Since new knowledge opens new possibilities that could not have been imagined in the absence of that knowledge, the most capable learners face the highest level of uncertainty in anticipating the future course of development.
>
> (V. Ostrom 1982a, 34)

A society that is rapidly expanding its stock of knowledge not only makes long-term social planning and long-term social forecasting impossible but also it makes any long-term comprehensive planning, an impossibility, too. If one wants to make social planning the key element of social change, the sole possible solution is simply to stop or dramatically reduce the growth of new knowledge.

> Creatures who are capable of generating new knowledge and of creating new possibilities are necessarily foreclosed from long-term comprehensive planning if they are to take advantage of the new knowledge and new possibilities. Planning can be an essential strategy for organizing information in an assessment of alternative possibilities so long as time horizons are limited and crude magnitudes of uncertainty can be specified in relation to the obsolescence of old knowledge and the generation of new knowledge.
>
> (V. Ostrom 1982a, 27)

The impossibility of planning – defined not as a result of some externally induced natural ignorance about the environment and of the human incapacity to overcome it but as a result of precisely the human capabilities to generate new knowledge – is an important challenge to be dealt with in constructing social order. The ability to cope with the future is a necessary condition for any institutional design. But it is one thing to hope that more knowledge will reduce that uncertainty and something else to realize that while new knowledge may reduce uncertainty in some areas, it may increase it in many others. One needs to know not only how to reduce uncertainty in specific domains but also how to manage it in the aggregate.

According to Vincent Ostrom, the solution is institutional and may take two directions. The first has already been alluded to and is simply to block the advent of the growth of new knowledge in the society. In this case, routines based on specific and meticulous prescriptions for each activity become the norm. However, there is a second possibility: designing rules and institutional arrangements that let open to choice an entire range of learning and actions and at the same time try to channel that in the most beneficial direction. To make this point clearer, the domain of learning should be understood in broad terms. For instance, learning takes place in market through prices – profit and loss. Learning takes place also through organizational experiments, failure and success. Rules ordering the space of learning in markets ensure the ability of a society to cope with the twin problem of the uncertainty of future and (as induced by) the growth of knowledge. In a similar way, the principle of bankruptcy in the law system help society to deal with failed organizational experiments. These are just examples of rule systems that administer knowledge and implicitly manage uncertainty.

Yet, there is more to the notion than the challenge of uncertainty generated by ideas and knowledge as responded to by rules and institutions. The fact that the rules aimed at harnessing the knowledge and uncertainty processes have a chaos-containing role, is only one facet of the phenomenon. Containing the threat of chaos may be done by simply freezing and closing the society in a system of rigid rules. But, containing uncertainty means more than that: it means dealing incessantly with the ongoing threat created by a relatively dynamic and open society in which learning and knowledge production take place continuously. The notion that in order to maintain itself and flourish the social order requires rules able to cope with uncertainty, has an important corollary. One needs to be able to generate those rules that are best for this specific purpose. In other words, one needs the knowledge of rules or "a science of rules."

Such knowledge should "enable us to understand how rules constrain choice and affect behavior in ways that are likely to generate social pathologies under changing conditions of interdependency." At the same time, such knowledge might then be used to change rules and create new patterns of behavior to avoid those "pathologies." Knowledge of "the behavioral tendencies evoked by institutional forms" enables us to alter, reformulate or redesign institutional arrangements in order to "accommodate to the changing potentials inherent in the generation of new knowledge." If orderly change is to occur, considers Ostrom, "advances in human knowledge about institutional analysis and design must accompany the generation of those other forms of new knowledge which enable human beings to manipulate nature and alter the structures of events" (V. Ostrom 1982a, 27–29; 1971).

Thinking of institutions in terms of "rules of the game" evokes the notion that knowledge about how rules function improves the game, both as structure and as results. In conditions of uncertainty and in conditions when planning is impracticable, the sole solution is to rely on knowledge of how institutions and the rules they consist of, alter human decision making and human choices. A good understanding of rules and their impact is a precondition of a successful social organization and implicitly, of a successful management of uncertainty and social change.

To sum up, institutional arrangements could also be seen from the perspective of their function as mechanisms of coping with the threat of uncertainty. When a society is creating a growing knowledge pool, that function cannot be fulfilled other than by building a system that generates not so much a reduction of uncertainty (because that is impossible other than in relative terms) but a competent management of uncertainty. In order to do that, one needs to have a system of rules on the lines of those that define modern markets or complex modern regulatory and legal systems. That effort requires the development of a special body of knowledge. Institutional theory, broadly defined as systematic knowledge about institutions is a significant contribution to that effort.

The threat of ignorance and error

One important fact that should be remembered when one is dealing with the "threats" described by V. Ostrom is that they should be seen as facets of one complex phenomenon and not as separated categories. A good illustration of this point is the "threat of ignorance" that could be conceptualized as a conjunction between the "threat of uncertainty" and the "threat of tyranny" (V. Ostrom 1973b; [1980] in McGinnis 1999a). Despite its composite identity, it is useful to give it particular attention. Seen in this light, the problem of knowledge and its uses in society highlights an additional facet adding to our understanding of institutional order. The starting point is the already familiar problem of structural uncertainty and the incapacity to predict the future introduced in human affairs due to learning and imagination (V. Ostrom 1982a, 34; 1973b; 1990a; 1991b). But, and in addition to that, another aspect of the structural limits to the growth of knowledge is introduced. Social order increases and intensifies the division of labor, which leads to better use of skills and knowledge in society. But at the same time, it leads, by definition, to specialization, and specialization in a particular domain has a cost: the lack of specialization in others. If one defines the issue in cognitive terms then one can conclude that relative knowledge brings relative ignorance, "the limited mastery that each individual can attain in relation to the aggregate pool of knowledge" (V. Ostrom 1982a, 31). In other words, while the division of labor increases the overall level of knowledge in a society, it also increases the relative ignorance of its individual members.

Adam Smith in *The Wealth of Nations* (1981[1776], 734–735) was among the first to identify this downside, or "perverse effect" of the division of labor. Specialization means coming to know more and more about less and less. By means of specialization the pin-maker "naturally loses, therefore, the habit (of the exertion of his understanding), and . . . the dexterity at his own particular trade seems, in this manner, to be acquired at the expense of his intellectual, social and martial virtues." The threat of relative ignorance is not limited to the undereducated or to physical laborers. It is a general or structural problem deriving from specialization of any type of knowledge and/or any type of division of labor. For instance, Vincent Ostrom writes, one cannot avoid observing that intellectual specialization among scholars tend to produce a "learned ignoramus." It is perhaps a harsh description but the point is clear: even those that are supposed to be learned, keepers and producers of "pure" knowledge, could not avoid the increasing relative ignorance produced precisely by a functional order and productive division of labor that leads to the growth of the aggregate pool of knowledge (V. Ostrom, 1982a, 31).

In brief, individuals are necessarily limited in their capacity to master large bodies of knowledge. As the aggregate pool of knowledge increases, the relative ignorance of each individual about that aggregate pool of knowledge will also increase. The implications are two-fold. The first is cognitive. The more complex the institutional order, the deeper the division of labor; the deeper the division of labor, the less one single person can "see" or "know" the "whole picture." Out of that emerges a second implication – an operational one. In these circumstances, all decision making could be subject to error. Hence all decision makers are fallible. "No decision maker can know all of the consequences that flow from his decision and actions. A proneness to error will plague all human efforts" (V. Ostrom 1982a, 32; 1973b; 1990a; 1991b).

Far from being a trivial observation, it is vital for the way we approach the governance of complex societies and one needs to recognize its importance and the danger of neglecting it. There is a relationship between accepting a vision of the limits of individual and human knowledge and accepting the necessity of an open, pluralist and polycentric political system functioning on the basis of dispersed knowledge. Alternatively, there is a relationship between assuming the perspective of an "omniscient leader" and believing in the viability of monocentrism, centralism and comprehensive social planning. Decision makers and political analysts who assume that "they can take the perspective of an omniscient observer," that they can "see" the "whole picture," are always a potential source of troubles because their solutions or decisions will increase the predisposition to error, not to speak of the fact that their perception of their own capabilities may invite a tyrannical behavior.

> Those who have recourse to the perspectives of 'omniscient' observers in assessing contemporary problems, also rely on political solutions which have recourse to some single center of authority where officials can exercise omnipotent decision-making capabilities an dealing with the aggregate problems of a society [...] Somebody who takes the perspective of an omniscient observer will assume that he can "see" the "whole picture, "know" what is "good" for people, and plan or pre-determine the future course of events. Such a presumption is likely to increase proneness to error. Fallible men require reference to decision-making processes where diverse forms of analysis can be mobilized and where each form, of analysis can be subject to critical scrutiny of other analysts and decision-makers.
>
> (V. Ostrom 1973b)

In this respect it is worth mentioning that the principles of a democratic society are radically different from those of autocratic or oligarchic societies. In the latter cases, a single "sovereign" – an individual or a group – conducts a political experiment whose subjects are the rest of the members of society. In the case of a democracy, the things are different as the people themselves are supposed to set the conditions of government, and are both de facto and de jure artisans conducting and monitoring the experiment through time. Society has to cope with uncertainties and experiment with ways of dealing with it. Success depends on the intelligence and the efforts of those involved in the design and implementation of the experiments. That is why citizens in a democratic society "require a critical awareness of what they do in the discharge of their constitutional prerogatives as persons and citizens" and in "monitoring, and holding agents, who act on their behalf, accountable to a proper discharge of their public trusts in the conduct of public affairs" (V. Ostrom 1991b, 23).

This way of framing the problem of the "threat of ignorance" brings to the fore another facet of institutions and another insight into the nature of institutional and political order. If a society accepts that all decision makers are fallible, then it recognizes the need to create institutional bulwarks against error. That is to say, the necessity to try to reduce error proneness by building "error-correcting procedures in the organization of decision-making processes" (V. Ostrom 1982a, 32; 1973; 1990b). These error-correcting procedures are nothing else than organizational and institutional processes aimed at facilitating and speeding up the rate of learning. Learning is the quintessence of error-fighting mechanisms. Correcting errors is part of a learning process. In this respect, systems of organization, including systems of government, can be viewed as arrangements that either facilitate or stifle opportunities for learning to occur. The question is what kind of institutional and decision-making arrangements facilitate error-correction? Do those arrangements involve a dispersion of authority or a centralization of authority? Is the institutional system creating "opportunities for critical scrutiny and review and facilitates the pursuit of error-correcting strategies"? What kind of institutional and political arrangements "facilitate concurrent deliberation and action in response to diverse environmental conditions and to diverse communities of 'interest'"? (V. Ostrom 1982a, 31–32; 1973b). What could one learn from the comparison between systems, such as the American political system with its fragmentation of authority and overlapping jurisdictions, and the USSR system based on totally different principles, in terms of the structural conditions that facilitate the error-correction processes? How is the belief that when one becomes a top decision maker, one gets into a position to "see" the "whole picture" or how is the belief that long-term comprehensive planning is desirable and feasible, affecting the way institutional arrangements are structured and are functioning? These are some of the questions that emerge naturally and re-shape the agenda once the "threat of ignorance" is added to the other "threats" as drivers of institutional analysis.

In conclusion, the overview of the "threats" illustrates the tenuous and volatile nature of social order as an extension of the human condition "plagued by critical tensions" (V. Ostrom 1982a, 33; 1973b). The human capability for learning poses a "threat of chaos." The solution to that threat implies a "Faustian bargain" in which human beings are required to "use instruments of evil to advance their joint good." The threat of chaos and the creation of order from chaos, in turn, pose a "threat of tyranny" while in parallel the amplification of human capabilities for learning necessarily increase the "threat of uncertainty." These threats are compounded by a "threat of increasing relative ignorance" that accompanies modern efforts to stimulate the growth of new knowledge. To sum up, once the crucial tension between learning and constraints, ideas and rules is projected as a background, and once the complexity and diversity of the attempts of human beings to organize and find solutions to unavoidable threats generated by the very human condition are considered, a deeper perspective on the institutional and political order is opened.

Institutions as knowledge and decision processes

The mere shift of emphasis to learning, knowledge and ideas as main drivers of social order and social change puts in a new light the way institutions and institutional analysis are understood. One of the first outcomes is a renewed perspective on institutional diversity. The many functions institutions have, in order to meet the multitude of challenges they are supposed to be a response to, create institutional patterns that defy the standard conceptualizations. Only a cursory look at the variety and complexity of institutional solutions emerging as a response to the "threat of tyranny" or to the "threat of uncertainty" reveals in what measure a mere shift of accent could render the standard conceptualizations obsolete or irrelevant.

The real dimensions of the paradigmatic differences are fully revealed when the problem of knowledge gets to be considered and integrated in institutional theory. When institutions are seen primarily in the light of knowledge and decision processes, a fresh perspective is opened. Seen from this perspective, social order consists of organizational arrangements that "can be thought of as nothing more or less than decision-making arrangements" (V. Ostrom 1973a, 3). To elaborate on this observation, Vincent Ostrom builds on M. Polanyi's work and on the Hayekian problem of the uses of knowledge in society and combines that with a functionalist–decision-making oriented perspective. Individuals need to "draw upon the knowledge and skills of others as a complement to the limits that prevail in the competence of each individual." The tacit understanding that "accrues from the skills of citizenship associated with the practical experiences of dealing with particular exigencies applicable to the world of events in discrete settings," requires institutional solutions (V. Ostrom 1982a; 1990a; 1991b). Human beings depend upon the knowledge and skills of others, however imperfect these may be. The existence of societies, then, depends on an institutional system able to put together as effective as possible the pieces of relevant individual or local knowledge. The institutions of the market generating a price system reflecting all kinds of existing information about individual preferences are only one example of such a system. As a parenthesis, Ostrom noted that, in fact, if the public – private dichotomy that underlies the market–state dichotomy is circumvented, then one may realize that competitive markets are important "public" institutions "in generating common knowledge about prices as a measure of value, informative to any entrepreneur who may seek to take advantage of opportunities that are available" and as such for "establishing conditions of individual rationality" (V. Ostrom 1997a, 107).

If one looks at collective decision procedures, voting and other social choice mechanisms, one realizes the pivotal role of institutional arrangements for preferences and information aggregation and that the diversity of such mechanisms is very large and deserves to be studied as such. Each mechanism has its own strengths and limits: "finer degrees of distinction about what is preferred among the permissible options" are determined by the "particular institutional arrangements that enable human beings to communicate their preferences to one another" (V. Ostrom 1986a, 241). Information, knowledge, communication and coordination are some of the building blocks of the emerging vision of social order:

> Prices in a market economy provide signaling mechanisms to allow people to express their preferences for the array of options that are available in the very large realm of possibilities that meet the criterion of being "goods". Similarly, elections enable people to communicate some order of preferences in the taking of collective decisions about goods and services to be provided in the

public sectors. Debate in parliamentary proceedings, discussions in public fora and in the press, protest meetings, and many other institutional arrangements enable people to inform one another about their preferences and aversions and take one another into account under circumstances where no one need have fear of others, and where each acts in relation to general rules of conduct that take account of the interests of others.

(V. Ostrom 1986a, 241)

In a word, in an interesting twist, what is usually relegated to the status of an assumption or a second tier variable in mainstream theories – as illustrated by notions such as "common knowledge assumption" or "full information" – tends to assume a central position in this version of institutional theory. The common sense view that "communities depend critically upon communication" and that decision making works "tolerably well when people can keep one another reasonably well informed about their intentions and the way they relate to one another" becomes a key principle of institutional analysis (V. Ostrom 1986a, 242). Information and knowledge are building blocks of social order. Institutions have a function for "the elucidation and transmission of information so that human beings can constructively take account of one another's interests as they interact with each other" (V. Ostrom [1980] in McGinnis 1999a, 381). That doesn't mean that the standard problems are neglected in the new approach. On the contrary, problems such as the problem of common knowledge and asymmetries related to the generation and use of knowledge and information gain new and richer dimensions and an added empirical relevance (V. Ostrom 1997a, 107).

By using knowledge and the processes associated with it (such as learning and communication) as major principles for his social philosophy, Vincent Ostrom's approach entails in fact an interesting move on two fronts. The first was to conceptualize institutions in general in the light of the framework that is usually used to analyze markets. In other words, to extend the view of markets as knowledge processes (information producing systems) to other institutions. In this respect he was very clear that he was dissenting from the "Anglo-American economic theory that emphasizes the equilibrating features of competitive market economies" and was embracing "the Austrian economists that emphasize the information-generating features of institutions and the role of entrepreneurship, innovation and advances in knowledge and technologies." This move opened up not only the possibility to investigate institutions using information economics and market process theory (Austrian economics) but also was consistent with the notion of circumventing the analytical stereotypes and conceptual rigidities that plagued the mainstream approach (V. Ostrom 1997a, 107).

The second was to make the reverse move. To see markets in the light of the framework that is usually applied to other institutions. Instead of conceptualizing markets in broad abstract formulas, to define them in ways not radically different from the ways other institutional arrangements are seen. Markets are not only processes of knowledge and information but also systems of rules streamlining decision making, as any other institutional structure. Markets are one form of institutional arrangements among others, a special type of institutional configuration or aggregates of institutional structures. Studying markets is also a study of rules and their consequences. Understanding the operation of a specific market means understanding the institutionalization of rules in various arrangements related to factors such as the nature of goods, the extent and nature of the exchange system covered, the nature of market participants, etc.

Together these two specific analytical moves put the institutional analysts in the position not only to assert the diversity and complexity of institutional structures but also to make concrete steps toward crossing the "great divide" while formulating coherent and unitary modes of analysis. Yet, that unity is not a positivistic "unity of science" or "consilience"-inspired construct. It is an approach that pivots around human interactions within an environment that is created and continuously changed by human decisions and ideas, using words and rules as the main building blocks, and that implies at least a change of emphasis, if not a change of approach, in the way one is doing social research.

Artisanship and artifact

One of the most significant implications of all of the above is an increased awareness of the limits of applying the methods of the natural sciences to the study of social organization. Social organizations are not to be studied as "natural" entities, the way natural scientists study their topics. Instead, we should look at institutions as works of art or as artifacts and "understanding works of art or artifacts may require somewhat different perspectives than understanding natural phenomena" (V. Ostrom [1980] in McGinnis 1999a, 377–379). Two concepts are thus emerging as central in the architecture of this new vision: artisanship and artifact.

Vincent Ostrom defines an artifact as "anything created by human beings with reference to the use of learning and knowledge to serve human purposes." He also notes that "the task and processes involved in the creation of an artifact" are defined as artisanship. Artisans create artifacts and indeed, organizations and institutions could be seen as artifacts (V. Ostrom [1980] in McGinnis 1999a, 378–379). This view subtly, but profoundly, challenges the way one sees the relation between theory and practice, between ideas and action. Vincent Ostrom uses the analogy between manufacturing a pot and creating an organization to illuminate not only this view but also its implications. Materials and knowledge contribute to the artisanship of a potter. But an artisan does much more than to mix ingredients and transform them from one state to another.

> In shaping a pot, a potter has a conception in mind about the purpose to be served by a pot, a feel for his materials, and a sense of proportion about what constitutes a good pot. These considerations are built into the pot just as much as the material ingredients that are used. The knowledge, purpose, skill, and sense of proportion that are drawn upon by an artisan affect the way that he or she shapes and transforms the materials.
>
> (V. Ostrom [1980] in McGinnis 1999a, 378)

In the end an artifact is more than a combination of the material and technical knowledge. Something that might be called as "value" elements – i.e. "artisan's preference, standards, and sense of proportion are also involved and become an integral part of the pot. Both constitutively and epistemologically, ideas and values are part of an artifact. This relationship is defining all artisanship and all artifacts. Artisanship involves both facts – (the material side) and ideas (knowledge and values). Both become integral parts of any artifact; an artifact is a union of both. Artisanship is never a value-free or idea-free endeavor and artifacts are never idea free or value-free (V. Ostrom [1980] in McGinnis 1999a, 387).

The fact that artifacts contain ideas of artisans, or as Vincent Ostrom puts it "an artisan imparts elements of intelligibility to an artifact as he conceptualizes, shapes, and fashions it," has clear implications for the way we understand and study artifacts. "Each person can draw upon his own intelligibility to comprehend the purpose and meaning of the artisan who created an artifact" (V. Ostrom [1980] in McGinnis 1999a, 379). In other words, if the institutional world is artifactual, the place of analytical insertion into it, the first step in institutional analysis, and the main vehicle in doing that, are the ideas of the artisans of those institutions and of those that live within their rules.

> When organizations are viewed as natural phenomena, we are likely to neglect the role of artisanship in their development and use. The problem is what conceptions inform the design? Without knowing those conceptions, we are in the position of observing an experiment without knowing what conceptions informed its design. Theory and practice are intimately associated, both in the creation and use of artifacts and in the study of artifacts. The theory used by artisans in creating an artifact is an element in its creation. Scholars need first to learn the theory that informs artisanship before they can contribute to new potentialities of artisanship.
>
> (V. Ostrom [1980] in McGinnis 1999a, 389)

The analogy between pottery and organization building has undoubtedly clear limits. There are some common principles at work but there are also significant differences: "conceptualizing and designing a unit of government to function in a more general system of government is vastly different than designing a building." Organizations as artifacts have special features that distinguish them from other types of artifacts. Identifying some of the most important is a step further in building a theoretical understanding of institutions and political order. Organizations are artifacts that contain their own artisans, or as in Hobbes's words, human beings are both the "matter" and the "artificers" of organizations (Hobbes 1960, 5). Individual human beings are the designers and creators of organizations while at the same time are their key elements: organizations are "works of art in which human beings function both as their designers and creators, and as their principal ingredient." That by itself is an implicit restatement of a methodological individualist position. However, the accent is not purely on rationality as in the standard approach but on a more complex view of human nature where learning, innovation and choice are crucial (V. Ostrom [1980] in McGinnis 1999a, 381). Each individual imagines and assesses the consequences that can be expected to flow from specific courses of action. In addition, each individual has a capability to construe and weigh alternative possibilities. This means that human beings do rarely act as perfectly predictable automata (V. Ostrom [1980] in McGinnis 1999a, 381). And this also means that an ongoing internal dynamics, ongoing change and not stasis or equilibrium is the norm in organizations and institutions.

The second special feature of organizations seen as artifacts is that organizations are the result of *joint* artisanship. In some cases social order may depend on one blueprint shared by all and in other cases it may depend on the aggregate results of ideas and decisions of many. But, in all these cases there is an element of "jointness" involved. However, a special attention should be given to situations in which there is no single dominant artisan, idea, or design but many (V. Ostrom [1980] in McGinnis 1999a, 381). This creates individual and aggregate level tensions and raises very sensitive questions related to the nature and domain of "spontaneous order." Design and ideas imply the notion of planning – the uses of knowledge and information in order to organize future actions. The very implication of planning introduces potential tensions between the focus on ideas and design and an intellectual tradition that is profoundly interwoven in the Bloomington School's vision and theory, the spontaneous order tradition, as illustrated by Friedrich von Hayek's use of the concept of "spontaneity" (1973, 36–54), or Adam Smith's concept of the "hidden hand." The challenge is double:

> Are such terms to be applied to relationships viewed as "brute facts" or as "institutional facts" that reflect self-organizing and self-governing capabilities among knowledgeable and intelligible human beings? Can "hidden hands" be expected to work spontaneously in the constitution of order in human societies viewed as systems of natural order –"brute facts"? If Hayek's spontaneity and Smith's hidden hand depend on the intelligent use of the arts and sciences of association among the members of societies, we in the Public-Choice tradition bear a substantial burden in elucidating and making use of the sciences and arts of association.
>
> (V. Ostrom 1997a, 98)

One crucial element of the challenge is to decide in what measure the spontaneous order phenomena should be treated as artifacts, and in what measure the ideas of the actors that are the main artisans of these phenomena are relevant for their study. Design and ideas are part of intellectual order. Yet the problem is complicated by the fact that in conditions of uncertainty it is impossible to match individual intentions with aggregate outcomes. There are many instances in which intentions and outcomes diverge substantially. Consequently, there are two possibilities: on the one hand, it is possible that in specific circumstances the actions of social actors "generate results that are contrary to the motives of the individuals who are involved" and in many cases "this discrepancy between individual motives and organizational results may assume pathological proportions associated with institutional weakness or institutional failure." On the other hand, it is possible to have situations "where the discrepancies between individual motives and organizational results yield beneficial consequences." A competitive market is an example of this dynamic and the spontaneous order tradition emphasizes precisely these unintended aggregated aspects (V. Ostrom 1997a, 98–99).

This might be seen by some as a proof that a spontaneous order approach might in the end be able to neglect the role of ideas and design in human action. However, a more constructive interpretation is to see it as drawing attention on how important is to incorporate into the ideas and design principles used, the lessons learnt, from analyzing and understanding spontaneous order, and the discrepancies between intentions and aggregate level results. This is precisely the kind of "institutional design" suggested by Hayek's *Constitution of Liberty* that incorporates explicitly an understanding of these phenomena. And, that is precisely Adam Smiths' lesson about the free market and the conditions that determine its functioning. One may even say that there are two types of institutional design principles: principles that take into account spontaneous order phenomena and principles that do not take them into account. If that is the case, then the Bloomington School's effort should indeed be seen as an extension and contribution to the spontaneous order tradition: a contribution to the development of a framework for integrating in institutional design the spontaneous order phenomena.

As second crucial aspect, reemphasized by the discussion of the spontaneous order with its emphasis on individual and micro level decisions, is that ideas are present in any political and social process. Ideas apply not only to grand politics – constitutions, major reforms, national security policies, etc. – but also to daily situations. Examples abound: people in all walks of life have designs for dealing with their problems and institutional arrangements; they are able to coordinate, communicate and think solutions. The common-pool resources research shows that rural people or people in traditional communities are able to create resilient and effective arrangements based on ideas, learning, imagination and deliberation. It is inaccurate to say that design principles apply only to a small minority of institutions and organizations. In fact, they apply to a very large number of social arrangements. The view that only for some institutions could the ideas of their artisans be relevant for their understanding smacks of misplaced elitism. Definitely not all institutional aspects could be analyzed through this ideas-centered frame. Yet, it is false to say that the frame applies only to modern, sophisticated humans and great leaders and visionaries.

People usually do not act as machines, are not slaves of traditions, customs or incentives. People in all paths of life are able to organize and test ideas on social order and to structure their interactions accordingly. The notion that "that the mastery of ideas is required only for leaders or administrators" has not only theoretical and methodological implications but also a very clear normative dimension. In a democratic society, writes Vincent Ostrom, "the knowledge appropriate to the analysis and design of organizations is not privy to scholars or administrators alone." Knowledge "appropriate to organizational analysis and design is part of the public knowledge shared with citizens in a democratic society." Artisanship in organizational analysis and design in a democratic society should draw upon the same theory that informs citizenship (V. Ostrom [1980] in McGinnis 1999a; 1982). In other words, at least theoretically, in a democracy, ideas about the institutions and the understanding of the institutional processes are more salient than in any other system. Democracy is the system whose design is explicitly meant to accommodate the dynamics of multiple and competing ideas on an ongoing basis.

To sum up, irrespective of the nature of the system of order humans create, ideas both reflect and shape the institutional order. We should not expect the institutional order to be created and maintained by "muddling through devoid of knowledge, and intelligibility." One "cannot make bread or bricks without careful attention to appropriate conditions . . . No experiment ever conducts itself." "No product ever produces itself" (V. Ostrom 1997a, 8). To build social order "human beings have relied upon the weak thread of words." Therefore, "we need to give especially close attention to what it means to use words and ideas as the basic element that binds societies together" (V. Ostrom 1973b, 34). While identifying the work of the Bloomington scholars with the Toquevillian tradition of the "science of association," the practice of which is an "art of association," Vincent Ostrom is circumscribing in a new way the traditional notion that ideas or "design concepts" regarding the social order are the basic elements of that order. By underlying the fact that everything we attempt to do in the realm of institutions requires "knowledge and intelligibility," and by exploring the relationship between ideas as "design concepts," he identified and rearticulated a crucial research area: the analysis of "the relationship of ideas to deeds and the notion of systems of governance from reflection and choice." This brings to full limelight the issue of selection and adoption of ideas. With it, what may be called the problem of "epistemic choice" comes thus to the fore.

4   Ideas, language and meaning

An unorthodox approach to institutional order and institutional analysis

We have seen in Chapter 3 how, in the light of the social philosophy that Vincent Ostrom tried to elaborate as a basis for the Bloomington research program, ideas, language and learning processes are critical elements in understanding the institutional order. His argument that the ideas, beliefs, values and institutional designs of social actors should be at the forefront of social science investigations was in the 1960s, when he started to articulate it, both outdated and premature. Outdated, because in a context dominated by the behavioral and positivist revolutions it sounded as an echo of a previous stage in the evolution of social sciences. Premature, because it preceded by decades the new interest in cognition and belief systems that became a mark of many social science research programs in the 1990s. Yet, old-fashioned or premature, the attention given to the role of ideas gives the Bloomington programs a special, distinctive flavor. This chapter will further explore the distinctiveness of the social philosophy and social theory behind the Bloomington School of Institutional Theory by focusing on this specific notion that ideas represent both the ontological and epistemological keys of social order, a notion that even within the School itself has yet to be fully developed to its real theoretical, methodological and operational potential.

Institutional facts, ideas and social ontology

As Vincent Ostrom noted, when he started to explore the problem of ideas in social sciences, treating ideas as "pictures which concealed the reality of politics" was increasingly becoming "the operational mode of social scientists." Even outside the Marxist school ideas were labeled "ideologies" and reflections of "rationalizations" and "false consciousness" and as such were given only a negligible attention.

> Interests were presumed to dominate human activities. Awareness that the pursuit of interests in human societies turns both upon an architecture of authority relationships and the place of ideas (the use of theory) in the constitution of complex configurations of rule-ordered relationships in societies was increasingly lost. It was as though the play of the game of who gets what, when, and how in relation to whom so preoccupied attention that the conception, design, and conduct of great political experiments were lost . . . That the facts of human

activity might, in part, have been artifactual creations of the theory used to design a political system was neglected.

(V. Ostrom 1991b, 11)

Most of this way of thinking was due to the spell of positivism and to the mimetic application of modes of analysis copied from natural sciences. Those were trademarks of the "behavioral revolution" of the 1950s and 1960s. As V. Ostrom repeatedly noted, it was ultimately an issue of basic intuitions about the nature of reality. Despite the fact that the very ontology of the social sciences, "as distinguished from the 'reality' of the natural world, requires recourse to ideas, knowable regularities, and informed practices," social scientists tended to turn a blind eye to that. The assumption that "nature" and "human societies" are structurally similar for analytical purposes was informing the bulk of the work in political sciences inciting the authors to seriously look in their studies at anything but the ideas of social actors and their institutional expression. Yet, in the end all is about an observation of commonsensical simplicity: human beings "rely upon ideas and knowable regularities to create artifacts." Ideas, knowable regularities, and informed practices are part and parcel of political realities. It is hard even to conceive political order if you do not assume that people "create their own social realities by reference to some shared community of understanding (pictures in their minds) and live their lives within those realities as artifactual creations." If that was the case, then there was no doubt that the most serious mistake in the social sciences was to ignore the ontology of the social order, i.e. the role of "ideas, conjectures about regularities, and the careful use of informed practices that are constitutive of that reality" (V. Ostrom 1991b, 11).

Woodrow Wilson's (1956) classical contention that a "constitution in operation" is a very different thing from the "constitution of the books" was for Vincent Ostrom not only a clear illustration and symptom of the mode of thinking he was criticizing but also an indication of a turning point in the history of political thinking. That was the reason why Wilson's work was used persistently to illustrate the errors of the mainstream approach and to pinpoint the moment when the move towards dismissing and marginalizing the role of ideas gained strength. For Vincent Ostrom it was telling that this move took place couched as an interpretive challenge to one of the most unequivocal and elaborated attempts to base social order and government on explicit ideas and deliberation: the U.S. Constitution. For Wilson and his followers, "constitution in operation" referred to human conduct, and the "constitution of the books" to mere "words on paper." From here a distinction between the "façade" of political power and its "living reality" was just one step. Ideas and words are a veil: they are misleading. And thus the role of the theorist is to go beyond the words that obscure the "reality" and

> escape from theory and attach himself to facts, not allowing himself to be confused by a knowledge of what the government was intended to be, or led away into conjectures as to what it may one day become, but striving to catch its present phases and to photograph the delicate organism in all its characteristic parts exactly as it is today.

(Wilson 1956, 30)

Wilson assumed that the "facts" or the "living reality" will reveal themselves to well trained and careful observers who have freed themselves from theory and from the veil of words and ideology. In fact, as Vincent Ostrom noted in his powerful criticism, the approach was not really avoiding the recourse to ideas but just substituting personal theoretical conceptions while rejecting others and not even being aware of the substitution. It was ironic that in Wilson's case ideas were dismissed as irrelevant only to have them inserted "in the next breath" as a "totally unwarranted assumption": i.e. that "there is always a centre of power." From there to imply that the task of the political scientist was to determine "where is that centre?; in whose hands is self-sufficient authority lodged and through what agencies does that authority speak and act?" (Wilson 1956, 30) was just a small step with ruinous theoretical and practical consequences (V. Ostrom 1991b, 20–21; 1973a).

As V. Ostrom explains in his *The Intellectual Crisis in American Public Administration* (1973a) the Wilsonian analysis marked an important paradigm shift in American political science. The first dimension of that shift was in terms of understanding the U.S. political system. Wilson's assumption that there is always a single center of power in any political system was accepted as a basic postulate by many, and that gave them a distorted perspective on the U.S. political system. Due to it, their attention was concentrated on the central level. All other levels and forms of governance and association were neglected or considered marginal if they were not directly linked or associated with the "system of government" and its "center of power." Features that were considered of such salience and importance in Tocqueville's analysis were ignored. "The incommensurabilities between Tocqueville's portrayal of democracy in America and Wilson's portrayal were of radical proportions even though only fifty years intervened between those two presentations" (V. Ostrom 1973a, 20–23; 1991b).

The second shift was methodological, and it was a direct outcome of the marginalization of the role of ideas in political order. As such it was even more damaging. Once ideas were dismissed as ideologies, "superstructure" reflexes, or at best as a variable among others in the equation of political process, almost the entire energy of political scientists was channeled in a very restrictive direction. The distinction was lost between "institutional facts" and "natural" or "brute facts" or the intricate dynamics that takes place between ideas-rules-decisions-learning that drives social change. The effort to address the "living reality" by seeking to discover regularities in political and social phenomena became the core of a behavioral approach founded on the hope that generalizations based on regularities will sooner or later lead to a "positive theory." Treating ideas as "paper pictures," which concealed the reality of politics, also meant that a major preoccupation of social scientists was the development of methods to penetrate those pictures and dispersing them in order to understand the "living reality" behind them. In no way were ideas to be taken seriously. And because ideas were not taken seriously, institutional change by design was not seriously considered (V. Ostrom 1971, 10–11; 1991a; 1986b).

Addressing a research agenda that takes institutions and ideas seriously meant first of all an effort to reject the vision behind the Wilsonian mainstream approach of the 1950s and 1960s. As a matter of strategy, the Bloomington scholars did not find it difficult to identify real life examples contradicting the postulates or implications of that vision. However, this epistemological rationale was solidly rooted in the post positivist epistemology illustrated by John Searle's *Speech Acts* (1969), a work that represents a milestone in departure from positivism and as such was often quoted (V. Ostrom 1991b, 5–6). Once the spell of positivism was gone, the fundamental role of ideas in institutional order and institutional analysis reemerges as crucial. In his book, Searle elaborated the distinction between "institutional facts" and "brute facts." The epistemological implications of his argument for those whose creed in social sciences is to "go beyond the façade of ideas and language to the living reality" are devastating.

The point is that an understanding of the living reality in human societies cannot take place other than by an understanding of how rules are constitutive of social facts as "institutional facts." The game of American football was offered as a good example for distinguishing "institutional facts" from "brute facts." If American football were to be viewed by social scientists that are truly and accurately applying the positivist methodological recipe, they might discover the "law of periodic clustering":

> [A]t statistically regular intervals, organisms in like colored shirts cluster together in a roughly circular fashion (the huddle). Furthermore, at equally regular intervals, circular clustering is followed by linear clustering (the teams line up for the play) and linear clustering is followed by the phenomenon of linear interpenetration.
>
> (Searle 1969, 52)

It is hard to say that the discovery of the law of periodic clustering advances in any way the understanding of the phenomenon represented by the game of American football. Searle argues that football, as all other social phenomena, is an institutional fact and that "social realities are constituted, not by brute facts, but as institutional facts." Understanding the way that the rules of the game constitute and shape the structure and the play of the game is a prerequisite of any meaningful explanation or analysis. The phenomena lack any intelligibility outside a good grasp of the rules of the game.

Vincent Ostrom used Searle's argument to make the point that the observed "facts" do not speak for themselves and that they are in some sense "artifacts." This was a vigorous way to reinforce his own argument that what goes on in a society "requires a shared community of understanding about rule-ordered relationships among the members of that society." The student of that society should be as well steeped into that shared understanding of rules as any member of that society. The rules of the game are the keys to opening an understanding of the intentions, and choices of the players. The rules of the game are deeply embedded in complex contingencies of intentions, conceptions, calculations, choices, strategies and activities that operate at diverse levels. The "institutional facts" that are observed on the football field represent a complex array of decisions having recourse to intentions, conceptions, rules, calculations, choices, strategies, penalties and activities. The "artifactual" character of "institutional facts," thus, represents some union of ideas, knowledgeable calculations, and evaluative judgments (V. Ostrom 1991b, 6).

The implications of these conclusions for social research are considerable. Because rules could be seen as "linguistic entities that give expression to the way that concepts (ideas, mental pictures) are related to the ordering of human relationships in associations, organizations, and collectivities," a sustained focus on rules brings with it a necessary focus on the problem of language and ideas. A social science that is based on an epistemology that tries to understand those associations, collectivities and organizations without making recourse to ideas seems doomed to failure by definition. Only because so many social scientists' research is focused on their own societies, in circumstances when they have instant access with no special effort to the understanding of institutional facts, may explain the lack of awareness of how important the understanding of rules is as a prerequisite for any social analysis. Nonetheless, this lack of awareness is still puzzling because it is rarely, if ever, that the doctrine of pure observation is followed in practice by those societies.

Searle's distinction between "institutional facts" and "brute facts" restores, on solid epistemological grounds, the role of ideas in social science and explains why even positivists have to rely on the understanding of rules, common knowledge and language. But the restoration of the institutional fact brings with it a real theoretical challenge. Accepting that challenge means a research agenda that has to deal with more rather than less complexity. Taking ideas seriously means a renewed focus on the fundamental issue of choice. The very notion of choice based on ideas and the construction of options and deliberation as opposed to behaviorist or algorithmic rational choice requires an additional methodological and analytical dimension. If the conceptual universe is defined as deterministic, choice is a mechanical and algorithmic process and as such does not complicate issues. However, once choice is accepted as an ontological fact, as a process based on constructing possibilities and imagination, things get complicated.

> Human artisanship always occurs within realms of choice: choices about ideas, knowable regularities, informed practices that apply to economic endeavors, to authority relationships, and to competing conjectures in the realm of ideas pertaining to a theory of knowledge. These exercises of choices are constitutive of the artifactual realms created by human artisanship. How the diverse *realms of ideas* pertain to the diverse *realms of choice* and what gets created by *human artisanship* is, unfortunately, of mind-boggling proportions if viewed as totalities. Infinitely complex and detailed pictures in our minds exceed the limits of human cognition. Relating ideas to choices and to intelligible artisanship may open a way to enlightenment only if appropriately focused upon problematical situations.
>
> (V. Ostrom 1991b, 19)

To understand choices one needs to understand ideas; but, to understand ideas one needs to look at the context or action/decision situation. The problems confronted in the specific situation constrain both the ways the situation is perceived and the way the solutions are defined. In other words, a focus on ideas is not a naïve or idealist recourse to superficial investigative techniques. Instead it is indeed a radical departure from the methodological presumption "that human beings can observe societies as a whole while escaping from theory, attaching themselves to facts, and not allowing themselves to be confused by a knowledge of what was intended to be" (V. Ostrom 1991b, 21). A focus on ideas is a focus on the *relation* between ideas and their setting or context. Ideas are illuminating and are illuminated by context. The configuration of factors surrounding an act illuminates and is illuminated by ideas. The very existence of the factors that frame and constrain action allow the development of regularities: "Choice always implies selection. When selection occurs under constraint, patterns can be expected to emerge" (V. Ostrom 1991b, 19).

In other words, most of the regularities that the scientist is so interested in identifying are what could be approached and analyzed as the result of the interplay between choice and constraints. But these regularities (and the theories that are built around them) are not the monopoly of the political or social scientist: "practical men concerned with public affairs are political theorists whether they like it or not." Lay people in their daily activities operate with a cognitive basis for accepting some assertions and rejecting others. "The presumptive grounds we use in determining the plausibility of political assertions is our theory about political relationships." All of us "use some form of political theory when thinking about political problems. We all use certain elemental terms and postulate relationships to think through complex problems" (V. Ostrom 1973b, 1–2).

Political science could thus be seen as an outgrowth of the practical activities of human beings engaged in associative and organizational endeavors. The difference between practical thinking and theoretical thinking is one of degree, not of nature. Both require an understanding of rules and choices and of the consequences of choices within specific natural or institutional settings. However, the difference is one of technique, systematic effort and specialization. Political scientists specialize as part of the division of labor in cumulating and providing specific knowledge about such problems related to rules and choice situations. But ultimately, be it based on science or common sense, any definition of a "problem" requires a model and a conceptual diagnostic tool in the sense that when one considers "some current state of affairs to be sick or pathological" that relies on "presumptive knowledge to identify or diagnose the causal conditions that give rise to those pathological consequences." Even more important, people rely on this presumptive knowledge to advance proposals or to formulate prescriptions about how to alter the conditions that had generated the basic pathology. If that is the case, then any political action is grounded in a more or less articulated "political theory." The theory provides "the basis for diagnosing problematical situations and for considering alternative courses of action" (V. Ostrom 1973b, 1–2). In other words, political actions could be seen as nothing less than testing grounds for ideas. This brings into the picture a notion usually related to scientific endeavors: the notion of experiment.

Ideas and experiments

An interest in the notion of experimentation and its relevance for social life is the logical completion of the argument that starts with the reconsideration of the role of ideas and their place in institutional theory. The conclusion of the chain of inferences is clear: political action and political institutions building is seen as a continuous series of experiments based on ideas articulated as institutional designs or strategies. Only when the notion of experimentation is considered are the real dimensions of the paradigmatic shift, suggested by the type of institutionalism advanced by Vincent Ostrom, fully perceived. Applying a political idea also means to follow and assess the practical consequences of that idea. The two concepts, ideas and experiments, are thus intrinsically connected. An experiment is an "artifactual creation" that tests a conjecture about hypothetical relationships. The experiment is informed by a conception (idea, conjecture) about what would be expected to occur. Each experiment is unique in its spatial and temporal circumstances but its power emerges out of the very capacity of the human mind to imagine possibilities, combinations, counterfactuals and scenarios. As Vincent Ostrom put it, "we use the symbols of language to specify elements and relationships in computational logics to inform our thinking as a partial substitute for and complement to mental imageries." The pictures in our minds are "composable, decomposable, and alterable. Imagination has creative potentials. Ideas, conceptions, pictures in our minds can be used to design artifactual creations" (V. Ostrom 1991b, 19). Once designed and implemented these creations become natural experiments.

The Bloomington scholars were not the first to note the link ideas–action–experiments. In this respect they followed into the steps of authors like John Dewey, who in his *Logics: The Theory of Inquiry* (1938, 508) noted that "every measure of policy is *logically* and *should be* treated actually, of the nature of an experiment." Thus they concurred in the notion that the ideas or knowledge inspiring policies and the expectations about practical consequences based on that knowledge "can be treated as hypotheses and acting on the basis of an hypothesis can serve as an experimental test if accompanied by discriminating observation of the consequences that follow from its adoption" (V. Ostrom 1991b, 3–4).

The institutional analysis scholars did not limit themselves at theorizing the notion. They applied it in a very concrete way, by focusing on tangible cases and situations. For example, when devising rules for grazing rights, people act on ideas and experiment with the consequences of those ideas implemented through rules and institutions. Also, when organizing the access to water rights, people experiment with ideas about the relation between rules and allocation. Moreover, when implementing a social policy, people experiment with ideas about the causal connection between rules and behavior. And the list of cases studied may continue (Kaminski 1989; Herzberg 1992; McGinnis and Ostrom 1996; Agrawal 1999; Oakerson 1999; Schlager and Ostrom, and Blomquist and Ostrom in McGinnis 1999a; Sproule-Jones 2002; Sabetti 2004; Sawyer *et al.* 2004; Gibson *et al.* 2005; Polski 2005; Aligica 2006; Hess and Ostrom 2006).

But the most glaring example in this respect was the American political experiment itself. Among the Indiana School scholars, Vincent Ostrom dedicated a lot of attention to the study of the "American experiment in constitutional choice" seen as a paradigmatic case. While the experimental nature of various institutional arrangements in history was just implicit and post factum, in the case of the U.S. an ex-ante experimental dimension existed and was explicitly announced. The founding fathers were well aware of the experimental nature of their political enterprise and made repeated allusions to that. In this respect Alexander Hamilton's question of "whether societies of men are really capable or not of establishing good government from reflection and choice or whether they are forever destined to depend for their political constitutions on accident and force" was pre-defining a great experiment and as such it become one of the mottos of the Indiana School (V. Ostrom 1991b, 3). In a similar vein, James Madison, in *Federalist* 39, referred to "that honorable determination which animates every votary of freedom, to rest all our political experiments on the capacity of mankind for self-government." For Hamilton, learning from the experimental method was the "best oracle of wisdom" while *Federalist* 37 concluded that, if the design of the U.S. Constitution was based upon erroneous concepts, those errors "will not be ascertained until an actual trial shall have pointed them out." Finally, besides the textual evidence, the testimonies of authors like Alexis de Tocqueville recognized the experimental nature of the American system and its radical magnitude. "In that land, he wrote, the great experiment of the attempt to construct society upon a new basis was to be made by civilized man" and it was there for the first time, that theories hitherto unknown, or deemed impracticable, were to exhibit a spectacle for which the world had not been prepared by the history of the past. *Democracy In America* can thus be viewed as an analysis, assessment and progress report of the nature of the American experiment to construct society upon a well specified institutional design (V. Ostrom 1991b, 5–6). And if we take Tocqueville seriously, "we would expect the explanations offered in *The Federalist* to be grounded in a theory used to conceptualize and formulate the document known as the U.S. Constitution" (V. Ostrom 1971, 4–5).

To cut a long story short, if experimentation might have a post hoc, more analytical or metaphorical rather than operational application to most institutional arrangements in history (and as such be considered more as a heuristic device than as a positive theory), understanding the link between ideas and institutional structures in the case of the U.S. presents a situation where the notion of experiment is more than an analytical device. In it, one has an exemplary case of a political experiment based on more than a clear conceptual structure but on an entire theoretical system. A comparable example could be the Soviet experiment. The Soviet system and the theory behind it offer a good comparative basis that allows us to understand something important about the experimental nature of political order. Even if in history societies may have evolved and organized without clear institutional blueprints, the more a society develops and encourages thinking about political order, and the more that thought takes the shape of a "political science" the more the experiment metaphor becomes appropriate for the institutional evolutions in that society. The comparison between these two grand political experiments based on different theoretical foundations and having different consequences is a good reminder of that. Accepting the very notion of experiment introduces an entire series of problems and questions: "What theories were used to design which experiments? Who were the experimenters? Were the experiments appropriately conducted? What is the duration of an experiment? What constitutes an appropriate test of an experiment?" These questions help to transform the analogy with scientific experiments into a powerful analytical and heuristic tool (V. Ostrom 1991b, 8).

There is an additional reason why the notion of experiment is a pivotal concept in framing the domain of political science. The idea of experimenting with real actors and the very existence of outlier cases, reminds of the importance of the ethical and normative dimensions. With that, questions about the basis for ethics and moral judgment in political science loom large. Value-free science or neutrality is not possible in assessing or designing institutional alternatives or social order, because sooner or later that means "to compare some set of rules or rule changes with other sets of rules with which people have had experience" and like it or not one has, sooner or latter, to do that by reference to criteria such as "justice and liberty." Seeing social order as a series of human beings engaged in experiments, continuously learning and adapting, requires "appropriately informed criteria" to assess those experiments. And that, by implication, requires a special intellectual effort in the direction of building criteria and a "method of normative inquiry." Different forms of experiments should be assessed, not only on a strict functional basis (as structures setting up specific patterns of choice and specific consequences), but also as normative phenomena. Assessment requires recourse to normative criteria. Whether those criteria and that method are based on a theory of moral sentiments or on the concept of utility is a separate issue (Ostrom 1982b; 1986a). The bottom line is that by its very nature, the "experiment" as a social fact and as a concept implies not only an analytic effort but also a normative one.

To say that that the normative element is not part of political science is to say that political science is unable to produce what is most needed from it: an assessment of success and failure. Failure in design and implementation are part of the experimental process. One may see experiments that fall short due to an obvious failure of design – such as USSR – are flawed from the inception. Also, one may see creeping, ongoing derailment of an experiment in the direction of unintended consequences. These are very interesting situations and they require an even clearer understanding of normative criteria and their applications. To identify the dynamics and the pathology of a complex and evolving system is a difficult task. The success of what initially looked as a good design could be undermined by perverse effects. In brief, employing the notion of experimentation in the social and political sciences is not only a logical completion of an approach emphasizing the role of ideas and institutional artisanship; but also, it introduces a series of useful insights and analogies while projecting the entire approach on a different level, where the normative and dynamics or processual dimensions are intertwined. Needless to say, that is increasing rather than simplifying the task of the institutional analyst.

Ideas and institutional levels

The arguments outlined so far have a noteworthy corollary. That is, in order to increase the chances of a society or a community to adapt, grow and prosper, one type of knowledge should be encouraged as much as possible: the knowledge of social rules and their consequences. The better understanding and knowledge the members of a community have about the relationship between rules and behavior, the better the society will be organized. Among others this insight turns the lights on the role that social and political scientists have in the division of labor of modern societies. That role is given precisely by the mission of transforming that knowledge into a science of central importance for institutional design. Thus ideas and learning are reentering the game in yet another way: as meta-level ideas about social order, ideas or knowledge about the very manner social order is constituted. Modern societies have created the conditions for the emergence of a *science of* "knowable regularities, skilled practices, and conjectures about how problematic situations might be conceptualized, structured, and transformed" that explores how "rule-structures may transform individual behavior either in a perverse or benign way" (V. Ostrom [1980] in McGinnis 1999a, 390). One could conjecture that the success or failure of modern societies increasingly depends on the knowledge of how these rule-structures transform human conduct, at different institutional levels.

> Artisans need access to ideas, knowable regularities, and informed practices that apply to the objects of their action, to the systems of order that affect the organization and conduct of actors, and to the bodies of knowledge and cognitive processes of what it means to think about and organize activities. Each endeavor, thus, references patterns of economic, political, and epistemic orderings. These are complexly nested with reference to one another. They function in the configurations of all endeavors that go on in human societies. If citizens are to govern, the demands for intelligible artisanship are substantial; all processes of artisanship turn upon cooperative experimentation among colleagues who presume themselves to be fallible, who can learn from one another, and who advance the frontiers of knowledge in extending what is possible.
>
> (V. Ostrom 1991b, 20)

The emerging grand picture is one in which societies are constituted by the simultaneous operation of several institutional levels, shaped by experiments inspired by various types of ideas. That gives a fresh meaning to the notion that social order consists of complex systems of knowledge processes.

The focus on the type of knowledge relevant to the constitutive and institutional choices and the recognition of diverse levels and dynamics of human interactions introduces the notion of different levels of analysis, a notion specific to the Bloomington School. The levels correspond to levels of decision making regarding specific institutional structures (E. Ostrom *et al.* 1994, 46; Crawford and Ostrom 1995; E. Ostrom 2005; 1982). Three key levels are identified (Kiser and Ostrom

1982): (1) Operational level, the level of day-to-day decisions made by the participants in any institutional setting; (2) Collective-choice level, the level determining the operational activities and results through specific, domain-focused institutional and organizational structures and operational rules, and (3) Constitutional-choice level, the level that defines the broad parameters of social action and social order creating the foundations for the institutional arrangements and the rules to be used in crafting the set of collective-choice rules that in turn affect the set of operational rules (E. Ostrom *et al.* 1994). For each level, specific formal and informal institutional and organizational arrangements emerge to facilitate the coordination and cooperation of actors. But the emergence of these settings is rarely a matter of pure accident or the result of deterministic forces. The way they are defined and constructed requires human intelligence, deliberation and artisanship (E. Ostrom 1998, 8).

The arrangements of each level are a response to the challenges and problems of each corresponding arena and require specific and articulated ideas about their organization, structure and functioning. One could see why ideas about the institutions and the understanding of the institutional processes become vital. Following closely the Institutional Analysis and Development framework, one could classify these ideas into three categories, corresponding to the three levels. First, the operational level ideas: ideas about the day-to-day decisions made by the social actors, ideas about social and technological processes, and about the most common rules and institutional arrangements of production and exchange. Second, the collective-choice level ideas: ideas about the parameters of the operational decision, ideas about the immediate institutions and rules encapsulating the operational activities. For instance, these are ideas about the specific rules to be used in changing operational rules, the nature of specific organizational arrangements, the procedures and acceptable parameters of institutional change and in general about the social technology governing the operational level. Finally, the constitutional-choice or constitutive level ideas: ideas that define the meta-level creating a broad conceptual and normative framework within which interactions and institutions are to develop. They are crucial in determining the legitimacy of actors and the rules to be used in crafting the set of collective-choice rules which, in turn, affect the set of operational rules. Constitutive or constitutional ideas are the ultimate framework, the code of operation as well as the source of meaning of a social system. By implication, ideas and the knowledge that informs constitutional designs and policies are a rather special and heterogeneous class. It is a potential problem to identify constitutional choice narrowly with processes of constitutional decision making in constitutional conventions, constitutional referenda and constitutional amendments. A constitution is simply a set of rules that apply to the conduct of government. Some of these rules may be articulated in a document called a constitution. But such rules may also be articulated in legislation, court decisions, administrative reorganization plans, collective bargaining contracts, or conventional understandings (V. Ostrom [1980] in McGinnis 1999a, 391–392).

Although the boundaries between these levels are not always easy to draw, there is always a manifested difference between the constitutive level ideas and the operational level ideas as there is an obvious difference between constitutional choices and operational choices. Awareness of the role of different levels of analysis in the study of institutional arrangements is important both theoretically and practically as it "can reduce some relatively unproductive conflicts which occur when levels of analysis are confused." At the same time, the essential complementarities of different levels of analysis "can be an important source of stimulation in an interdisciplinary research concerned with guidance, control, and performance evaluation" (V. Ostrom 1986b).

Methodological implications: causality, rules and regularities in human affairs

An approach based on ideas and rules has several major implications: the first is that an emphasis on the "decisions–rules–consequences" sequence revamps a mode of thinking and doing social research that departs from the positivist recipe. The second is that this mode of thinking brings with it a more complex view of causality in social sciences. The two implications are obviously related. A focus on rules and institutions means that an important part of the social science enterprise is an attempt to specify the consequences that follow from different configurations of rules. This implies a specific view of causality in the social domain: "To assert that consequences follow from conditions is to say that effects have their causes" and the mark of a successful approach in social science is to be able "to indicate the conditions and consequences that derive from the choice of alternative organizational arrangements" (V. Ostrom 1973a, 2). Causality in social affairs operates differently from natural realm causality. The difference between social sciences and natural sciences is the distinction between "causal ordering" and "a quasi-causal ordering." In causal ordering "a cause impinges directly upon and determines an effect." On the other hand, a quasi-causal ordering depends on "the intervention of human actors who are capable of thinking, considering alternatives, choosing, and then acting." In other words, "one is determined; the other is constituted" (V. Ostrom 1973a, 2).

As it has already been discussed, the fact that a large part of social order is constituted by human actors' actions and decisions, and the understanding of the fact that the causality processes involved have a special nature, constitutes the epistemological basis of the social sciences methodology. The presence of actors and their cognitive and decision processes requires the social scientist to consider "how individuals view themselves, conceptualize their situation, and choose strategies in light of the opportunities available to them." The rule-ordered relationships that are constitutive of human organization function as soft constraints that are themselves subject to choice. In this view, analysis in the social sciences is built around strategic thinking in quasi-causal orders (V. Ostrom 1973a, 2).

As we have already seen, it is not a surprise that this approach to causality and its methodological implications ran in large measure against the mainstream of the day in social sciences, dominated as it was by the notion that the methods applicable to the natural sciences were also applicable mutatis mutandis to the social sciences.

That dominant idea, wrote Vincent Ostrom, was founded on an analogy. And in this case, using reasoning by analogy loses all that is specific to human social relationships. The fact is that there is a notable and undeniable specific difference between social and natural orders and the goal of social science is to capture precisely that difference. A social science inquiry "is focused upon the constitution of order in human societies and not upon the constitution of order in general" (V. Ostrom 1982b, 17–18; 1986a). This doesn't mean that a general meta-theory of order shaped on a natural sciences model is not possible. However, that theory will miss exactly the specific difference between the "social" and the "natural" forms of order.

The same problem could be approached from yet another, slightly different angle. The effort made by modern social scientists to ignore or to reduce to a mechanical understanding the place of rules in ordering human social relationships, despite the fact that each investigator had some level of awareness that his or her own life was pervasively organized with reference to rules, was no accident. A focus on rules would have opened a Pandora's Box of methodological and epistemological challenges. And that was the last thing somebody emulating the Newtonian model of science wanted. Yet, understanding the nature and function of rules is crucial for the task behind the social science enterprise. The very fact that social order means rules puts in a different light and, not a very flattering one, the effort "to discover regularities of a universal character that hold for all societies and through all time."

> Having denied the relevance of factors that give order to his own life, the social scientist has no basic foundation for beginning his inquiries. One point is as good as another for initiating the search for universal regularities in human social relationships.
>
> (V. Ostrom 1982b, 19)

The identification of regularities remains one of the critical tasks of social science but the nature of regularities to be identified emerges as the contentious point in a discussion of the epistemology and method of social sciences. What kind of regularities is social science looking for? What kinds of regularities are identified? If "some semblance of regularities are discovered in human social relationships," the question becomes whether these regularities are "grounded in universalities; or are they simply artifacts of some set of ordered relationships which have been created from a structure of rule-ordered relationships?" (V. Ostrom 1982b, 19). The overwhelming probability is that the regularity will be of the latter nature. But, separating the two is of crucial importance for social sciences both as a scientific enterprise and as a policy relevant effort. Yet irrespective of the kind of regularity one is looking for, there is only one way one could answer that question:

> to proceed on an assumption that social orders are artifactual in nature, that social relationships are value laden, and statements of a factual character about such relationships are not value-free. The social scientist would then be required to use his or her capabilities as a social scientist to come to a

sympathetic understanding of the basic criteria that inform normative distinctions in a society, how these criteria relate to one another and are taken into account in the choices that people make in a position to discover how the conception of basic values in a society informs choice, generates tensions, and biases social relationships in certain directions.

(V. Ostrom 1982b, 19)

This approach is equally valid if one is in search of universal regularities or of society (or context) specific ones. If one is looking for universal regularities, it ensures a method to identify them as universal patterns of response evoked from a similar human nature, by similar challenge: "human societies confront similar types of problems and difficulties in ordering social relationships and the particular way that resolutions are attained might then be compared for similarities and differences." Such a strategy of inquiry "would permit the recognition of patterns of regularity and variety in different systems of social order" and would also "permit generalizations to be made about underlying patterns that may reflect a basic similitude of thoughts and passions in human experience" (V. Ostrom 1982b, 20). On the other hand, one may look, by applying the same approach, for more specific patterns and regulation. The understanding of their emergence might in most cases be more relevant than broad generalizations, presumably leading to the discovery of "social laws." Also, the specific differences and their variety are especially relevant for policy purposes. The artifactual nature of various social arrangements could be ultimately traced back to human choices. Therefore "we would expect to find differently structured systems of social order to the degree that choice exists." In most cases one may "expect societies to reach different solutions, to the same problem" and that has important consequences for the level of generalization intended in the social scientific inquiry (V. Ostrom 1982b, 18–20).

Methodological implications: sympathetic understanding, motives, intentions

Irrespective of the level of generalization intended, identifying regularities should start by accepting the "possible plausibility" of the actors' conceptions, and only then to look at that more general pattern that might emerge without actors being aware. Social scientists, writes Vincent Ostrom (1982b, 21), should resist the temptation "to substitute their own conception of the nature of that order" without "giving plausibility to the conceptions used by those who shared in formulating the design for the constitution of particular order." The analysis will be always torn by the tension between fundamentally different conceptions. But the solution is not to assume that one of them is a priori the correct one:

It is entirely possible for persons participating in processes . . . to be in error and not to have given satisfactory consideration to grounds for the choices made. On the other hand, it is possible for social scientists to be at error in the formulations they advance.

(V. Ostrom 1982b, 21)

The significance of the fact that the social scientist should operate accepting the assumption of ignorance and fallibility could hardly be overstated. Only when the problem is singled out as such, does one realize how much of the social science enterprises are usually conducted with an attitude totally opposed to that spirit. Social scientists assume that they posses a knowledge, a technical virtuosity and a methodological insight that sets them far apart from the people they are studying. It is easy to defend this attitude in the name of scientific objectivity and discipline. However, once that attitude is relaxed, the notion that the subjects of social inquiry must be allowed to speak for themselves may come to be recognized as a fundamental prerequisite that springs not from a methodological blueprint but from a deep spirit of understanding the place of knowledge and ignorance in social research. This means that the conceptions, belief systems, and basic criteria for making normative distinctions must be sympathetically understood rather than being dismissed as myths or ideologies. The fruitfulness of this approach was demonstrated by Elinor Ostrom's empirical studies of the limits of prisoner dilemmas' models in real life common-pool resources management cases.

The thesis that "the method of sympathetically taking the perspective of others" should be accepted as a key element in social sciences is in a sense a restatement from a different perspective of a principle already introduced and discussed from different angles in this part of the book (V. Ostrom 1982b, 30). However, it is worth delving into a little more in the context of this discussion about methodology. The first requisite for social inquiry, argues Vincent Ostrom, is one of sympathy. The reason is that related to it is the assumption of the unity of humankind and of the unity of understanding. This is not in any way an innovation of the Indiana School. In fact, one is talking about the same basic method implicit in Hobbes's and Smith's work that relies on a proper consideration for the place that beliefs and passions have in human action and the role sympathy has as a vehicle to unearth them. Smith talked about the capacity of an individual to take on the perspective of another and potentially to function as an "impartial observer." And Hobbes's analysis functioned on the presumption that a "similitude of thoughts and passions" characterizes all mankind. Both of them noted that there is an underlying similitude that enables one person, to understand via introspection or self-understanding how others think and feel. Both implied that a "political science" is unconceivable other than under the assumption that this similitude exists and could be used as a vehicle in social research by scientists. It is not an accident that this specific aspect of social science was of special interest to Vincent Ostrom. In fact, that is the assumption behind the method of studying human artifacts. In studying them, he writes, the researcher has "to rely upon the presumption that human beings share a basic similitude of thoughts and passions." By taking the perspective of other researchers, "attempt to understand the basic structure and logic of their situation and infer the strategy that they are likely to pursue. This is essentially the strategy that is inherent in methodological individualism" (V. Ostrom [1980] in McGinnis 1999a, 381).

Advocating "the method of sympathetically taking the perspective of others" doesn't present it as an easy street for social and political theorizing or as the panacea of institutional analysis. On the contrary, his work reverberates with the uneasiness that comes with the keen awareness of the complexity and challenges of a mode of analysis focused on ideas. His was a clear understanding of the methodological problems that come up from adopting such a perspective. Besides the epistemological problems of interpersonal comparisons and inter-subjectivity, there are very concrete, technical aspects that needed to be dealt with.

For instance, the very task of "construing motives and ideas as operational elements of analytical process" needs to be dealt with. Could that be done without distortions? (V. Ostrom 1971, 13). Even if the ambiguities of language are overcome, there is still the problem of correctly identifying motives. There are errors, ambiguities, and reservations in the arguments and ideas advanced by one actor or another at one time or another. How is one supposed to deal with them? Moreover, deliberations have a life of their own and "it is entirely possible for individuals to modify their opinions in light of calculations that had not been taken into account and were clarified in the discussion." Besides that, there are the contradictions between positions taken by different actors. When looking at groups and communities one should remember that groupthink is a relatively rare phenomenon and that usually not all ideas are shared by all members. Finally, one should distinguish between different types of ideas. The concept of "idea" covers a very diverse class: beliefs, world views, values, motives, intentions, causal beliefs, operational codes etc. Each type of idea requires a different understanding and has different institutional implications (V. Ostrom 1971, 13–16). All of the above are just a sample showing that dealing with an ideas-centered approach is anything but straightforward and simple.

There is yet another set of problems. When one thinks of ideas as institutional design a potential trap is set up that introduces automatically the notion of motive or intention. And focusing on motives sets up another potential trap: the temptation to insist in identifying the "true" motives of those who are exposing an idea or another. The problem with that is once motives take center stage, there is a tendency for them to overshadow ideas:

> Ideas are then judged on the basis of motives attributed to authors rather than on the merit of the ideas themselves. Motives or intentions are assumed to drive human action without regard to beliefs about the way that conditions affect consequences. This runs the risk of being an *ad hominem* argument that diverts inquiry from fundamental issues . . . to what can be fruitless speculations about human motives.
>
> (V. Ostrom 1971, 13)

But the truth is that there is "no way to resolve issues that turn upon determining the true motivation and secret views of other human beings." This is a fundamental fact of social science: to get an understanding of social order and regularities one needs a relatively reliable understanding of human action, beliefs and intentions. However the task of doing that will always be uncertain, and as a result the social scientist has to operate with the consciousness of the limits and fallibility of his enterprise.

> I cannot deny that human action is purposive. Actions are motivated by thoughts and preferences that reflect both meaning and intentionality. My response is to advise caution in judging motives as grounds for construing the meaning of terms . . . The search for truth is much too difficult to presume that I can know the truth either in relation to other people's motives or opinions or in relation to the beliefs that I hold as a scholar.
>
> (V. Ostrom 1971, 15)

This entire attitude and approach is well illustrated in Vincent Ostrom's *The Political Theory of a Compound Republic* (1971). A central issue in the book is how to construe the passage in the opening paragraph of Federalist formulating the issue of "whether societies of men are really capable or not of establishing good government from reflection and choice, or whether they are forever destined to depend for their political constitutions on accident and force."

> I consider this issue to be of fundamental importance to political theory. This same passage can be lightly dismissed as meaningless rhetoric intended to deceive people by "pulling wool over our eyes." I know of no way to resolve such an issue other than to give other human beings the benefit of the doubt so that we can consider the merit of ideas for the implications that they yield. The issue posed by Hamilton has implications that are of epochal proportions for human civilization. I prefer to give credence to such a possibility; but to do so in an effort to understand the conditions that are logically necessary to realize such a possibility.
>
> (V. Ostrom 1971, 15)

Analytical strategies focused on ideas and motives are indeed very complicated. Motives and ideas are not easily distinguishable. Even more, ideas come in different forms, different levels, different functions, and different contexts. There is no algorithm or process that could match a specific idea to a specific method of dealing with it. Yet, at the bottom line, there is one simple, essential approach: trying to understand the idea, the logic of the argument that describes the institution or institutional design in point.

> In exploring the merit of ideas, the burden is upon me to take, first, a sympathetic attitude and attempt to understand the basic argument being advanced and to state that argument to the best of my ability rather than speculating about motives. It does no good in judging the merit of ideas to treat them as either propaganda or ideology. I happen to have a broad area of agreement with the arguments being advanced by Hamilton and Madison as I understand those arguments. If I were to expound Lenin's theory of constitutional choice, I would have the same obligation sympathetically to understand and articulate that argument even though I might have great doubts about the appropriateness of the logical inference in some aspects of the argument.
>
> (V. Ostrom 1971, 16)

The elusive foundations of social order: language and "The mystery of being"

The discussions in this chapter draw attention to the relevance of intangible and sometimes even unnoticed conditions or assumptions that shape both action and analysis in the institutional domain. Studying the institutional reality means discovering in human action, language, cognition and culture the springs of the institutional processes. Both the existence and functioning of institutions and the analytical framework meant to study them are based on language (V. Ostrom 1993b). Although it might sound obvious, writes Vincent Ostrom, the fact that the existence and survival of communities depends on language as well as the role language has in human cognition, communication and the emergence of human forms of organization, needs to be reminded, again and again, to social scientists. Language is the main tool of human artisanship. All social coordination and social organization goes through language. Teamwork requires coordinated actions through the use of language. Specialization and division of labor imply mutual understanding and, as such, a language to convey it. Furthermore, language ensures the transfer of knowledge and skills over the intergenerational cycle of life (V. Ostrom 1993b). In brief, "as an effort to introduce order into the structure of human relationships . . . human beings have relied upon the weak thread of words to build order into relationships with one another." That means that "if we are to understand the human condition and its potential, we need to give especially close attention to what it means to use words and ideas as the basic element that binds societies together (V. Ostrom 1993b).

The analysis of language as a foundational element of the institutional order could take many forms. One way would be simply to view language as a "thing" and ascertain its "nature" as a "good." Following the standard analysis of the nature of goods one could reveal some interesting and important aspects of the role a language plays in that respect. Thus, language could be seen as a public good: the use of a language does not subtract from its use by others and it is very difficult, almost impossible to exclude others from its use. Viewing language as a "thing" that has the characteristics of a pure public good is one way of recognizing the foundational and yet clearly definable role of language. Yet language has, besides this "functional" nature, a "constitutive" nature. It is not only a public good but an essential ingredient in the constitution of identities, social structures, patterns of association and communities, ways of life and in what gets done "in all aspects of the constitution of order in human societies" (V. Ostrom 1993b, 5–6).

Useful as it may be to employ "institutional analysis as a metalanguage to inquire about the problems of languages," any effort to deal with language as a "thing" or to abstractly analyze it is severing it from its context and misses exactly its constitutive facet. The language is intertwined with the culture, the way of life in a society, thus, having "structured continuities in which individuals come and go." That means that "diverse relationships are mediated by and bound together through language usages that permeate all aspects of life among intelligible beings" (V. Ostrom 1993b, 6–9). This relationship between individuals, languages, shared communities of understanding, and ways of life is often identified as the core elements in characterizing societies:

> The political artisan, or the designer of political institutions, is concerned with the use of language to order relationships among human beings. Human beings have a way of not staying in place like steel, concrete, bricks, mortar, boards, and nails that an architect has reference to in conceptualizing the design of a building. Words themselves do not have meanings except as human beings share communities of experience with one another in communicating through the use of words. We give meanings to words from the experience we share in communicating with one another.
>
> (V. Ostrom 1971, 70)

Language shapes conceptualization and the way reality is approached. Vincent Ostrom's criticism targets, as usually, those who try to imitate natural sciences. Aware of neither language's critical role in the architecture of human societies nor of how it operates as a factor of social change, they nevertheless insist in advancing agendas for institutional design or institutional change. Even harsher words are meant for those who having a natural sciences background, become advocates for specific policies:

> Distinguished physical scientists can proceed on a presupposition that putting mandatory language on paper will suffice to solve global problems with minimal awareness about what is required to make words in rule-ordered relationships binding in human conduct. It is as though words bind human conduct without reference to language, shared communities of understanding, and agency relationships pertaining to monitoring conduct, enforcing prescriptions with reference to diverse dimensions embedded in systems of authority relationships. A sorcery of words can easily be presumed to be sufficient to achieve fantasies about what ought to be.
>
> (V. Ostrom 1993b, 9)

Without understanding the science of association and the way language is functioning in generating rules, authority and coordination, the natural scientists masquerading as social scientists fall into a "sorcery of words." The "pollution" of the physical environment "is dwarfed by comparison to the potential for the pollution of the human mind created by these mistakes encouraged by their misplaced authority" (V. Ostrom, 1993b, 13).

There is yet another example of the relevance of intangible and sometimes unnoticed conditions or assumptions of the institutional order. Human beings have a propensity to achieve coherence in understanding the world. That means something more than having a set of more or less plausible causal explanations. It also means "efforts to relate microcosms of consciousness to cosmos" and an effort "to achieve intelligibility, meaning, and identity" (V. Ostrom 1993b, 6–9). Such efforts bring to light the problem of existential meaning and religion. The failure of social science to appreciate the role in human life and social order of belief systems in general and to derive out of that the analytical implications was translated as a failure to appreciate the role of a special set of beliefs, the religious beliefs. Social sciences operated for almost the entire twentieth century under the Weberian assumption of the increasing and unstoppable secularization of the modern society and the "disenchantment of the world."

That was, argued Vincent Ostrom, an analytical fiasco rooted into a deeper failure to appreciate "the place of the mystery of being as an ontological necessity." How could one speak of social order and human organization without taking that into account? Humans have beliefs. Some of those beliefs are of a deeper nature – beliefs regarding the nature of existence, the meaning of existence or "the mystery of being." People, besides being maximizing opportunists, are shaped by passions, cultural traditions, language. But they are also facing and trying to deal with the challenge of understanding the meaning of their existence. Not always, not all the time, not with similar intensity, but sooner or later each human being has moments in life when they confront that experience. The way they answer to that, the way they rationalize that or they avoid that, shapes the way they see themselves and their communities and consequently the way they act: "A deep awareness about the mystery in the mystery of being is an ontological necessity and a necessary epistemological contingency." The mystery materializes "in how we act and what we do in living and working with others" as well as one's understanding of what it means to participate in the larger order of Creation (V. Ostrom 1997a, 81–86).

The issue is confused by the dogmatism of the debates and the confusion is compounded both by "the opportunities for fantasies and free associations about such a mystery," and by "the dogmatism with which beliefs are held about the characteristics associated with that mystery or with which the existence of such a mystery of being is denied" (V. Ostrom 1997a, 179). However, irrespective of the concept used to define it (world views, metaphysical beliefs, religion) what shapes the way people think about themselves, their relationship with others, and the nature of their universe is an essential ingredient in shaping each society. To sum up, basic presuppositions about the transcendent character of order associated with the "mystery of being" are essential elements in constituting human societies (V. Ostrom 1997a, 187; Allen 2005).

It is not necessary to be a religious person to appreciate the importance of those beliefs. Whether a person believes in a transcendental order or not is not in question. Neither is demonstrating the existence or nonexistence of such an order. This is ultimately not a religious or philosophical problem. It is a factual one.

> My own presumptions about human fallibility and the propensity to err do not take one very far . . . Being a philosophical agnostic is no resolution to the problem of gnosticism as pertaining to faith. What I comprehend turns, then, on my efforts to use my intelligibility to construe what is being said about the mystery of being, which must, in some fundamental sense, be and remain a mystery. Yet I presume that there is a mystery that must of necessity be

accepted as a "reality" – an ontological necessity – and that such an ontological necessity is an epistemological contingency.

(V. Ostrom 1997a, 179, 197)

That is to say, we are dealing with a fact of human nature and of social life. There are belief systems or metaphysical presuppositions that cannot be proved but that in daily life provide the foundations for standards of judgment of actions and institutions. To argue this point, Vincent Ostrom illuminates the link or the path from religion to secular religions and ideologies. The starting point of his argument is that

> a manifestation of the mystery of being occurs as an essential feature among those who deny or repudiate the idea of religion. If religious presuppositions are ontological necessities and necessary epistemological conditions in the constitution of systems of knowledge in communities of being, we would expect those presuppositions to manifest themselves among those who explicitly reject a belief in religious presuppositions.

(V. Ostrom 1997a, 189–90)

By forgetting the challenge of the mystery of being to which religion is a response, we forget the importance and the need of meaning for human beings. The dynamics of the process is straightforward. In the absence of a way to deal with the "mystery of being," to escape the meaningless, to escape the isolation and helplessness of individuality, many may take refuge in slogans and ideologies. Humans need system of beliefs in order to be fully functional socially. If the need or the demand exists and if for some reasons traditional ways could not answer it, then we would "expect to *find prophets of new secular religions*" rising to meet or take advantage of that need. Secular religions are a test and demonstration of the need and ubiquity of foundational belief systems. And from here grows the very interesting problem of those systems of order that

> were constituted under circumstances of explicitly *rejecting* religion as a necessary feature in their constitution. We have the potential, then, of those who reject religion becoming the *prophets* of new *secular religions*. What we call "ideologies" may be the source of the most profound pathologies in human personal and social disorders.

(V. Ostrom 1997a, 190)

The power of these beliefs in history could hardly be overstated. As one of the major factors of social change, the magnitude of their impact in modern times was of epical proportions:

> The religious fervor associated with the French Revolution, Russian Revolution, Chinese Revolution, and numerous other "revolutionary" movements have become human tragedies. Can the cultural and social sciences afford to dismiss the realms of ideologies as fictions of the mind that have

little to do with political and social realities? If they do, are they neglecting "a grim, terrific force of nature, a newfangled monster, red of tooth and claw" to quote from Tocqueville, which is capable of "destroying political institutions," abolishing "civil institutions," and undermining "the social order." . . . Scholars who presume that ideologies are purely fictions of the mind see no essential connection between a theory of sovereignty and the forms of holocausts and genocide practiced by rulers pursuing fantasies of an idealistic character in relation to their own people.

(V. Ostrom 1997a, 192)

To further illustrate that argument, Vincent Ostrom is using Tocqueville's analysis of the historical role of religion in America, as an exemplary case study focused on the constitution of the American system: "Religion in America takes no direct part in the government of society, but it must be regarded as the first of their political institutions; for if it does not impart a taste for freedom, it facilitates the use of it." Tocqueville devotes a large effort the principal causes that tend to maintain democracy in the United States and while doing that he practically writes an essay on religion as a political institution. The essence of his argument is that "if the human mind be left to follow its own bent, it will regulate the temporal and spiritual institutions of society in a uniform manner, and man will endeavor, if I may so speak, to harmonize earth with heaven." That means that "by the side of every religion is to be found a political opinion, which is connected with it by affinity" (Tocqueville 1945 [1835]; V. Ostrom 1997a, 184–189; Allen 2005).

Human beings strive to deal with patterns of order in coherent ways. Presuppositions regarding a spiritual or transcendent order will be accompanied consciously or unconsciously by principles used to constitute and justify arrangements of political orders. Vincent Ostrom concurs:

If there is to be a political science, then the place that basic precepts about the mystery of being have in forming the foundation for conceptualizing systems of order also need to be included in efforts to understand and explain the constitution of order in human societies. Religion not only influences "the habits of the heart" as people relate to one another but "the habits of the mind" as people articulate their intelligibility in their use of knowledge in the constitution of order.

(V. Ostrom 1997a, 186)

The fact that belief systems or social phenomena that are usually associated with the notion of religion are "establishing standards of judgment not motivated by envy" but by "a faith grounded in precepts to honor God above all else, love thy neighbor as thyself, and do unto others as you would have others do unto you" is of no minor consequence for the institutional order and its analysis (V. Ostrom 1997a, 190). For instance there may be one important ingredient explaining why the theoretically predicted destructive logic of rational choice prisoners' dilemma or tragedy of the commons is not happening in reality in most cases. What is called "religion," is something that checks, balances and normatively encapsulates the actions of the individuals, creates premises for trust and association. It offers a rationale for "the give and take and the renunciations and sacrifices required by any social organization." As such, it is a critical ingredient in a complex system of checks and balances between self-seeking rationality and the altruistic concerns regarding other members of the community.

Framing the function of religion in this way may suggest some solution but it also brings with it a series of challenges. How important is the specific doctrine of a religion in this respect? It may well be the case that "the fruits borne by ontological presuppositions turn more on fundamental principles used in constituting ways of life than on the names of particular religious doctrines" (V. Ostrom 1997a, 196–197). But if that is the case, then, in this functional approach to religion, the question is, why should the *specific content* or doctrine a religion is espousing matter as long as the function it fulfills could be meet by any alternative doctrine? This raises yet another set of questions: Do the two dimensions of religion (substantial and functional) converge? Does that matter? Are there more "socially functional" religions than others? Is there a "religion" better suited for democratic self-governing systems than the other religions? If yes, is that religion the most functional by other political and institutional criteria? What is the relationship between the "mystery of being" and the "functional" dimension of religion? Can the functions of religion-type belief systems be substituted with other types of belief systems?

These are in no way theoretical or speculative questions. All of the above raise fundamental questions about the very enterprise of creating a "theory of institutions" and "a science of association." A science of institutions, or the science of association, cannot avoid the normative challenges and therefore it has to confront not only theoretically but also practically the problems of religion, ideology, values and meaning as associated to its identity and social function. Institutional theory or the science of institutions is a contribution to the belief system of a society. What is the relationship between belief systems and "a science of association" or a "theory of institutions"? Is there any overlap between their functional roles? Is, for instance, the notion of a "science of liberty" a too normatively loaded concept to deserve the name of science? Should it be considered an ideology? How is the role of a science of association, a theory of institutions different from the functional role of religion or religion-like belief systems? What is the relationship between a normatively loaded social science (such as "a science of liberty") and secular or standard types of religion? Is the project of a normative analysis or normative science a viable one? All of the above not only show how important the clarification of the normative element in institutional analysis is, thus validating Vincent Ostrom's preoccupation with "the method of normative inquiry," but also show how complex the task of building a theory of institutions, and together with it a "science of association," is.

Part III

The Bloomington School in its intellectual context

A family of themes and schools of thought

A review of the foundations of institutional theory as seen from the perspective of Vincent Ostrom's ideas, confronts the reader with a paradox. On the one hand, the ideas he exposes seem somehow unfashionable. In no way do they betray the feverish eagerness to be at the "cutting edge" of "recent advances in social thinking" displayed by so many others. Yet, on the other hand, these ideas have a refreshing flavor. They seem to bring to the picture something genuinely familiar and yet new. Or, to put it differently, while they keep a balance between the old and the latest styles of doing social science, they seem to point towards "new approaches and frontiers of knowledge." The key of the paradox is that the type of institutionalism that Vincent Ostrom's work inspired bears the mark of an intriguing intellectual experiment. It is an attempt to contribute to a "revolution" in social sciences. But one is talking about a "revolution" that requires a "restoration" – a return to and a revival of a tradition of social theorizing, of a mode of thinking that is coextensive with an influential current in Western intellectual and political history that runs from Hobbes to the Public Choice movement of the twentieth century. And thus, the Bloomington School has found itself in the middle of the major social science debates of the twentieth century and, at the same time, has tried to transcend them by presenting itself as a comment and an extension of a 500-year-old intellectual tradition. This part of the book will explore this captivating facet of the Bloomington School. The following chapters will provide an overview of the Bloomington program from the perspective of its intellectual context. In doing that, this part will illuminate several of its facets which otherwise may escape scrutiny and will offer the perspective needed for a correct interpretation of its place in the broader picture, including other schools of thought coexisting in its intellectual neighborhood.

5 Competing disciplines, methodological divides and emerging research agendas

The Bloomington School in its interdisciplinary setting

The earlier chapters internally explored the Bloomington School providing an in-depth overview of several of its foundational themes. This chapter adopts a different strategy. It explores the key elements of the School within the thematic and intellectual context that dominates the academic environment relevant for its evolution. Consequently, this chapter will shift the focus from the in-depth discussion of the arguments and views expressed by the key authors of the Bloomington School to a birds-eye-view of its intellectual setting. That is to say, it will use an indirect approach that employs as reference points a set of controversial themes in social sciences which help us put in clearer perspective the nature and relevance of the approach developed by the Bloomington scholars.

Polycentricity, spontaneous order, anarchy

We have seen how, in examining the decision rules within municipal governments, Vincent Ostrom (first in joint work with Tiebout and Warren and then on his own) developed the concept of polycentricity. In developing the notion of polycentricity, Vincent Ostrom combined two traditions: the tradition of spontaneous orders and the tradition of constitutionalism. "Polycentric connotes many centers of decision making that are formally independent of each other" and its organizational arrangements and performance are a function of rules of the game at the "constitutional level" (Ostrom *et al.* 1961). Following Polanyi, he emphasized the general system of rules "providing a framework for ordering relationships in a polycentric system." Whether governance can organize as a polycentric system, it is argued, will "depend upon whether various aspects of rule making and rule enforcing can create polycentric structures" (V. Ostrom [1972] in McGinnis 1999a, 58). Given all of the above, there is no doubt that the Indiana School should be seen in the larger context of preoccupations with the relation between spontaneous dynamics of social order, and rule-guided behavior and rule systems. M. Polanyi, F. A. Hayek and the Scottish Enlightenment tradition are undoubtedly its natural family.

The connection between the notion of spontaneous order and polycentrism has already been discussed in the earlier chapters. In fact, as shown already, there is a natural relation between the two. One can see in M. Polanyi's work the unequivocal bridge that unites them, as well as the lines of continuity between Hayek's work,

German ordoliberalism and the Indiana agenda. Given the Bloomington emphasis on the artefactual dimension of social order, the first reaction is to think of the potential tension between the two. But it is critical to recall that the notion of spontaneous order does not jettison purposeful action on the part of individual actors. In stark contrast, as the ordoliberals remind us, a spontaneous order is the outcome of purposeful, rule-guided behavior. At the highest level, it is clear that no central planner could purposefully design a complex system of polycentric governance to function in the way that it does in fact operate. The notion of spontaneous order is not intended to mean that a system arrives at some fixed equilibrium in the absence of purposeful human action. Rather, the main idea is that there are unintended consequences to purposeful human action. These unintended consequences play a significant role in constituting the overall order of the system. As a result, what is needed is a set of institutions that allows individuals to act purposefully and make adjustments to the unintended consequences of those actions.

One can envision the Bloomington School as operating in the broadly recognized "two kinds of order in society" theory. The first is what Hayek called "organization" – through actions that are consciously thought out and implemented. The second type of order is spontaneous in that it is independent of anyone's oversight or direction. It is critical to keep in mind that the claim being made is not that all complex phenomena must be spontaneous. Rather, the more complex the order, the more we will have to rely on spontaneous forces to generate that order. Given this dichotomy, one can see that polycentric systems of governance clearly display both types of order. But it is important to note that the very notion of spontaneous order expunges any notion of a static equilibrium and requires an emphasis on the mechanisms that allow individuals to deal with unique situations that arise. The emphasis on these mechanisms for dealing with unintended consequences pervades the Ostroms' work on polycentric systems of governance. Given the objectives and targets of their work they did not delve too much into these issues. Once the notion of polycentricity was clarified, they did not consider it necessary to go beyond this point. Yet, the nature of their position, and how it plays within the larger traditions of constitutional theory and spontaneous order theory (or as W. Ropke put it, in a unified "ordered anarchy" tradition), is unambiguous. This means that as a topic of research one must not only address the self-regulating of social order and social cooperation, but also the constitutional craftsmanship of self-restraint and binding rules.

When exploring the concept of social order via polycentrism, the Indiana School is placed in its intellectual milieu. However, there is yet another important tradition that deserves special attention because, willingly or not, the Indiana scholars have contributed to it in a very substantial way: the problem of "anarchy" or "social order without the state." Given the prima facie controversial nature of this statement, one has to be prepared to explain it. The rest of this section will be dedicated to this task.

Economic theory, since its first systemic treatment in Adam Smith's *An Inquiry into the Nature and Causes of the Wealth of Nations*, had established a presumption toward voluntarism in human interaction on consequentialist grounds. Individual liberty was not only right from a moral perspective, but would yield greater social benefits as well. However, from the beginning of economics it was argued that these benefits of voluntary exchange could only be realized if the presumption toward voluntarism was suspended in order to create the governmental institutions required to provide the framework within which voluntary exchange can be realized. Precisely how much the presumption toward voluntarism would need to be suspended in order to provide the framework for voluntary exchange has been one of the most contested issues since the late nineteenth century. The theory of public goods, monopoly and market failure all contributed to expanding the acceptance of coercion and qualifying the presumption toward voluntarism among mainstream economists. It is important to remember that each of these arguments for qualifying the presumption have been met with counter-arguments which have demonstrated that so-called public goods can actually be privately provided, monopoly is not a natural outgrowth of voluntary exchange but the result of government intervention, and that the root causes of market failures are themselves legal failures and not the consequence of unfettered exchange. Although a dominant line of research has pushed against the presumption of voluntarism, another line of research suggests that the presumption should be upheld more consistently if peaceful and prosperous social order is to be achieved. It is out of this thesis that the Indiana School has contributed to in a substantial way to the second, alternative line of research, even if, probably, the label under which we present it may not be considered the most fortunate by the Bloomington scholars. Our emphasis will be on what we'll call "positive analytical anarchism" and the evolutionary potential of these ideas as a progressive research program in political economy in the contemporary setting of social science. While not arguing that the Indiana scholars advance "anarchism," we think that our perspective and our understanding of the Bloomington research agenda gains an additional dimension if it is seen making an important contribution to this research program.

The idea that the voluntary presumption should be held in a consistent and unwavering manner has not been absent in political economy. It has, however, been consistently argued by the mainstream of political and economic thought to be an impractical ideal. In *Leviathan*, referenced repeatedly by the Bloomington School, Thomas Hobbes argued that the social order in the absence of an effective government would devolve into a war of all against all and life would be nasty, brutish and short. John Locke was not so pessimistic in his judgment of society without a state, but he argued that such a natural state would not be as effectively organized as a society governed justly would be. As we have already seen, Adam Smith argued that commerce and manufacturing could not flourish outside of a state of just government, and while David Hume argued that we should model all politicians as if they were knaves, he still insisted that an effective government was required to realize the system of "property, contract and consent." In histories of political and economic thought we often pass over the anarchist writers too quickly. There are, however, some good reasons for this. Anarchist writers have always been minority figures, and have often waxed lyrical about worlds of post-scarcity and populated by transformed human spirits. But, not every anarchist thinker in the history of political economy should be so easily dismissed. The historical anarchist discussion can be divided into three major categories: (1) Utopian – following in the tradition of William Godwin's *An Enquiry Concerning Political Justice* (1793). (2) Revolutionary – following in the tradition of Mikhail Bakunin and the First International, 1864–76. (3) Analytical – in the tradition of Murray Rothbard's *For a New Liberty* (1973) and David Friedman's *The Machinery of Freedom* (1973). Our purpose of discussion has to be limited to analytical anarchism. The reasons for this are straightforward. However historically important utopian and revolutionary anarchism may be, both traditions are decidedly devoid of social scientific content, whereas analytical anarchism is grounded in economic reasoning.

Thomas Carlyle described nineteenth-century *laissez faire* as "anarchism with a constable." Rothbard and Friedman were the first modern economists to ask whether the services of the constable needed to come from a monopoly provider. The challenge that Rothbard and Friedman represented to the mainstream of political philosophy and public economics did not attract the attention it deserved, but it was recognized by two major figures – Robert Nozick in political philosophy, and James Buchanan in public economics. Nozick (1974) argued, using the invisible-hand style of reasoning that is closely associated with the discipline of economics, starting in a world of anarchism one can derive a minimal state without violating the rights of individuals due to the natural monopoly character of law and order. Nozick, in a fundamental sense, harked back to Locke's argument and argued that civil society was possible absent the state, but that certain goods and services required for a more prosperous social order could only be provided by a monopoly supplier. Buchanan (1975), on the other hand, relied on social contract theory to escape from the anarchist state of nature and in so doing explicitly harked back to Hobbes's argument that in the absence of a sovereign the social order would be meager at best. The discussion of analytical anarchism in academic literature tailed off after Nozick and Buchanan.

Buchanan distinguished between the protective state, the productive state, and the redistributive state. The argument against Rothbard and Friedman made by Buchanan was intended to establish the necessity of the protective state (court system, and domestic and national security) and the desirability of the productive state (public goods such as roads and libraries). But, Buchanan warned of the expansion of the state via rent-seeking through the redistributive state. The puzzle in Buchanan's work moved from escaping from anarchism to effectively constructing constitutional-level constraints in government so that the protective and productive state could be established without unleashing the destructive rent-seeking tendencies of the redistributive state. How can a minimal state be kept in check and not evolve into a maximum state? Anarchism represents one side of the social dilemma, with Leviathan representing the other.

Researchers in the field of political economy have sought to provide an answer to the paradox of government as put by Buchanan and any approach to the Indiana School that misses this intellectual context, which is an important part of the significance of the School. The work of Barry Weingast (1995) on what he terms "market-preserving federalism" is an example of similar attempts that might be used for a comparative illustration. Weingast argues that the paradox of governance can be solved through a federalist structure where political authority is decentralized, economic regulation is limited to the local level, and competition between the different levels of government is ensured. In such a political structure, a common market, Weingast reasons, is cultivated, resulting in the expansion of the markets (and with that the corresponding division of labor). The political institutions of constitutional constraint and the organization of federalism, where the political ambition of some is pitted against the ambition of others through structural design, lead to the economic growth and development of nations. When this structure breaks down in times of crisis, market-preserving federalism collapses as the delineated authority is violated and economic regulation becomes centralized. The ties that bind the ruler's hands are broken, and the limits on government give way to an increase in both the scale and scope of government. State power, rather than restrained, is now unleashed. That is indeed a relatively pessimistic perspective. The quest for constitutional constraints that will forever bind rulers is in vain, though it might be an example of a noble lie. One has thus an example of an approach that illustrates the pessimistic side of the family of ideas out of which the Indiana School is a somewhat more optimistic member.

While the discussion is abstract and normative in intent, it also has a clear and practical dimension. The ideal of a limited government that cultivates a market economy is a normative benchmark against which real-world political economies are judged. This normative exercise emerged as practically relevant in the wake of the collapse of communism in East and Central Europe and the former Soviet Union in the late 1980s and early 1990s. The original stage of transformation began with the recognition that socialist economies were shortage economies and thus the first policy moves had to be focused on *getting the prices right.* But getting the prices right proved to be more difficult than simply freeing up the trading process. In order for a market economy to operate, the rules providing security to market participants must be instantiated. The transformation discussion moved to a focus on *getting the institutions right.* The difficulty of getting institutions to "stick" in the transforming societies proved to be much more difficult than merely manipulating formal institutions of governance. For rules to stick they must be to a considerable extent self-enforcing. Thus, we have entered a different stage of discussion in transition analysis, where the focus is on *getting the culture right.* The discussions surrounding social capital, trust and civil society all relate to the idea that you need some underlying set of shared values that reside in the everyday morality of the people, which legitimate certain institutional structures and patterns of social intercourse and ultimately enable the gains from peaceful cooperation.

This quick detour through almost 20 years of transition political economy demonstrates that we have moved from the normative ideal to the description of the underlying conditions necessary to realize that ideal. The social world is not so malleable that we can impose whatever social order we desire wherever and whenever we want. But there is another side to this evolution of intellectual interests. Precisely because our ability to impose exogenously the institutional structure that will effectively govern society has proven to be so weak, we must open up our analysis to the evolution of rules from games of conflict to games of cooperation.

Instead of designing ideal institutional settings that we can exogenously impose on the system and thus provide the "correct" institutional environment within which commerce and manufacturing can flourish, we have to examine the *endogenous* creation of the rules by social participants themselves. The science and art of association is one of self-governance, and constitutional craftsmanship should factor in that. And herein lies the contribution that contemporary research on anarchism can make to modern political economy and the point where the Bloomington School contributions become very relevant.

In this respect the Indiana School's studies were opening a new territory even before the focus on endogenous rule creation in commercial societies started to receive serious attention during the late 1980s (McGinnis 1999a; 1999b; 2000). Important studies in this respect were conducted by Bruce Benson (1990) and Avner Greif (1989), whose approach and conclusions converged with those of the Bloomington researchers. Benson provided an examination of the law merchant and how a body of law governing the commercial transactions of traders in an international setting had developed spontaneously to provide the security for the expansion of trade. The development of international trade and the expansion of the division of labor did not require governmental institutions, but instead developed on the basis of endogenous rule creation by commercial parties as they sought to minimize conflicts and realize the gains from exchange. Greif's work explained how trading partners functioned in medieval Europe without the sanctity of government enforcement of contracts. He provided a detailed historical account and used the analytical lens of modern game theory to analyze how reputation mechanisms facilitate cooperation among traders outside of state enforcement. Benson's argument is one where self-interest drives the development of a body of non-state law that parties agree to so that they can realize the gains from exchange even among socially distant individuals. Greif, on the other hand, shows how reputation mechanisms can serve to ensure cooperation among traders who are socially near. Greif's work is not as optimistic as Benson's about the ability of self-interest to generate endogenously rules of social intercourse once we move beyond small group settings where reputation mechanisms are effective, but both authors offer excellent examples of the growing body of literature to which the Indiana scholars have also been contributing, being in a sense its pioneers in the 1960s.

Benson and Greif are but two prominent examples of a literature that seemed to explode on issues of self-governance in the late 1980s and 1990s. Janet Landa's (1995) study of trading networks, Lisa Bernstein's (1992) study of the extra-legal rules governing trade in the diamond industry, and Robert Ellickson's (1991) examination of the resolution of conflicts between ranchers and farmers in Shasta County, CA all point to a growing recognition among social scientists that advanced cooperation without command can indeed occur and does occur in a variety of social settings. Social order is not necessarily a product of governmental institutions; instead, peace and prosperity can emerge outside of the structure of state enforcement. To sum up, the key messages of the Indiana School, as well as its approach, resonate with larger movements in current social sciences. Thus, irrespective of the label use ("anarchism" may not be the most fortunate, while polycentricity has proven to be cumbersome) one could see how its research is not only a pioneering contribution to the new "positive analytical anarchism" but also one of the most substantial and advanced contributions to the long standing tradition of thinking and analyzing the nature of alternative governance systems.

Economics, sociology, interdisciplinarity

One of the most salient features of the Indiana School has been its interdisciplinarity. From the very beginning it tried to bridge the divide between deductive and inductive research and to combine in its studies theories and methods from different disciplines. A closer look at the disciplinary frontier between economics and sociology in contemporary social sciences will offer an opportunity to better understand the position the School occupies as an intellectual experiment in interdisciplinarity.

There has been a growing interest in the past decade or so in the intersection between economics and sociology. Much of the literature on this derives from a perceived disappointment by either economists or sociologists of the traditional approach to social questions of the other. On the one hand, there is the economists' perception of the lack of rigor in sociology. Social questions, it is argued, are too important to be left to poor methodological treatment. Thus, economic imperialism and rational choice sociology result. On the other hand, sociologists criticize economists for ignoring the social dimension within economics. Economic science is sterile and, as such, cannot address the real issues it purports to examine. The treatment of individual actors as disembodied from institutional and historical context fails to account for how the social environment shapes individual desires and perceptions. Socio-economics is proposed to replace neoclassical economics. Given this context, the interesting thing about the Bloomington research program is that it suggested an approach to social thought which sought neither to colonize sociology with economics nor eliminate universalistic economics with sociological analysis. Instead, without making a big fuss about it, economics and sociology as well as other social sciences are simply combined in a pragmatic manner in the IAD framework. A closer look at this disciplinary divide will put in a clear light the contours of this position.

When Gary Becker (1975) first decided to use economic tools to examine subjects that were the domain of sociologists, such as discrimination, his work was met with great skepticism. Becker provided something which traditional sociology did not – a theory grounded in the rational behavior of individuals. Discrimination, crime, politics, family relations and social interaction in general all came to be examined using the tools of economics. The economic approach became synonymous with the study of human behavior in all walks of life and realms of society. Becker defines the economic approach as the relentless and unflinching use of the combined assumptions of maximizing behavior, market equilibrium and stable preferences (1976, 5). But Becker's economic imperialism has been criticized for having an "undersocialized" view of the individual. Classic Durkheimian and (Karl) Polanyian themes of social systems of rules and values, the embeddedness of culture, etc. have been resurrected in a modern sociological critique of the neoclassical view of the individual. Non-rational processes, it is argued, form the basis of our choices. The influence of our parents, our situation within the community, and the religious morals of that community form the basis of human behavior, not rational choice (see, for example, Etzioni 1988). With this shift away from utilitarian rational choice, comes an entire package of reassessment of the social sciences, from methodology to discourse within the polity to public policy. Mark Granovetter's alternative approach, for example, focuses attention on the social structures, organizations and groups within which economic activity is embedded, including the state in its capacity of shaping ownership, authority and financial relationships between business groups. Granovetter's intent is to overcome both the problems of the undersocialized and oversocialized view of the individual that is evident in standard economics and standard sociology. Granovetter's approach is quite consistent with the Weber–Mises formulation of methodological individualism, but Granovetter's actual argument proceeds more often than not as if the arrow of influence runs in only one direction – from the social context to the individual. That individuals are the source of institutions is not an avenue that is pursued, and, thus, the meaning of these structures remains incomplete.

However, with the Bloomington School's approach in mind, one could say that a sophisticated version of methodological individualism would see institutions as both the product and shaper of individual choice. In this perspective, the problem with the modern discourse is that while sociology asks the interesting questions, it remains hobbled by a lack of analytical structure. On the other hand, while economics possesses an analytical structure, it remains hobbled by an undue restriction of the questions it can ask and answer. Good social science reasoning requires a more flexible form of thought, which does not mechanically "close" the system as in equilibrium styles of reasoning, but nevertheless enables us to establish the boundaries of action. The task before us is one of simultaneously broadening the questions and yet retaining structure. Granovetter's concern with embedding individual action within a social context is an important first step, but it is neither enough in itself nor is it unique to him. At its best, one is caught between "dismal science" and "worldly philosophy" without becoming exclusively either. The approach of the Bloomington School is one which recognizes that the best contributions in political economy combine the analytical rigor of economic theory with methodological and philosophical sophistication of sociology and political theory. In the intersection between politics, philosophy, sociology and economics – whatever the ideological perspective – the truly interesting work in the social sciences takes place.

We better understand the position of the Indiana School if we see it in the context of the typical challenge in social theory: to steer a course between either an undersocialized or oversocialized view of the individual. Whereas the undersocialized view eliminates the social context within which preferences are formed and choices are made, the oversocialized view eliminates the power of human agency to shape the social world. Neither approach is very fruitful. The classic historicist/old institutionalist critique of economics is that culture and history are core concepts that have been eliminated in the strife for universalistic explanation. What standard economists assume to be characteristics of human nature are instead behavioral regularities that are specific to time and place and persist because of enculturation. Solutions must be found in the historical and cultural practices of the time and placed under consideration. Culture and historicity are the core concepts of social analysis, and work not based on these concepts will be faulty and misleading. Again, with the Indiana School approach in mind, one could say that the major problem with relying only on culture and historicity as the core concepts is that it slights the simple fact that in order to understand a people and their culture and history, we must presuppose the validity of some universal propositions about human behavior. The question is never one of theory versus no theory, but articulated theory versus unarticulated theory. The gulf between historicism and economism simply reflects the classic social science dichotomy between the "thick" and "thin" description. Economists possess a penchant for "thin" description (and the scientific value of parsimony), while area studies scholars and historians value "thick" description (and the scholarly value of thoroughness).

The social scientific methodological question for over a century has been whether meaningful "thick" description is possible without the guidance of "thin" description. On the one hand, "thin" description unconcerned with the underlying reality conveyed in "thick" descriptions describes little of relevance to our daily lives. On the other hand, "thick" description unaided by an articulated theory cannot help but bring on board theoretical baggage that defies critical scrutiny. The social world is far too complex to access directly; our understanding of necessity must be theoretically driven. We need, in other words, both "thin" and "thick" descriptions for our social theory to possess both meaning and relevance – coherence and correspondence, so to speak. To put it bluntly, if there were nothing universal in the human experience (the basis for "thin" description), then even our "thick" description of different people would remain beyond our ability to understand. Alien cultural practices would forever remain alien and inaccessible to others. At the same time, if all there was to the human conditions was the universal, then culture and history and area studies in general would disappear. Both extremes of exclusivity in social explanation are to be avoided.

It is precisely at this juncture – between "thick" and "thin" – that institutional individualism of the manner promoted by the Bloomington scholars offers an alternative to either atomistic individualism or naïve holism. "Rationality" in this formulation of individual action incorporates notions of instrumental rationality and must be understood as being entirely individually subjective and forward-looking. An open-ended notion of human agency can subsume the Weberian categories of action – valuational, emotional and traditional – under the rubric of the purposive – rational, which in turn is simply "meaningful action." The essence of the sciences of human action lies in "grasping the meaning of action." The universalistic approach is based on purpose – rational action is made possible by introducing degrees of typification, including the most abstract anonymous typification to the more concrete typification of historical agents. The point to emphasize is that it is the institutional context of choice that gives meaning to individual choices within a social system, and provides the basis for the scientific ability to grasp the meaning of human action both through discursive reasoning (conception) and through empathetic intuition (understanding).

One of the most interesting achievements of the Indiana scholars was to demonstrate practically that functionalist or social systems theories are not necessarily in conflict with rational choice theories. In fact, they pointed out that one of the most ambitious enterprises in contemporary sociology is the one associated with James Coleman's attempt to bridge the gap between rational choice and functionalism (Coleman 1990). Seen in comparison to Coleman's work, the Indiana approach is less ambitious in its promises but more substantial in delivering. Coleman approach suffers from serious problems. First, it does not eliminate the problem of under- and oversocialization, but rather constructs an oversocialized view of the social system from an undersocialized view of the individual. Second, as a result, the approach cannot adequately deal with either social embeddedness or human agency. The wonder of social life as individuals steer a course between alluring hopes and haunting fears is lost to the analyst, and with that his/her ability to understand the human condition. A precise set of propositions about maximizing entities and social forces not subject to human will is produced, but in a fundamental sense the analyst is blind to humanity.

This offers us a nice transition to a theme very dear to Vincent Ostrom. The criticism of the strict assumption that individuals maximize their behavior is on the ground that it eliminates the conscious component from the choice problem faced by individuals in a world of uncertainty. Choice is instead reduced to a simple exercise within a given ends–means framework. The individual's attempts to discover not only which ends to pursue but also the appropriate means to use in pursuing these ends is left out of the equation. The maximizing assumption eliminates not only the social construction of individual preferences, but also the individual's own construction of preferences through time (Buchanan 1979). The rationality postulate can only generate formal proofs of equilibrium if the future (with its novelty, uncertainty, and ignorance) is excluded. A static conception of rationality is inconsistent with the passage of real time (O'Driscoll and Rizzo 1985, 52–70). If an understanding of economic and social life requires the examination of both the passage of real time and rational behavior, then modeling human interaction in a fashion which excludes either of the two drains the explanation of essential details, to the detriment of social scientific thought.

To sum up, once projected in the context of these debates, one could see how the discussion of the position taken by the Bloomington School reveals that it is part of that family of efforts done by various scholars which attempted to grapple with some of the most important problems emerging at the disciplinary boundaries between social sciences. At the same time, the conjectural history of the Scottish moral philosophers, Toqueville's analytics and the interpretative sociology of Max Weber are the general framework for a social theory that attempts to steer between under- and oversocialized views of the individual, between individualism and holism, between neoclassical and behavioral and hermeneutic models of rationality (Boettke 1990). And thus, seen in this light, the Indiana School seems to represent a constructive step in the right direction of what Max Weber called "a science concerning itself with the interpretive understanding of social action and thereby with a causal explanation of its course and consequences" ([1922] 1978, 4).

Approaches, methods and perspectives

There is yet another way to situate the Indiana School within the context of the main debates and evolutions in social sciences during the last fifty years or so. The last half of the twentieth century was dominated by a systematic attempt to rewrite social sciences into the language of mathematics so as to eliminate the vague assumptions that underlay debates among social scientists of previous generations. Restating economics in the axiomatic language of mathematics, Samuelson argued, would force economists to make explicit assumptions that they had previously held implicitly. But the techniques of mathematics available to authors like Samuelson that pushed this agenda in all social science disciplines required well-behaved and linear functions; otherwise, results would be indeterminate and the promised precision would not be achieved. In order to fit behavior into mathematical language, the real world had to be drained of its complexity. The problem situation of social actors had to be simplified drastically so as to yield the precise formulations.

This formalist research program was one of the main reasons that led many social scientists to eliminate the conscious component from the choices facing individuals in a world of uncertainty. Choice was reduced to a simple determinate exercise within a given ends–means framework, "something an automaton could master." The task of discovering not only appropriate means, but also which ends to pursue, was left out of the equation. Moreover, it was forgotten that market institutions and practices arise in large part precisely because of deviations from the perfect-market model. The imperfections of the real world give rise to the essential institutions and practices that make economic life possible. The complexity of both institutions and individuals is impossible to model precisely, so it was pushed aside by simplifying assumptions.

The huge gap between the older view and the new use of equilibrium models can be illustrated by considering the reception of Ronald Coase's work on transaction costs. Viewed as a practitioner of counterfactual thought experiments, what Coase was focusing on (in both his 1937 paper on the theory of the firm and his 1960 paper on the problem of social costs) was the origin of actual market and legal institutions as mechanisms for coping with real-world positive transaction costs (Coase 1988). Without transaction costs, Coase argued in 1937, there would be no need for firms. Transactions in spot markets would be all that would be necessary to coordinate production. In addition, without transaction costs, Coase argued in 1960, there would be no need for property law. Voluntary negotiations between economic actors would resolve all conflicts over property rights. The actual existence of firms and the law can be seen, therefore, as evidence of the ubiquity and intractability of transaction costs. Coase's project, however, has been largely misunderstood by formalists. Instead of highlighting the functional significance of real-world institutions in a world of positive transaction costs, Coase's work has been interpreted as describing the welfare implications of a zero transaction-cost world. The "Coase theorem" has been taken to hold that in a world of zero transaction costs, the initial distribution of property rights does not matter; for as long as individuals are free to transact, resources will be channeled toward their most highly valued use.

Coase's theoretical insights into the role of institutions of property and contract are just an example of all that was buried by the formalist revolution. Historical work on the complex web of institutions that undergird capitalist dynamics produced by the earlier generation of neoclassical scholars, such as Knut Wicksell, Frank Knight, and Jacob Viner, as well as Hayek, was swept aside in the rush toward formal theorizing. The real problem was that the medium was becoming the message, as the strictures of formalism denied scientific status to realistic theory. Ideas that defied the techniques of formal analysis came to be considered unworthy of serious consideration. Even when an idea was thought to be interesting, if it could not be translated into an appropriate model, there was not much that could be done with it. The substance of economics was displaced by mathematical technique, and fundamental knowledge was setback – despite the obvious progress made in the precision with which economists could say what was left to say. Formalism drained economic theory of institutional context, and the econometric approach to empirical economics eliminated historical detail. Parsimony won out over thoroughness. Economics moved at this time from one side of the cultural divide (the liberal arts) to the other side (the sciences) – or at least that was the self – image of economists who equated science more with precision than accuracy.

The most important casualty of the formalist revolution was the historically and institutionally rich tradition of political economy still evident in the 1930s. Case studies of particular industries, for example, had been common. After the development of formalism and econometrics, however, the case-study approach was discarded in favor of large-sample data analysis. The best of the earlier approaches combined an appreciation for the particularities of institutional context with theory grounded in the generalities of choice under conditions of scarcity. Individuals always face tradeoffs, in this view, but the manner in which they weigh their choices is contingent upon the particular context of choice. This is the context in which an important part of the contribution of the Indiana School should be seen: a return to the earlier tradition but an approach that did not reject the formalist revolution but simply absorbed and dealt with it in a critical but meticulous way.

We have seen that an essential ingredient in the Indiana research program is a demand to connect real-world problems with the "human condition." This is indeed a firm departure from formalism. To gain access to these problems, fieldwork, experiments and detailed case studies are utilized. Water supply, irrigation systems, police, indigenous institutions addressing common – pool resources, and the process of economic development in less developed economies have all been the focus of institutional analysis by scholars associated with the Bloomington School. The analysis proceeds from context to the action arena to incentives to patterns of interactions to outcomes, which are evaluated and, in turn, influence the interactions. The context is defined by the physical and material conditions existing in a society, the attributes of the community in question, and the rules that are in use in that society. The different action arenas generate incentives which, in turn, engender a pattern of social interactions. The pattern of interactions results in outcomes that either reinforce the context of choice or conflict with it. This has been an extremely productive research program and has successfully challenged not only formalism but also the artificial division of the disciplines in the social sciences. Moreover, in addition to that it is noteworthy that it has also questioned the increasing bias against the normative dimension of social analysis by going beyond the positive institutional analysis of existing social interactions, identifying dysfunctional situations and suggesting policy changes to affect social change.

At this juncture a larger point regarding the normative dimension in social sciences is in order. The Indiana School's perspective has adhered to the notion that in social sciences there are two forms of analysis: positive and normative. Positive analysis "uses theory to draw inferences about consequences to be anticipated." These inferences "can be used as hypotheses to guide empirical research and test the predictive value of theory." The value of a theory is given by its ability to indicate "consequences that can be expected to flow from specifiable structural conditions" (V. Ostrom 1973b, 2). A second form of analysis derives from the first. In this type of analysis the relationships between institutional arrangements and consequences are assessed in the light of their contribution to human welfare. But in order to be able to do that, one needs to be engaged in normative analysis. "This method of normative inquiry provides a foundation for establishing the meaning of value terms and for setting, using, and judging criteria of choice and standards of performance." The creation of tools for diagnosis to identify "organizational arrangements that are detrimental to human welfare" and the different alternatives or forms of remedial action, require systematic assessment criteria (V. Ostrom 1973b, 3). The implications are that criteria for assessing choices and, for that matter, introducing the problem of rules and institutions are crucial. Treating social pathologies, institutional weakness and institutional failure depends on "modifications in the structures of decision-making arrangements inherent in different institutional forms." A change in decision-making arrangements transforms patterns of human interaction from "unproductive pathological relationships to productive relationships." But if that is the case, then one also needs solid criteria to determine what is pathologic and what is not. In other words, the "science of norms" that Vincent Ostrom advocates, should be seen not only in a positive way (rules of the game and the mechanics of their implications) but also as an exercise in thoroughly thinking about human values and criteria for decision and action.

The presence of the normative element at the core of human action has consequences for the way social science is conducted. The standards for determining the "plausibility of causal assertions about human social relationships" need to take account of "the normative criteria that inform the ordering of relationships in human societies" (V. Ostrom 1982b, 17–18). These foundational aspects rule out the possibility of a value free social science that is just a replica of natural science. Vincent Ostrom was very clear about where the Indiana School should be placed in relationship to the debates regarding the normative factor in social sciences. To allege that "the nature of social inquiry is value-free," he wrote, one "runs the risk of cutting social inquiry off from essential levels of understanding" (V. Ostrom 1982b, 17–18). And yet, the history of twentieth-century social thinking seems to be the story of a series of attempts to purge the "essential levels of understanding" from its inquiries. A revolt against the traditional approaches brought new and fresh insights but also a mode of analysis avoiding difficult and relevant theoretical and methodological questions. And, because of that, it is also unrealistic and impractical in its applied implications:

> The cult of modernity leads the "modern" intellectual to reject the terminology of an earlier generation as archaic. Value terms in particular were apt to be identified as meaningless. With the rejection of value terms as meaningless comes a denial of the artifactual nature of political and social phenomena and a demand that methods of the natural sciences be applied to the study of such phenomena. Value terms are at the core of rule-ordered relationships, and rule-ordered relationships are at the core of political order and social relationships. An intellectual tradition that rejects value terms as meaningless cuts itself off from the essential nature of political and social phenomena. If citizens were to accept epistemological positions taken by many modern scholars, they would be devoid of the appropriate moral and metaphysical grounds for functioning as intelligent constitutional decision makers.
>
> (V. Ostrom 1984, 434–435)

Before ending this brief overview of some of the issues and themes defining the intellectual locality of the Indiana School's research, briefly note one additional theme. Moving to the institutional level of analysis, we learned that we cannot simply construct and impose whatever institutional design our theory suggests, wherever we want it. In the public finance literature there is a warning against "flypaper" theories of taxation – taxes do not just stick wherever we impose them. Similarly, institutions do not just stick wherever we hope they may. So we are drawn into the intellectual game of focusing not only on incentives but also on the elusive concept of getting the culture right. If a culture accommodates the right institutions, the right prices will emerge and economic stabilization and performance will be achieved. In short, one may say that individuals will respond rationally to the incentives they face and these incentives are a function of the institutions that are effectively operating in that context. But as Douglass North, a pioneer of institutional analysis, has emphasized in his recent writings, claiming that individuals respond rationally to incentives is to say nothing at all unless you can explain how individuals represent those incentives. In other words, we could see that the Indiana School is not unique in this interest and that there is increasing pressure for questions of social meaning and interpretation of social signs to move to the forefront of any analysis of how alternative institutional arrangements impact on economic, political and social decision making (North 2005). Beliefs and other carriers of social meaning flood back into the analysis and we are, as Vincent Ostrom anticipated, confronted in the twenty-first century with the basic social science dilemma which nineteenth-century thinkers such as Max Weber had to grapple with – namely how to deal with the ideational variables (the ideas factor) to explain the nature, structure and change of a social system. Thus in this respect, imperfect as it may be, Vincent Ostrom's contribution was a move in the right direction.

Conclusions

Political economy was born out of a mystery and a puzzle. The mystery is, how did a complex division of labor among socially distant individuals emerge and serve as the basis of the wealth of modern civilization? In exploring this mystery economists came to highlight the mutual benefits of voluntary exchange and its self-reinforcing nature. However, this raised a serious puzzle. There was a presumption toward voluntarism in human affairs; but, in recognition that our nature is divided between a cooperative nature and an opportunistic nature we must figure out a way to curb our opportunistic side if we hope to realize the fruits of our cooperative side. While our cooperative nature is reflected in our propensity to truck, barter and exchange (which no other specie actually exhibits) as well as our natural propensity toward the "art of association," our opportunistic side is revealed in the warring nature witnessed throughout human history. Political economy claimed to be able to solve the puzzle by suggesting that we could sacrifice in a small way the presumption of voluntarism in order to create a government which will curb our opportunistic side and enable our cooperative side to flourish. But was that a viable solution? How should one investigate the issue? Are there theories and concepts that could help us? What are the best methods and approaches? What makes some theories more viable than others in this respect? This is indeed an extensive research agenda with an entire range of vital theoretical, methodological and normative dimensions. The nature and significance of the Bloomington research program could be really understood only when seen in the context of the discussion raised by these questions.

6 Public policy analysis, Public Choice and the old "new science of politics"

From the Bloomington School's perspective, the social sciences are a worthwhile enterprise not so much in themselves (though knowledge for knowledge's sake is valued as well); but rather, because they are the conceptual mold and the precondition of the more applied discipline of policy analysis. Policy analysis is the practical facet of theory. Without it, social sciences become an irrelevant game. A distinctive feature of the School is its insistence on the fact that social scientists should try to think not only in terms of creating theory but also of applying it. Given these assumptions, it is no surprise that the evolution of the Bloomington agenda, while rooted in the "Public Choice" movement, has also been linked to the evolution of the emerging disciplines of "public policy" and "public administration." This chapter will further illuminate the contours of the School by exploring its position within the perimeter defined by "policy analysis" and "Public Choice" while simultaneously projecting them in the broader picture of the evolution of political economy in the last hundred years.

Public policy analysis – an interpretation

The work of the Bloomington institutionalists is pervaded by the notion that the difference between policy analysis and political science is one of accent, not one of nature. Both of them are dealing in one way or another with ideas, human behavior and institutional designs and with their consequences. As such, write the Indiana scholars, they share not only a mode of analysis but also a history. Despite the fact that policy studies as a discipline emerged and was institutionalized in the post-Second World War period, it is important not to forget the fact that the practice as such was not new. In fact, if one follows these arguments, it has been something done in a natural way by human beings during their entire history. At one point in history, the reflection on that practice generated the beginnings of a science working to make "diagnostic assessments of the source or sources of perceived difficulties and consider alternative contingencies which, if altered, might yield more favorable consequences" (V. Ostrom 1991b, 1–2).

Modern policy analysis is one step further in the evolution of the practice, i.e. a more informed, systematic approach. It takes advantage of the specialization in the intellectual division of labor by focusing on the implementation dimension. That is to say, the growth of knowledge in this domain meant a gradual transition from the practice of humans organizing their relations in more or less intuitive modes of transmission and accumulation of knowledge, to explicit conceptualization and systematization of this knowledge in the "disciplines" of policy analysis and policy science. In brief, the modern approach is an attempt to develop, understand and assess the application of knowledge about institutional design in a methodical way.

Policy analysis (and the public policy discipline) has gained a specific place in the contemporary intellectual and political landscape. But that happened not only because the modern intellectual division of labor encourages an increasing special-ization that reaches every corner of the human endeavor, but also because of the "threat of relative ignorance" on policy issues that is generated by precisely that specialization. The danger, writes Vincent Ostrom, is that people acting on pre-sumption of knowledge step in with an epistemic authority gained in other fields, and engage in policy analysis in conditions of relative ignorance without under-standing that policy analysis may require in fact an increasingly specialized disci-pline and preparation.

> It is possible for learned scholars in a specialized field of scholarship to be naively ignorant about other realms of knowledge. When such scholars func-tion as policy analysts, they may combine the confidence of a knowledgeable expert with the intuitive fantasies of vacuous minds moved by passionate anx-ieties about other realms of life in human societies. Intelligible communication among persons engaged in critically rational efforts at problem solving can be abandoned for the slogan-shouting and drum-beating of self-proclaimed activists who view rage as a virtue.
>
> (V. Ostrom 1991b, 21)

To avoid that, one has to cultivate policy analysis as a discipline, despite the fact that ultimately that discipline will be based mainly on the knowledge produced by the other disciplines participating in the intellectual division of labor as well as on the commonsensical assumption that "choices informed by knowledge would pre-sumably be better choices than those not so informed." Indeed, in the end, the dif-ference between the traditional approach to policy and modern policy analysis is just one of degree. Given the fact that policy analysis is rooted in political science and the two are structurally similar, there is no wonder that the two are sharing not only the broad questions, but also their methods and approaches. But irrespective of the knowledge base, or analytical sophistication, both traditional and modern forms of policy analysis are by their very nature dealing with the same old problem of collective action. "Policy analysis," writes Vincent Ostrom, "is an effort to address problems impinging upon members of societies and requiring collective choices with commensurate effects upon collective actions." Indeed, this effort is based on the presumption that "appropriate forms of collective choice and collec-tive action will contribute to a more effective resolution of common problems and an advancement in the aggregate well-being experienced by members of collectiv-ities" (V. Ostrom [1990a] in McGinnis 1999a, 394).

Policy analysis may be depending on a theory of collective action yet its defining feature is that it is very specific and problem-oriented. It refers to concrete, public affairs problems confronting specific communities or groups. Its objectives are not abstract and theoretical but applied and aimed at problem solving. In the end, they are the ones that frame and define broader and more general questions about what policy analysis is as a discipline (V. Ostrom 1991b, 21). Policy analysis "is variable with problematical situations" and "any diagnostic assessment must necessarily be conjectural." Policy analysis is an interplay of ideas-conjectures and data gathering (V. Ostrom [1990a] in McGinnis 1999a, 411). Without knowledge well grounded the *problematic circumstances* of a collective action "policy analyses are likely to be misspecified." That may seem commonsensical but most policy failures are the result of formulating and implementing general solutions in total ignorance of the local conditions. It goes without saying that knowledge of the institutional environment is crucial. A diagnostic assessment "is complexly linked to the institutional facts" (V. Ostrom 1991b, 25–26). Even more, due to the very specific and contextual nature of knowledge required for the assessment of a case, "in finite time and place exigencies," the need to get the local knowledge, and perceptions and ideas of the actors involved is even more stringent.

> A policy analyst cannot be an external observer of an "objective reality" that has no relationship to ideas, knowable regularities, and informed practices. Actions are informed by thought. The world of human habitation is essentially related to communication, ideas, material conditions, tools, informed practices (artisanship), and the consequential state of affairs evoked by these efforts. The analyst may take the perspective of an external observer but is required to develop an understanding of any social reality that gives the observer access to the community of understanding that prevails among those being observed about the constitutive character of institutional facts that create social realities.
> (V. Ostrom 1991b, 23)

This is an important point that reintroduces the sensitive problem of values and norms. As we have already discussed in the earlier chapters, the Bloomington institutionalists have always been aware that the values embedded in institutions mean that scientific inquiry is a chimera. By their very task, social scientists are deeply involved in clarifying the meaning and place of values in the development of human institutions. An understanding of values, or a normative inquiry, is a prerequisite to perform the task of policy evaluation. Moreover, if one wants to design or assess decision rules, one needs criteria. Then the question is: what kind of criteria for those rules? How we construct (or for that matter assess) those rules depends on the criteria used. The task of the policy analyst is not only to use values as entry points or vehicles for analysis but to apply them. These values are not "given." One has to derive criteria for choosing one alternative over the other and to assess their consequences. In other words, the applied dimension presses the problem of norms not only at an analytical level but also at the decision making one. The world of policy analysis is in the end the world of implementation – i.e. the world of action and decision, and therefore is the world of normative commitments.

We have already seen the many ways the Bloomington School has analyzed the link between lack of understanding of institutional diversity and complexity (that implies polycentrism) and the monocentrism assumption. In discussing public policy analysis, as one may expect, an important theme of the critique of the mainstream approach is the treacherous link between the lack of interest in institutions and the ubiquity of monocentricity assumptions in policy analysis. They simply made the point that from there to the idea of universal models and solutions in public policy design was just one step. In other words, the criticism of the way policy analysis was thought for the most part of the twentieth century, is the criticism of the same logic that defined the standard approach in political science: the absence of institutions, the monocentric vision, and as a result of that, one universal solution implemented by one center of power and decision – the (national) state.

> Much of contemporary policy analysis appears to be largely institution-free except for abstract allusions to the Government, or the State (meaning nation-states) . . . Policy formulations presume a clean slate as though the failure to proclaim a General National Policy implied the absence of an Energy Policy, an Urban Policy, a Housing Policy, an Educational Policy, or any other specifiable policy. It is as though all political systems were unicentric, hierarchical in order, and run from the top down. The same modes of analysis and policy prescriptions can presumably be used anywhere in the world.
>
> (V. Ostrom 1991b, 2)

This logic and its implications are not accidental but a basic paradigmatic problem. As such, it is prone to persist as long as policy analysts continue to conceptualize social order using just two ideal types – Markets and Hierarchies – and believe that all societies could be described by reference to them, thus ignoring the "diverse nestings of institutional arrangements in time and place specificities." But once the theoretical lenses of polycentricity are used, policy analysis is forced to give more attention to institutional analysis driven by analytical methods and to problem-solving using "variable policy formulations" based upon "different presuppositions."

But, before discussing the idea of presuppositions, one needs to mention the link made by the Bloomington School between experiment and policy. As one may expect, in the light of its general position on social artifacts and natural experiments, from its perspective "every measure of policy can be treated as an hypothesis and that the experience accruing from acting on the basis of such an hypotheses" (V. Ostrom 1991b, 1–2). That means in order to fully assess a policy, one needs to go back to the theory that shaped its original core hypothesis. Any policy is a theory laden experiment. The "political doctrine" used to formulate "basic demands and expectations" typically "set forth in constitutions, charters, and formal declarations, might be treated as relevant hypothetical conjectures." To assess a policy as an experiment, one needs to not only know what the theory behind the experiment is but also to monitor the implementation and the consequences of the policies designed as inspired by those theories. Failure is as important as success because learning occurs from both failures as from successes. "These are the necessary foundations for mobilizing knowledge to inform choices about public affairs" (V. Ostrom 1997a, 104).

Policy analysis: concepts, assumptions and language

In his writing on public policy, Vincent Ostrom tried to remove the problems of public policy out of the realm of intellectual triviality. Policy is not a pure technical exercise of adjusting means to given ends fixed in function of "obvious" problems. The very notion of a "policy problem" is infused by deeper philosophical or normative speculations related to human nature and the human condition. One sees a policy issue not only through the theoretical and methodological background of the institutional theory and political science but also in the context of the social philosophy vision associated to them. The full dimensions and the complexity of the problems are fully revealed when normative concepts "collide with natural conditions of human beings." For instance, sexual asymmetries abound in nature. However, only human beings have "the potentials for viewing such asymmetries as being 'unjust'" and strive to "liberate females and attempt to achieve equality among the sexes." But what "equality" or "freedom" mean in these circumstances, and how critical rationality is to be achieved in addressing some aspects of such asymmetries when such problems defy "the bounds of rationality is itself problematical" (V. Ostrom 1991b, 25).

The definition of the problem in policy analysis and public policy is in the end a natural extension or expression of the social philosophy inspiring the analyst. As such, it should not be a surprise that two fundamental issues, language and assumptions, play a large part in this respect. Consistent with the overall social philosophy he articulated, Vincent Ostrom gives a special importance to the role of language in policy analysis and design. Precisely because language is the vehicle of coordination and communication and the basic building block in the construction of social reality, it could also be very dangerous. That may explain the special concern with the framing function of language and the assumptions that it surreptitiously plants in policy analysis. An intellectual construct is like a pair of spectacles, writes Vincent Ostrom:

> We see and order events in the world by looking through our spectacles and by using intellectual constructs to form pictures in our mind's "eye"—an intellectual vision. Yet we tend to neglect a critical examination of the spectacles or the constructs themselves.
>
> (V. Ostrom 1973a, 11–14; [1990a] in McGinnis 1999a, 394–396)

An important task of the policy analyst is to identify the situations when language and conceptualization drive policy making in the wrong directions. The very concept of "government" is such an example where the very notion is in many cases the source of a misleading assumption in public policy. The following quote not only expresses this point but also reveals the intellectual sources inspiring it:

> Any presumption that policy analysis applies to some proposed course of action to be taken by the "Government" is likely to be the source of profound errors. Not all systems of governance can be conceptualized abstractly as the

"Government." Such an abstraction obfuscates, rather than facilitates, analysis. Policy analysis conducted only by reference to goal setting on the part of the Government or the State strips away (1) reference to time and place exigencies that are essential considerations in all forms of human artisanship (Hayek 1945; Lachmann 1978), (2) the essential discipline required of any analyst for offering a diagnostic assessment of what it is that is problematical (Popper 1964; Albert 1977; Radnitzky and Bartley 1987), and (3) the neglect of the human and social capital that is available in the particular time and place exigencies of problematical situations to help people formulate and cope with problems (Schultz 1960; Machlup 1962; Becker 1975; Coleman 1988).

(V. Ostrom 1991b, 25–26)

The Bloomington research produced an entire list of cases where the assumptions drive the analysis in questionable directions. Some of them are already familiar and relate to the general theme of the (mis)conceptualization of the authority and decision in political and policy systems. In fact, they are just a variation of the same foundational themes: "If policy analysis is grounded in a presumption that a policy decision can be taken by a supreme authority to achieve some policy goal" we reduce the entire set of options to what Adam Smith recognized, as "the command and control presupposition that people in a society were pawns on a chessboard to be moved at the will of a sovereign." If, however, "the great chessboards of human societies involve circumstances where every piece has a principle of motion of its own, human beings will not be perfectly obedient pawns" and the range of policy options increases exponentially (V. Ostrom 1991b, 25–26).

Other examples of wrong assumptions in policy are more concrete. For instance, the notion that "money is the solution" and, its corollary, that the lack of financial resources is the cause of most policy problems are but two examples of mistaken assumptions. But money could not create by itself social bonds, institutional structures and patterns of rules and order. All of them depend on interpersonal relationships. Policy based on the presumption that "moving money solves problems may be destructive of both human and social capital" and instead of solving problems may aggravate them. Money, writes, Vincent Ostrom, "may be an especially poor substitute for the bonds of reciprocity fashioned to assure the helping hands and capabilities afforded by family, colleagues, friends, and neighbors." People "who fail to invest themselves in fashioning bonds of family, kinship, friendship, collegiality, neighborhood and other associations" are unlikely to be able to use the money in ways able to solve their problems (V. Ostrom 1991b, 25–26).

The link between assumptions and the institutional reality is transparent. Allusions to "the nation's schools" may, for example, "convey impressions that proprietorship and authority over schools reside in "the nation." "National authorities" may presume themselves to be competent to oversee and manage "the nation's schools" (V. Ostrom 1991b, 24). A vicious circle is thus created: a problem is identified as "national." "National solutions" are then identified. Then the implementation of the "national solution" fails and the cycle starts anew. Such conjectures can easily be associated with the increasing dominance of the national government in public affairs. Framed by such a language and guided by the leading assumptions beneath it public policy might degenerate into magic and sorcery.

> Decision-making processes are, in the technique of modern political mythology, transformed into rites where magical words are reiterated. Faith is reaffirmed by the frequent reiteration of slogans as magical words. In such decision-making rites, evil forces are exorcised as impediments to the realization of an ideal state, and the faithful reaffirm their devotion to the struggle for social imperatives. Modern rhetoric associated with the "war on poverty," the "urban crisis," the "environmental crisis," and "comprehensive planning" is acquiring a status of political mythology. Decision-making processes associated with this mythology are also taking on the characteristics of rites. Comprehensive, over-all solutions are called for. Sources of evil are associated with those who have "special interests" in contrast to the "public good" of the greater community. Those who resist the comprehensive over-all solutions called for by "omniscient observers" are identified as exploiters and obstructionists who are unwilling to assume the burdens of poverty, congestion and the general erosion of environmental quality in urban living.
>
> (V. Ostrom 1999; see also 1997a, 74–76)

A critical and discriminating use of language may thus be among the necessary conditions for having a sound public policy. Even more important is the language in social and political sciences, given the role those disciplines have in framing the political discourse and the public policies of modern societies. And in this respect a special attention should be given to the deficiencies of the language of discourse in policy analysis with its "split between intuitive impressions and inappropriately generalized models." Political science and policy analysis share twin temptations: on the one hand to distance from "reality," or on the other hand to get lost in descriptive and intuitively appealing details. This is to say that the problems of the policy analyst and political scientist are similar: the tension between general abstract models and the multilayered complexity of facts (V. Ostrom 1991b, 19).

As is frequently the case, the main concern is that the reliance on the "generalized models aimed to have universal applicability" creates a distance between analysts and social reality. And so, although great developers and employers of models, we find the Bloomington scholars very emphatically cautioning on the limits of using models in policy analysis. "Absurd doctrines can meet standards of logical rigor and mathematical proof but yield disastrous consequences when used to inform actions" (V. Ostrom 1991b, 97). Relying on abstract models of "markets" and "states" and building the entire discourse around them means that "the language used cannot capture the empirical reality." The problem is not only theoretical and empirical (in the world there are many systems of governance put together in different ways) but also a practical and policy one in which language implicitly promotes an unrealistic or even dangerous role for the government. This is an indication of how intricately even the most abstract modeling subtly inserts in modes of language assumptions into analysis and diagnosis.

In policy analysis, as in political science, the suggested solution is the same: flexibility – using multiple perceptions and adjusting the approach to the circumstances of the case in point. Implicit in all this discussion is the crucial issue of conceptualization or problem definition: the "data" might be conceptualized in "an indefinitely large number of ways." This is not a theoretical speculation but an operational one regarding the approach to very concrete policy problems. The way of conceptualizing the problem or the actors involved is not an exercise driven by arbitrary and pure subjectivity. To limit conceptualization in function of natural constraints or the facts of reality is of critical importance. In policy making that makes the difference between success and failure. Moreover, an analysis based on a narrow conception, might be not only institutionally dysfunctional but also politically dangerous. Such observations were already in the air by the time they were published in the 1960s. Yet their application to the cases in point was very challenging for that time:

> An attribute, such as homelessness, race, gender, or money, may be accurately identified with problematical situations. The existence of some attribute in some nexus of relationship may fail to identify elements in the structure of that situation that are tractable to problem-solving strategies. Pointing to an attribute, which may from some perspective be the source of a puzzle, is insufficient for offering an explanation or in providing leverage for resolving some problem. Pointing to attributes, such as homelessness, race, gender, or money, may misspecify problems. Any effort to alter states of affairs directly associated with some such attribute may aggravate rather than relieve the perversities that may accrue in societies.
>
> (V. Ostrom 1991b, 25)

Last, but not least, are the examples of inference one can draw from general impressions. The modern state is again one of the favorite examples. The same problem is now tackled from a slightly different angle: because modern state is so obviously out there, there is the tendency to think of every policy issue in terms of it and to forget that "human societies might be put together in different ways." In policy, people do that on a constant basis.

The bottom-line of this long criticism of the policy analysis practice is this: one should never forget that instead of relying upon intuitive impressions, unanalyzed assumptions and overly abstract universal models, it is possible to build better "languages of discourse" specifying "elements and relationships that are constitutive of diverse levels of social reality" (Ostrom 1991b; 1991c), and in doing this create a better basis for dealing with collective action and public policy problems. The various configurations of these elements (actors, situations, rules, beliefs, the manners and customs of the people – the habits of the heart and mind – at different levels and units of analysis) give a more operational account of social order than intuitions or abstract models.

> Where do these elements fit in the scheme of policy analysts? Until we have a language that is appropriate to an understanding of what it is that is constitutive of democratic societies, people cannot learn how to maintain such societies in

a world of increasing complexity and interdependence. A new science of politics for a new age calls for a language that can be used to penetrate social reality and perfect our understanding of how ideas relate to practice in the exigencies of human experience.

(V. Ostrom [1990a] in McGinnis 1999a, 413–414)

And thus, based on an assessment of the deficiencies of the mainstream political science-policy analysis set, a call for a "new science of politics" whose basic building block is a careful language of policy definition and policy analysis comes as no surprise.

Public Choice and the new science of politics

Policy analysis has developed as a discipline and as a language, building on the accumulated knowledge from many historical experiments. Its history is the narration of the evolution of human capacities to understand the nature and consequences of their institutional and policy experiments. Yet, the Bloomington scholars considered that the progressive historical move in the direction of building that science, after accelerating from the seventeenth to nineteenth centuries has slowed down close to a standstill. The rise of the state-centered discourse has brought progress almost to a halt. Important elements and insights about the assessment of institutional arrangements and experiments were neglected or lost.

A new science of politics combining the traditional and contemporary approaches should remedy the entire sets of deficiencies of the standard policy analysis. It indeed implies that the language traps, the assumptions, and the misleading conceptualizations should be cleared. This further implies a recognition of the fact that "a theory of the state is no longer sufficient for the world in which we live." As a parenthesis one should note that, today, when the nation state is being eroded by new and powerful economic and political forces, the echo of the Bloomington scholars to the challenge that Tocqueville identified a century and a half earlier, is as pressing as ever: "A new science of politics is needed for a new world" (Tocqueville 1945 [1835]).

Amid the developments of the 1960s there was a ray of light. What was considered by many as an "intellectual revolution" was brewing. For scholars like Vincent Ostrom the growth of the Public Choice movement might well have been not only the revival of an old tradition of formulating problems but also the much needed infusion of new methods and concepts into the stalling intellectual climate. One of the most powerful arguments in this respect was made by his book on the crisis in American public administration (1973a). The growth of a science of politics on the lines defined by Hobbes, Hume, Smith and Tocqueville, he argued, was derailed by diverging beliefs about the nature of political inquiry. As a result, public administration, and consequently the practice of public policy, got into a dead end. The problem was foundational: political science was employing the wrong paradigm. What was needed was a different paradigm, a different way of looking at the world, a way that better reflects the twentieth century's social and institutional context. The key was in the new Public Choice theory of political economy.

Ostrom's book on the crisis in American public administration contained a robust elaboration of that idea. Its starting point was the observation that "the profession no longer has confidence in what it professes." Thus, urban issues, environmental crises and race problems seem without solution or at least that administrative and policy theory has no solution to offer. The cause was that political science and administrative theory are shaped by a state-centric monocentric vision originating in the writings of Woodrow Wilson and legitimized by the theories of Max Weber. These views assumed a bureaucratic paradigm, centralized control, homogeneity of administrative structures and the separation of the political from the administrative. As such they neglected two important aspects of public organization. First was the fact that different circumstances require different decision-making structures. Second, the fact that multi-organizational arrangements might be possible within the same administrative systems. This paradigm was framing both the analytical and practical approaches in ways that not only were unable to offer solutions but were unable to even identify problems. Seeking an alternative became a vital task.

And the alternative was to be found in the work of those political economists concerned with *institutional weaknesses* and *institutional failures* in non-market economies. By comparing and contrasting the approach of, on the one hand, these political economists and, on the other hand, of bureaucratic theorists he concluded that in the political economy, Public Choice approach "yielded the insights able to revive the science of public administration." Several major reasons made Public Choice yield that potential: first, the concern with the provision of public goods and services. The theory of public goods was the central organizing concept used by Public Choice in conceptualizing the problem of collective action and implicitly in analyzing issues of public policy and public administration. The mainstream theory of public administration used the theory of bureaucracy as its indispensable framework. But that theory has limited explanatory potential once the central problem in public administration is viewed as the provision of public goods and services. Moreover, from a policy perspective, the extension and perfection of bureaucratic structures has slowly come to be seen as a solution of low impact or even as a pseudo-solution. Bureaucratic structures are necessary but not sufficient for a productive and responsive public economy. Alternative forms of organization are available for the performance of those functions and they should be studied as such. Public Choice points to the study of the relationship between decision (and administrative) structures and outputs by asking the key question: "what structures most effectively allocate public goods?"

In other words, Public Choice asked the right questions that pointed out the crucial issue of choice among forms of organization, institutional frameworks or systems of rules. The implication was that there is no one organization or institutional arrangement that is "good" in all circumstances. The goal of a wise public policy or public administration is to search for the optimal arrangement, that which "minimizes the cost associated with institutional weaknesses or institutional failure." Public Choice implies a pluralistic theory of administrative and organizational life and of institutional arrangements. That, concludes Vincent Ostrom, together with its methodological individualism made it the best set of ideas that could lead to the reconstruction of a paradigm for public policy and thus a candidate for the "new science of politics."

James Buchanan's Public Choice – an intellectual family member and a benchmark

Public Choice as a policy analysis approach re-linked modern political science to the tradition of the eighteenth and nineteenth century's political thinkers and at the same time it served as an illustration of the process of growth and accumulation of knowledge on institutional design and assessment taking place in Western democracies. But the influence of Public Choice was also due to its contribution to the major debates of the day. If market failure was the theme of the day, Public Choice showed that failures in market arrangements could not be corrected simply by recourse to bureaucratic governmental decision processes. It demonstrated that it was at least as appropriate to talk about government and bureaucratic failure as it was to talk about market failure. By challenging the state-centered assumption, Public Choice had the capability to bring a fresh breath of air into the public policy studies by redefining the ways the structure of decision making and performance in the "public sector" was understood.

By the time Vincent Ostrom reached those conclusions, Public Choice was a marginal movement at the boundaries of economics and political science. In fact it is important to remember that Vincent Ostrom was one of the founders of Public Choice Society and identified up to a point and in a constant way his work with this intellectual movement. A closer look at Public Choice as developed by its most salient author, Nobel Prize winner James Buchanan, could set in a better light the specificity of the institutionalist approach developed by the Bloomington scholars. Looking back at the beginnings and at James Buchanan's original vision, one could see the common roots and the common themes going through the Virginia and Indiana Schools. And looking at the potential for further evolutions in the field, one could also see why Vincent Ostrom, later in his career, felt compelled to take some distance from the new mainstream of Public Choice and why that move was in fact consistent with the core, initial vision shared with Buchanan. In other words, there is no better way to get a better understanding of the Bloomington School in the context of its closest intellectual family member than to briefly overview some of the main themes of Buchanan's work.

The basic propositions which guide Buchanan's research programme can be summarized neatly (Buchanan 1979, 280–82):

1   Economics is a "science," but it is a "philosophical" science, and the structures against scientism offered by Knight and Friedrich Hayek should be heeded.
2   Economics is about choice and processes of adjustment, not states of rest. Equilibrium models are only useful when we recognize their limits.
3   Economics is about exchange, not about maximizing. Exchange and arbitrage should be the central focus of economic analysis.
4   Economics is about individual actors, not collective entities. Only individuals choose.

5   Economics is about a game played within rules.
6   Economics cannot be studied properly outside of politics. The choices among different rules of the game cannot be ignored.
7   The most important function of economics as a discipline is its didactic role in explaining the principle of spontaneous order.
8   Economics is elementary.

From his early critique of social choice theory and welfare economics to his most recent writings on constitutional design, Buchanan's Public Choice stresses these eight points. It is important to recognize the methodological schema that Buchanan employs to address questions in political economy and how this schema allows him to weave these eight propositions into a coherent framework for social theory. The common roots of the Bloomington IAD approach and Buchanan's Public Choice are evident.

Buchanan emphasizes that we must distinguish between pre- and post-constitutional levels of analysis. Pre-constitutional analysis concerns the rules of the game, while post-constitutional analysis examines the strategies players adopt within a set of defined rules. Political economy, properly understood, involves moving back and forth between these two levels. Successful application of modern political economy to the world of public policy demands a constitutional perspective. In this regard, Buchanan, as the IAD framework does, introduces the vital distinction between "policy within politics" and systematic changes in the rules of the game. Lasting reform results not from policy changes within the existing rules, but rather from changing the rules of governance. Thus, far from being conventional intellectuals, Buchanan and Ostrom, as founding members of the Public Choice movement, were intellectual radicals seeking to get at the root cause of social and political ills.

According to an ancient legend, a Roman Emperor was asked to judge a singing contest between two participants. After hearing the first contestant, the Emperor gave the prize to the second on the assumption that the second could be no worse than the first. Of course, this assumption could have been wrong; the second singer might have been worse. The theory of market failure committed the same mistake as the Emperor. Demonstrating that the market economy failed to live up to the ideals of general competitive equilibrium was one thing, but to gleefully assert that public action could costlessly correct the failure was quite another matter. Unfortunately, much analytical work proceeded in such a manner. Many scholars burst the bubble of this romantic vision of the political sector during the 1960s. Before Public Choice, economic theory frequently postulated an objective welfare function which "society" sought to maximize, and assumed that political actors were motivated to pursue that objective welfare function. The critique developed by the initial Public Choice pointed out: (1) that no objective welfare function exists, (2) that even if one existed societies do not choose (only individuals do), and (3) that individuals within the political sector, just as in the private sector, base their choices on their private assessment of costs and benefits.

The major insights all flow from these three elementary propositions – the vote motive; the logic of dispersed costs and concentrated benefits; the shortsightedness bias in policy; and the constitutional perspective in policy evaluation. Politics must be endogenous in any reasonable model of economic policy-making. But the intellectual spirit of the 1950s and early 1960s was one of zealous optimism about the nature of politics. Buchanan's warning of democratic folly, and the need for constitutional constraint, did not sit well with the intellectual idealist of the day. In the wake of the Vietnam War, and then Watergate, as well as the failed economic policies that emerged from both Democratic and Republican administrations, it is now difficult to imagine a non-cynical view of politics. This is not an endorsement of apathy and malcontent with politicians. Nowhere in Buchanan's Public Choice or Indiana IAD is it suggested that politicians are any worse than the rest of us. Rather, their work simply stressed that politicians are just like the rest of us – neither sinners nor saints, but a bit of both.

One of the most important issues regarding Buchanan's work – an issue that is critical for understanding both the evolution of Public Choice as a school of thought and Vincent Ostrom's position towards it – is the problem of subjectivism and the elemental principles of economics. Ironically, modern economists were reluctant to accept the "economic way of thinking," in particular, the central role of exchange and the notion of subjective tradeoffs. In his 1963 Presidential Address to the Southern Economic Association, Buchanan (1979, 17–37) argued that economists should put the contribution of constrained maximization in perspective. Resource allocation was not the central problem of economics. Economists should, Buchanan urged, concentrate on the human propensity to truck, barter and exchange, and the institutional arrangements that emerge as a result of this propensity. If this step is not taken, it is too easy for error to sneak into economic analysis and become embedded at the most fundamental level. The allocation definition of economics "makes it all too easy to slip across the bridge between personal and individual utility of decisions and 'social' aggregates" (Buchanan 1979, 22–3). Economists know that crossing the bridge is difficult, and Lionel Robbins was successful in keeping many from summing utilities in order to get across the bridge. But Robbins was only partially successful, as economists still thought that as long as they specified their social welfare function they could "maximize to their own hearts' content." Buchanan pointed out that this intellectual exercise is illegitimate; economists should not engage in this activity.

The Buchanan critique of optimizing models is not about the introduction of value judgments via the social welfare function; nor is it a critique of formalization per se. Rather, the critique is that the subject matter of economics is lost in these exercises in applied mathematics, and that where the subject matter seems to creep back into the analysis it is mischaracterized. The mutual advantage that can be realized through exchange in specified institutional settings is the one important truth of political economy, Buchanan insists; modern economics has threatened our ability to understand this truth. Again here, one could see the common vein running through the Virginia and Indiana schools as well as the overt radicalism of the beginnings of the Public Choice movement.

Subjectivist economics compels theorists to avoid the pitfalls of abstraction. It grounds economic analysis in the choices of individuals, and demands that empirical analysis pay attention to the institutional context of choice and how agents perceive their institutional constraints. The mechanical model of allocational computation and its corollary (the model of perfect competition) eliminates genuine choice from study, just as the focus on aggregate data ignores the ideas, desires, beliefs and cultural practices that motivate historical actors. In other words, looking back at the works of Buchanan and Ostrom one could identify a streak of intellectual radicalism that goes beyond what the conventional wisdom teaches about the nature of the Public Choice revolution. Vincent Ostrom's arguments do not seem eccentric anymore.

The project advanced by Buchanan, where the subjective half of the 1870s revolution in value theory is emphasized as strongly as the marginalist half, leads to a different sort of economic science. In a broad brush summary, it leads to a conception of economic science as a philosophical science, and not a technocratic one. Unlike other critics of modern economics, the subjectivist tradition retains a commitment to universality, an emphasis on marginalism, and seeks to study how a systematic order emerges as the unintended consequence of individual choice.

Subjectivism demands a major restructuring of economic theory. Cost, Buchanan insisted, must be understood as the subjective assessment of tradeoffs by individuals if it is going to have any meaning in a theory of decision-making. In addition to a renewed appreciation of the nature of choice, the context of choice comes to occupy a central stage within the subjectivist research program. There can be little doubt that Buchanan approach was a powerful attempt to resurrect a broader notion of political economy; a conception grounded in an appreciation of the subjective nature of choice and its implications for social order. One should keep that in mind when we'll return to discuss V. Ostrom's assessment of the current state of Public Choice and its prospects. Because that puts a new light on Ostrom's interest in the role of ideas and meaning in social sciences.

Before doing that, lets focus on another aspect of the work of James Buchanan, a feature that relates to the IAD perspective and that further demonstrates the affinity between the Virginia and Indiana Schools. Positivism and formalism promised to lift economics from its immature past when ethical concerns and the ambiguities of philosophy and natural language clouded the thinking of its leading figures. Submission to empirical reality would compel those with a scientific mind to surrender ideological beliefs, and mathematical reasoning would eliminate the ability of theorists to slip in unwarranted assumptions. But, wrote Buchanan on a similar note with Ostrom's position, these promises were misleading. Empirical reality is complex and must be sifted through a theoretical lens for us to make sense. In addition, mathematical reasoning might be precise but irrelevant, Mathematical modeling ensures syntactic clarity, but it does not guarantee semantic clarity. The model may be logically precise, but lacks meaning. Both the empiricist and formalist aspiration were misapplied in the study of man. One cannot cast out of scientific court the very things (beliefs, desires, expectations) that motivate the subject of study without distorting the object of study. To put it another way, while eliminating anthropomorphism from the physical sciences was a noble cause, eliminating anthropomorphism from the study of man eliminated the very thing that was supposed to be studied.

Buchanan fought persistently against the disappearance of man from economic analysis. By insisting that economic processes always exist within a political/legal/ social context, Buchanan begged economists to focus attention on the rule structure within which individual strategies would manifest them. Reform, he insisted, would not come from tinkering with individuals and their strategies, but only from changes in the rules of the game. By introducing the methodological schema of pre- and post-constitutional analysis, he was able to demonstrate the positive-scientific value of social philosophy for economics. He proposed both a positive analysis of normative issues and a recognition that political economists engage in normative analysis whether we want to admit it or not.

Buchanan (1991) has argued that classical political economy discovered that as long as the state provided and maintained appropriate rules of the game, individuals could pursue their own interests and simultaneously enjoy the values of liberty, prosperity and peace. The vision, however, was never implemented, and it failed to capture the imagination of intellectuals for more than a generation or two. One could see the theme of reviving a tradition, a theme that runs through the IAD School, too. Yet, Buchanan elaborated beyond this point. He conjectures that this failure was due to the absence of a theory of justice in classical liberal political economy. Attempts in the twentieth century to develop a model of social justice in order to correct this weakness have generated failed experiments in socialism and the social democratic welfare state. The failure of socialism and the welfare state can be directly attributed to the incentive incompatibility of the rules of these games with the strategies of the work ethic and personal responsibility, behavior associated with economic prosperity and social cooperation.

Buchanan shared the frustration of the Ostroms with the growth of the state in the twentieth century, indeed. In his view a large part of the growth of the state had to do with the Romantic vision of politics that had captured the imagination of American liberals and the growth in numbers of those that are "afraid to be free." In addition, from a technical perspective many arguments for government intervention were grounded in a poor understanding of economics and an even worse understanding of the political processes. Much of the critique of the market was generated by those who failed to grasp the basic principles of spontaneous order analysis. Buchanan believed that rational analysis and the construction of the appropriate institutions of governance could emerge from the pens of economists and could reform the system in a "desirable" direction. Freedom was to be found in the constitutional contract.

To sum up, by focusing attention on the rules of political economy, Buchanan has opened up the discourse in economics to again deal with moral questions and the tradition of political philosophy. He pursued a subjectivist research program when the majority of the profession lost sight of the subjectivist roots of the neoclassical revolution; he rejected the formal models of utility maximization and perfect competition when these models represented the tool-kit of any respectable economist; and he reintroduced moral concerns into economics at a time when economists were content to worship at the shrine of scientism. When Buchanan won the Nobel Prize in 1986 the Public Choice movement that he pioneered reached its final recognition. What started as a challenge to the mainstream has become mainstream. But was it the same? How was it perceived by founding figures like Vincent Ostrom?

From Public Choice to Epistemic Choice

Once we have reviewed James Buchanan's foundational contribution to Public Choice we are now in the position to understand Ostrom's arguments in the context of this movement of ideas and its immediate vicinity. Seen in this light, his criticism and his speculations about the future of the Public Choice research program may be seen less as an eccentric deviation from the tradition but as a natural continuation of the core initial ideas and themes shared with at least one of the salient figures of the program. As one of the founders of the Public Choice movement, quite unsurprisingly, Vincent Ostrom was enthusiastic and hopeful in the 1960s . This is why his assessment, three or four decades later, after Public Choice gained public recognition, when he revisited the issue and asked how does one assess the prospects for the next generation, is very illuminating. Needless to say, this assessment offers the elements for better understanding of not only the evolutions of the Bloomington School within the Public Choice movement but also implies some interesting evaluation criteria for the rational choice approach in general.

As expected, Vincent Ostrom's assessment is not focused on the academic or public successes and recognition gained by Public Choice but on its contribution to the more important goal of paradigm change and especially its contribution to the old "new science of politics" project. Quite expectedly, first and foremost, Ostrom (1997a; 1997b; 1993a) is keen to argue that Public Choice needs to thoroughly detach itself from the contamination of the mainstream conceptualization of social order in terms of "markets" and "states."

> The specter of simplified allusions to "the Market" and "the Government" [State] haunts a large proportion of the work in Public Choice theory. An allusion to something called "the Government" does not clarify what the term refers to. Concepts of "States" and "Markets" are not effective ways of articulating the intellectual revolution that is stirring in our midst. As intellectual constructs, they are too gross to be useful; they run the risk of being misleading and are the source of serious forms of deception and misconceptions.
>
> (V. Ostrom 1997a, 111–112)

But his most significant criticism is even more foundational. His verdict is straightforward:

> My conclusion is that the most important potentials have been associated with diverse thrusts on the peripheries of work in the Public Choice tradition rather than with efforts at the core of the tradition to apply "economic reasoning" to

"non-market decision making," as the Public Choice approach has been conceptualized by the mainstream of Public Choice scholars. The "core" of the Public Choice tradition involves economic reasoning that places primary emphasis on a nontuistic, self-interested, rational actor. . . . Work on the peripheries is where important advances at the frontier are most likely to occur. The leading contributors to the Public Choice tradition have never confined themselves to a "core" built on extreme rationality assumptions. Perhaps the important challenge for Public Choice scholars is to address how basic anomalies, social dilemmas, and puzzles can be resolved in human affairs, rather than to apply economic reasoning, narrowly construed, to non-market decision making.

(V. Ostrom 1997a, 89)

The question then becomes how to fit these efforts at the periphery of the Public Choice approach with the rest of the Public Choice enterprise. Are they "only miscellaneous idiosyncratic accretions" or are "cumulative contributions" to diverse "levels of analysis that are complementary to one another and that meet standards of scientific warrantability?" The challenge is to find ways to keep the field together while at the same time to grant the legitimacy they deserve to the experiments at the periphery. Wisely enough, Ostrom's chosen examples in this respect are difficult to challenge: Gordon Tullock's (1965) filtering and distortion in the transmission of information for deception and for error in organizational settings, James Buchanan's (1979) emphasis on the artifactual character of human individuality, or James Coleman's (1990) concern with norms.

Of special relevance in this context is Douglass North's (1990) conversion of many Public Choice elements into institutional theory. Ostrom uses North's work as a vehicle to make the point that rules, cognitive processes, values, learning, are not residual in a theory of social action and social order. To understand how people solve social dilemmas one needs to go beyond rational choice theory. The search for a social science of collective action and social dilemmas, could not rest solely or primarily on rational choice theory but in a theory of rules and institutions. Without a theory of institutions, rational choice theory is impotent. However, the theory of institutions, relies on a theory of ideas and the associated domain of language, knowledge and learning processes. To understand collective action and social organization, one has to go back and forth between all these dimensions but always return to recharge and readjust to the theory of ideas. In brief, Ostrom's criticism although sharp, is presented in a velvet glove and has a constructive note.

What is even more interesting and important than the criticism (after all similar arguments were made by other authors during the last decades) are his conjectures about the future intellectual developments. In his view there is one emerging notion that could be a potentially powerful unifying concept of this literature: Epistemic Choice. This concept illuminates the various choice dimensions – operational, public and constitutional – but at the same time emphasizes that choice in institutional matters is ultimately a choice of ideas and is intrinsically linked to learning and knowledge. One should never forget that social scientists and policy analysts are contributors to a knowledge base (consisting of ideas, theories and models) for better decisions in institutional affairs. Hence Epistemic Choice seems to be the best candidate to epitomize at a certain level of generality covering all choice dimensions. Yet while there is an element uniting these dimensions, there is also something special about the choice of ideas, principles and beliefs.

> The principles of choice applicable to the warrantability of knowledge are different than the principles of choice applicable to a choice of goods in market and public economies. These are different than the principles of choice applicable to the constitution of rule-ordered relationships in accordance with standards of fairness. Principles of consensus among participants can apply to each, but the criteria of choice vary among different types of choice.
>
> (V. Ostrom 1997a, 90)

That is to say that the concept of Epistemic Choice has several functions. First, it is functioning as an element of unity among the different approaches, between the core and the multitude of periphery components of the Public Choice family of ideas. Second, it is adding a complementary element (usually neglected) to this set of approaches, i.e. the very notion that a choice of institutions or organizational arrangements is ultimately a choice of ideas. To that, one additional function should be added. An emphasis on the intellectual, epistemic element ensures continuity with older traditions in which the Public Choice approach is rooted. The hope is that based on the notion of Epistemic Choice, "an intellectual apparatus can be developed to give complementarity to the diverse thrusts in inquiries pursued over the last three or four decades." And we might also expect "to achieve a greater coherence among much longer traditions of inquiry in the social or cultural sciences":

> Thomas Hobbes, David Hume, Adam Smith, and others give us foundations for dealing with language, learning, knowledge, communication, artisanship, and moral judgment in the exercise of choice. In considering the problem of Epistemic Choice, the contingencies of language and their relationships to knowledge, choice, and action are at the focus of attention. A new approach not only opens potentials for future work but allows for a better appreciation of how to select from and build on prior achievements. Problems of Epistemic Choice – the choice of conceptualizations, assertions, and information to be used and acted on in problem-solving modes – must necessarily loom large. If the Public Choice approach will continue to contribute to the advancement of knowledge, that future depends on meeting the requirements of Epistemic Choice.
>
> (V. Ostrom 1997a, 91)

If Vincent Ostrom is correct, the 'Epistemic Choice' turn in Public Choice or a related field such as institutional theory is apparently unavoidable. Public Choice has outgrown its neoclassical mold. If it continues to rely and behave like an extension of standard, neoclassical economics, it will become sooner or latter an intellectual dead end. Its initial contribution was useful as one specific stage in the revitalization of policy analysis (overcome market failure obsessions and bring back the inquiry on rules and choice in political studies) but the program should not stop with that. It is vital to not get fixated on the economics core precisely because this core is too much tied to the abstract intellectual enterprise of the neoclassical economics, and too dependent on the presumption of perfect competition in which fully informed actors who maximize individual self-interest interact in strictly predictable ways. The challenge is then to understand how people solve those problems instead of the formal speculations and hypotheses about the underlying mechanics or rationality. The implications are clearly pointing out to the periphery of Public Choice program. Public Choice and neoclassical economics got the maximum possible out of the application of economics models postulating perfectly informed actors (participating in competitive markets) and operating in unitary States directed by a single center; or of variations on these themes. They managed not only to reach the limits but to push them into new territory. But today, in order to make progress, "we need to go back to basics to reconsider the human condition and what it means to be a human being relating to other human beings in the world in which they live" (V. Ostrom 1982a; 1993a).

That shouldn't be read as a rejection of rational choice theory. The point is that one should not stop with the orthodox way of applying "economic reasoning" to non-market decision making. Instead, it should take it as a starting point and use the concrete cases of uncertainty, social dilemmas, anomalies, and puzzles as vehicles that allow for basic advances in knowledge and "opens important new frontiers of inquiry" (V. Ostrom 1997a, 114; 1993a).

In the end, following Ostrom's logic, all could be translated as a problem of language. Constructing one language, the language of rational choice economic reasoning, is a powerful scientific tool as long as it is not blocking other possible ways of scientific reasoning. A rigid adherence to the mainstream economics rhetoric blocks the perspective and stalls the advances at the "frontiers of inquiry." The contribution of that rhetoric should be considered just the beginning, a first stage in a strategy. The language of rational choice should be seen as a vehicle aimed at, and part of an effort of constructing new levels of analysis and new, additional (and complementary) conceptualizations. In other words, it should be seen in a purely instrumental way: one tool in the intellectual toolkit. The promise and the dangers of rational choice draw attention to the fact that social scientists "need to be sensitive to the artifactual character of language and the intellectual constructions that are used to frame inquiry." Never forget that they are our intellectual constructions. A pluralism of conceptualizations is natural (V. Ostrom 1997a, 98–100). The intellectual enterprise requires moving back and forth across frameworks, theories, and models "so as to appropriately fit limiting conditions, opportunities, and hypothetical contingencies into the multidimensional facets characteristic of the artifactual nature of human habitation" (V. Ostrom 1997a, 105).

To sum up, advancing the agenda of the old "new science of politics" should be built by drawing on the early non-orthodox insights and the early work of Public Choice scholars but at the same time should not reject the "hard core rational choice" mainstream solidified at the center of the discipline in the latter years. However the real long term contribution of Public Choice lies not in the mere application and replication of economic models to non-market settings and situations, but in reviving a tradition of inquiry on institutional and constitutional decisions and arrangements and pushing it to new territories. And in order to do that it has to recover and explicitly incorporate the epistemic element:

> In my judgment, the innovative thrust in early Public-Choice efforts was to bring together concerns about "methodological individualism," "the nature of goods," and "decision-making arrangements" [institutions] as distinct elements to be taken into account in addressing market and non-market decision making (V. Ostrom [1973] 1989). These were elements of a general framework that could be used to specify the logic of prototypical situations in human societies. An epistemic element –the place of common knowledge and communities of shared understanding in decision situations – was neglected.
>
> (V. Ostrom 1997a, 102)

All these directions of development may be subsumed to the overriding concept of Epistemic Choice. The interplay between institutions, decisions and actions is, in the end, a matter of acting on ideas in an idea framed setting. Institutional choice or policy choice are ultimately forms of "epistemic choices." Learning is a problem of epistemic choice. While still vague, under-defined and under-explored, the emancipation of this concept and the approaches implicit in it seems to be a promising avenue. From Public Choice, to Institutional Analysis, to issues of Epistemic Choice is a straight fine line and a natural path to follow. The future of the intellectual revolution stirred by Public Choice, and the latter embodied in the new institutional theory, depends on making the right steps on that path:

> The future of Public Choice will be determined by its contributions to the epistemic level of choice in the cultural and social sciences and to the constitution of the epistemic order with which we live and work. . . . Rationality is affected by access to knowledge and communities of shared understanding; every individual is fallible; and everyone endures the costs of choices made under ignorance, misconceptions, deceptions, and strategic manipulations. Both the systems for making epistemic choices and those for making market choices contribute to the elucidation of knowledge and information essential to systems for making public choices. A key question is how variable structures among market arrangements affect conduct and performance. If the range of inquiry is extended to the epistemic realm, our concern is with how variable conceptions [ideas] affect the design of structures, the organization of processes, patterns of conduct, and performance.
>
> (V. Ostrom 1997a, 115)

To study the interplay between ideas and institutional structures and to approach institutional arrangements in the light of their function of knowledge processes and decision frameworks, "an alternative mind-set – a paradigmatic shift in perspective" is needed. Public Choice and institutional theory were a move in that direction. But a next step is required and that step should be more powerful and bolder. One could speak of an unfinished revolution. Yet that would betray the impatience of a short term vision. In the long run, that paradigm shift would be part of a historical or even evolutionary process of learning and growth of knowledge, and serve as yet another example of adaptability and ingenuity on behalf of human mind in its ongoing confrontation with the treats of chaos, tyranny and uncertainty.

Conclusions

A science of association, a science of citizenship, a science of liberty

At the core of the Bloomington School of Institutional Analysis lies a paradox. We have seen that, on the one hand, time and again it makes recourse to Alexis de Tocqueville's assertion that "a new science of politics is needed for a new world." Yet, on the other hand, the School is trying to revitalize and extend into the new millennium a traditional mode of analysis in Western political and economic thinking. This paradox could be reconciled if one sees the Bloomington School as an attempt to synthesize the traditional perspectives with the contemporary developments in social sciences and, thus, to re-ignite the old approach in the new intellectual and political context of the twentieth century. This synthesis that combines technical aspects of contemporary social science with the insights and accumulated experience of a lineage of thinkers of great distinction, preeminence and impact, could be described with reference to another of Tocqueville's ideas, the notion of "a science and art of association." According to Tocqueville, we are talking about "the mother of action, studied and applied by all" so important that "the progress of all the rest depends upon the progress it has made." Following the author of *Democracy in America* the Bloomington scholars were convinced that their contribution to the development of "the science of association" is a contribution to the development of "the foundation of a free and democratic governance" (V. Ostrom 1993b).

This synthesis of old and new, of traditional and contemporary ideas, attempted by the Indiana scholars, grew out of an actual public policy debate on the issue of governance in metropolitan areas and ultimately was meant to contribute to the improvement of the systems of governance in modern urban settings. Yet, very soon the relevance of its agenda for issues and areas that went beyond the metropolitan reform became evident. In the grand perspective outlined by Vincent Ostrom, the School's contribution may be seen as one stage or a step in the ongoing evolution of learning in human societies, an evolution coextensive with the evolutions of societies themselves. If histories are "accounts of evolutionary paths associated with the uses of language and knowledge and with the conduct of artisanship in problem-solving ways of life," the School is a deliberate effort to make a step forward in the growth of knowledge on human artisanship. A science of association is emerging in this historical process and the School's significance should be seen as a part of a collective effort to the further development of this science. Yet, seen from the shorter term perspective of the specific historical circumstances in which this research program emerged, one could interpret it as a counter-reaction to what was perceived as an important transformation in the American society triggered by a change in "the habits of the hearts and minds," in the ideas and principles used to understand and design its institutions.

> Instead of functioning as a self-governing society where people have recourse to covenantal methods for constituting civil bodies politic appropriate to diverse communities of relationships, the society is becoming highly national-ized. . . . Instead of presuming that human beings are fallible creatures of lim-ited comprehension, human beings presume to be omniscient observers capable of comprehending society as a whole. . . . The central government, referred to as "the government," is presumed to be a universal problem-solver. Citizenship is equated with voting and democracy is equated with majority rule. Winning elections is presumed to convey a mandate to rule; law is viewed as command and good citizens are viewed as obedient subjects. All societies are presumed to be nation-states in which "states" rule over societies. Democratic societies are transformed into sovereign states where a sole, simple, provident and creative power is presumed to rule over society. Such a power is viewed as the source of law, above the law and cannot itself be held accountable to law.
>
> (V. Ostrom [1990a] in McGinnis 1999a, 404–405)

Based on this diagnostic, the Bloomington scholars sought to fight back against the trend. Their diagnostic and willingness to fight back were not unique during the middle of the twentieth century. To give only one example, F. A. Hayek dealt extensively in his work with this state of affairs and its possible remedies. As in the case of all the other authors struggling to understand the sources of this historical transformation, investigations were to point out, sooner or later, to one specific area: the realm of ideas or the "climate of opinion" as shaped by influential intel-lectual and political elites. The Bloomington scholars themselves identified the source in a double intellectual evolution. First were the developments in social sci-ences where people were striving hard to imitate natural sciences (or what was per-ceived their "scientific methodology") in a search of universalism in explanation that overshadowed any real interest in the crucial relevance of the particular, spe-cific and contextual in human affairs. All that was followed by the fact that the con-cept of "the state" and the ideas of command and control system of organization it represented become accepted by the intellectuals and elites as the paradigmatic institutional and governance models (V. Ostrom 1993b, 18–20).

   That meant that one form of social organization, one form or way of constituting social order, one institutional design (i.e. the one associated with the modern state) become the framework through which almost everybody perceived social reality while that very perception was extensively theorized in modes that mimicked the natural sciences. All policy problems and their solutions were defined using the vocabulary of the mainstream theory in ways not only assuming the existence of a "state" (which in a sense was an empirical fact) but also the state was elevated to the status of the main tool for collective action and as a precondition or instrument for any conceivable policy solution. That meant that any other alternative form of organization or conceptualization was either considered irrelevant or marginalized.

If everything is centered on the notion of state and everything is thought through the lenses of a state mindset, the idea that political science is "the body of knowledge that properly informs the choices that human beings might make in formulating the design for institutions of government as embodied in constitutions" becomes almost meaningless. Once all acceptable institutional design has to fit within the state-centered conceptual framework, the notion of exploring "arguments about conditions and consequences used to inform constitutional choice" as they were "tested as hypotheses in empirical inquiries about political experiments" becomes almost irrelevant. Before the rise of Public Choice and new institutionalism, twentieth-century social science managed to almost bring to a standstill the tradition of thinking about governance and constitutional and institutional alternatives.

> Indeed, I have reason to believe that modern scholarship in the twentieth century involved a radical break with the ways of thinking about political relationships that applied to the design and modification of the American constitutional system in the late eighteenth and during much of the nineteenth century. Constitutions in the modern era are dismissed as formalities having little relevance for construing political experiences. The methods of the natural sciences are assumed to be the appropriate methods to apply to the study of political phenomena. Works like *The Federalist* are treated as propaganda, or as an ideology, without relevance for a political science.
>
> (V. Ostrom 1971, 20)

But, if arguments and ideas about the conditions and consequences of institutional and constitutional arrangements should be the core of our preoccupation, then recovering that way of thinking and doing political analysis is mandatory. One prerequisite of that effort is to go back "at least to the seventeenth and eighteenth centuries to a great ferment of discussion, debate, and violent struggles bearing upon basic constitutional issues" illustrated by authors like Locke, Montesquieu, David Hume, Adam Smith, Hamilton and Madison, and to understand and reappraise the mode of analysis they developed. Their task was of no minor historical significance. The challenge that they, and especially the Americans, faced was to formulate an alternative solution to the one developed by Hobbes to the riddle of human governance. Hobbes implied that the institution of government (i.e. the Sovereign) dominated society from a single center of authority, and was basically above the law. The task that the American thinkers and statesmen faced was, as defined by Vincent Ostrom, to formulate an alternative to Hobbes and to conceptualize "how a system of government with multiple centers of authority reflecting opposite and rival interests could be held accountable to enforceable rules of constitutional law" (V. Ostrom 1971, 20–23). Moreover, they had to engage in a political experiment to demonstrate that it was workable. The contrast between Hobbes's formulation and the American experiment is radical. In Hobbes's design one single center of authority exists, the Sovereign. In the other, no single center of authority dominates; all authority is confined by rules, and governance structures coexist. New governance arrangements corresponding to new communities of interests are constituted "as political entities enjoy concurrent and autonomous existence" in a "federal system of government." Those studying Hobbes's theory of sovereignty "might have concluded that the absolutism inherent in that formulation offered such a small probability to achieve a just and prosperous commonwealth that alternatives merited consideration and experimentation." However, "Locke, Montesquieu, Spinoza, Hume, Smith, Adams, Hamilton, Jefferson, Madison, and many others might be viewed as drawing upon their critically rational capabilities to conceptualize, design, and establish the experimental foundations for different systems of governance" (V. Ostrom 1973a, 22; 1971; 1990a; 1990b).

The great explorations in constitutionalism and governance and the boldness and complexity of the American experiments in constitutional choice, thinkers fuelled, were reflected and reconfirmed in Tocqueville's work. Tocqueville did not limit his observations at the national level of constitutional arrangements and policies but looked also at the American constitutional system as a whole and that meant the inclusion of the institutions of local government. His analysis confirmed the viability of the American experiment based on the theory of a compound republic as opposed to that of an extended unitary republic and made clear once for and all why the political theory of a compound republic was not to be confused with traditional theories of sovereignty (V. Ostrom 1971, 25–27).

The review of the intellectual challenges and solutions before the emergence to preeminence of the nation state based perspective illustrates how fundamentally different the approaches to the organization of governance in human societies could be. The scholars of the twentieth century that turned their back on earlier traditions of inquiry were not only challenging scholarship but also policy practice. The reform principles of the twentieth-century policy scientists and reformers were the antithesis of the design principles used to formulate the American experiments in constitutional choice and the ways eighteenth-century thinkers approached the issue of alternative institutional designs for political order. The way government was seen in the twentieth century was a fundamental challenge to the political theory of a compound republic and its underlying premises exploring "what it means for human beings to design and create systems of government based upon reflection and choice." And thus the debate in political science in the twentieth century became a battle to determine what intellectual tools were appropriate to determining the future of the American experiment in constitutional choice and, with it, the political future of the world. The Bloomington scholars were among those that identified and explored the nature of the challenge, and, in turn, challenged the challengers. Starting small, from the local level, by participating in the much applied policy debate on metropolitan governance, they managed to reconstruct an entire intellectual system on longstanding foundations. At the core of the system was a bold conclusion and challenge:

What is required is an alternative mind-set – a paradigmatic shift in perspective . . . The focus upon States governing Societies has stripped much of human consciousness about what it means to be a human being coping with the exigencies of everyday life. Before we can come to terms with potentials for change and reformability in human societies, we need to understand how human beings come to terms with the constitution of their ways of life in the microcosms of everyday life. . . . Concepts of States governing Societies are inadequate for the peoples of the contemporary world . . . The illusion that democratic Republics can be fashioned under circumstances where States govern Societies is also a serious delusion. States cannot solve the problems of Societies or Mankind. [And] until we rethink the basic place of language in the political economy of life . . . [g]iven the languages of the cosmopolitan manipulators of the symbolism of mass media, we can reasonably expect the twenty-first century to be seriously plagued by times of trouble.

(V. Ostrom 1993b, 24–25)

The Bloomington School's message is in the end a challenge to liberate ourselves from the intellectual idols of our time and an invitation to explore, using the power of reason, imagination and of a solid exposure to the empirical reality, the various possible institutional alternatives available to us today. And thus, in the end, one could read in between the lines of the works of the Bloomington scholars' one ultimate message: a call to free our institutional and political imagination. As Vincent Ostrom (1990a) put it, in order to do that, we need to return to the idea that government cannot be the universal problem solver because "there can be no universal problem-solver capable of addressing diverse problems as applying to societies as wholes." Rather, "human societies require diverse patterns of association to cope with problems of varying scales under variable time and place exigencies." To explore those patterns is the task of the "science of association." And that science is also "a science of citizenship" and a "science of liberty."

Postscript

Rethinking institutional analysis and development. Dialogues with Vincent and Elinor Ostrom

Vincent Ostrom: rethinking the terms of choice

Vincent Ostrom: Probably the best way to characterize our approach would be to start with one of our most influential themes: the idea that broad concepts such as "markets" and "states," or "socialism" and "capitalism," do not take us very far in thinking about patterns of order in human society. For example, when some "market" economists speak of "capitalism," they fail to distinguish between an open, competitive market economy and a state-dominated mercantile economy. In this, they follow Marx. He argued that "capitalism" has a competitive dynamic that leads to market domination by a few large monopoly or monopoly-like enterprises. But what Marx called "capitalism," Adam Smith called "mercantilism." Similarly, many authors who write about "capitalism" fail to recognize the complexity of capitalist economic institutions. They overlook the rich structures of communal and public enterprises in societies with open and highly competitive market economies.

Instead, we should expect to find some combination of market and non-market structures in every society, and we should recognize the complex configuration of institutions behind labels such as "capitalism." We might usefully think about combinations of private and public economies existing side by side. However, it's important to stress that not all forms of public enterprise are, or need to be, state-owned and operated. Various forms of communal or public ownership may exist apart from state ownership. Markets are diverse and complex entities. Markets for different types of goods and services may take on quite different characteristics. Some may work well under the most impersonal conditions. Others may depend upon personal considerations involving high levels of trust among trading partners. In other words, the options are much greater than we imagine, and we can see this is true if we don't allow our minds to be trapped within narrowly constrained intellectual horizons.

Q: The Workshop in Political Theory and Policy Analysis is the organizational expression of the Bloomington research program. What does the Workshop do, and how do you do it?

VO: The Workshop was organized with distinctive teaching and research goals in mind. We called it a "workshop" to communicate a commitment to artisanship and collaboration. Colleagues and students work with one another in conceptualizing the task to be undertaken and in the conduct of inquiry itself. One of the main objectives of the Workshop is to challenge the prevailing emphasis on government as a unitary command structure. The first programmatic articulation of the argument was in a paper I wrote with Tiebout and Warren, "The Organization of Government in Metropolitan Areas: A Theoretical Inquiry" (1961). During the 1960s, several very important works with similar emphases were published contemporaneously: James Buchanan and Gordon Tullock's *The Calculus of Consent: The Logical Foundations of Constitutional Democracy* (1962) and Mancur Olson's *The Logic of Collect Action: Public Goods and the Theory of Groups* (1965). Buchanan and Tullock were concerned with the logic of constitutional choice in establishing the legal framework for collective action. Mancur Olson clarified the logical dilemma entailed in collective action and public entrepreneurship. My work as an advisor to the Alaska Constitutional Convention, and Elinor's dissertation work on "Public Entrepreneurship: A Case Study in Ground Water Basin Development" (1965), added to this burst of theoretical and conceptual creativity regarding theories of goods, public economies, and the constitution of order in human societies. My books *The Intellectual Crisis in American Public Administration* (1973a), and *The Political Theory of a Compound Republic: Designing the American Experiment* (1971), and Elinor's *Governing the Commons: The Evolution of Institutions for Collective Action* (1990) resulted from the intellectual stimulus created by the organization of the Public Choice Society.

One of the distinctive features of our approach is our method for evaluating institutional performance. In our first generation of studies, conducted by graduate and undergraduate students, we compared performance of police in neighborhoods served by Unigov, the consolidated government of Indianapolis and Marion County, with the performance of police in three municipalities in Marion County that had remained independent. This led to a decade of work on policing and governance, including a major study of 80 metropolitan areas sponsored by the National Science Foundation. This work was later extended to include other issues, governance systems and geographical areas.

The possibility that systems of governance could be organized in different ways and yield different patterns of performance could be verified only by empirical analysis. So, we formulated the various positions on the issues as competing hypotheses, gathered empirical data, and created a database that would support in-depth statistical analysis. As the project expanded in scope, we paid very close attention to the way we gathered data and the way we structured it in our databases so that we could derive useful statistical measures. We've since faced a number of similar challenges in gathering data and organizing databases. We've studied the organization of irrigation systems in Nepal, and institutional arrangements for forest management in Nepal, East Africa and Latin America, to name a few examples. We were able to take the results of these studies and model the institutions formally in game-theoretical terms. These formal results were then used in turn to design laboratory experiments that help to clarify the logic of choice confronting persons in different institutional structures.

Q: Is there a specific approach in the mode of analysis employed by the Bloomington School?

VO: We try to combine formal approaches, fieldwork and experiments in order to "penetrate" social reality rather than to use formal techniques to "distance" ourselves from it, as Walter Eucken once expressed the difference. We seek to find a fit between the conceptual framework used by the researcher and the framework used and shared by the people we are trying to study. The researcher or observer needs to take into account the way people think about and experience themselves and their situation.

If a human group is bound together by a shared purpose or identity, then it has a set of understandings that order the relationships among the members of the group in common. No such group is entirely freestanding; each embraces or is embraced by other groups and other configurations of human relationships, and these configurations each have their own structure or logic. We use these structured social relationships – these overlapping sets of shared understandings – to coordinate our behavior over space and time. It follows that all human choices and actions will be to some extent socially or culturally conditioned. But this does not prevent us from identifying certain human universals, or from drawing comparisons across cultures. There are aspects of human nature, and certain features of social interaction, that can be expected to show up in all human societies. The analysis of particular groups or associations, then, can be placed in a comparative context. We can seek to understand how culturally singular groups come together and strive to solve universal problems.

As I said, we need to address problems of institutional analysis and development with methods that allow us to penetrate social reality rather than distance ourselves from it. A critical dialogue between the observers and those being observed can reduce the potential for observer error. Rethinking the terms of choice that apply both to observers and to the observed remains a continuing challenge for exploring the relationship of human institutions to potentials for development. Working with both students and visiting scholars from different parts of the world is essential to our understanding of the constitution of order in human societies.

Q: Your work and the work done at the Workshop illuminates complex institutional configurations only partially captured by the standard ways of thinking and talking about institutions in public discussion and even the social sciences. For instance, you have repeatedly warned of the limits of approaches analyzing social reality exclusively in terms of polar concepts such as "market" and "state." Does that mean that your approach could be described as an attempt to go conceptually beyond "states" and "markets?" In other words, is your vision the foundation of a sort of theoretical "Third Way?"

VO: I would be very reluctant to say that. I see my approach as a set of theoretical lenses. They are better lenses, I hope, than those that compel us to perceive social reality in terms of just two ideal types: states and markets. Dichotomies should be avoided in the social sciences. Regarding the market, in my view, the market has a crucial and unique role in a complex social order. The perspective developed by the Workshop, helps, I hope, to better locate and understand the market in the context of the broader, complex social order. Competitive market structures play a vital role in achieving high degrees of commensurability in the use of money as a measure of value. In the absence of those conditions, money prices give distorted information regarding commensurabilities. This is a fundamental issue. Price provides diagnostic tools for social change and adjustment processes which lead to development. Using price signals, individuals can begin to understand why problems of distortion in pricing arise and thus solve the problems generating those distortions.

Q: In your approach, market prices and the opportunities and choices they signal, should be seen in the broader context of an entire universe of choices and opportunities. The implication is that while keeping an eye on the market processes, we should pay equal attention to the rest of that universe of opportunities and choices and the institutions and processes they engender.

VO: Indeed. Modern society is remarkably complex. For instance, there are millions of different variations in economic goods. Each variation is the result of a particular kind of production process by which factors are transformed into products. The way human beings relate to one another in the production, exchange, and consumption of diverse goods and services requires an extraordinary variety in patterns of organization.

We should understand this broader way that prices signal opportunities and avenues of choice. When we set about to choose institutional arrangements, we are thus confronted with establishing how price signals indicate the relative advantages of the available institutional alternatives. Price, in its most general sense, can be defined as the terms on which alternatives are available. Some estimate of the terms on which alternatives are available, or might become available, is necessary before one can begin to estimate the demand for alternative institutional arrangements. Rather than choosing on the basis of money prices for discrete commodities, the choice here is at a different level. It is the choice of configurations of rule-ordered relationships – the choice of institutions – that is at stake. The relative merits of alternative institutional arrangements are much more difficult to assess than are those of commodities on the market. Nevertheless, choices regarding institutions still need to be made.

When people exercise their prerogatives as citizens under a properly constituted system of government, they are able to take into account how their decisions may affect the productive and consumptive possibilities that will be available to them under the institutions they fashion. This implies that individual choice is not limited to choice on the basis of price in a market, but involves a broader range of calculations extending to the choice of terms on which alternatives become available under diverse institutional arrangements, including both market and non-market institutions.

Q: Turning from the issue of the "market" to the one of the "government," I think it is safe to say that you approach the "government" issue using the same broad vision that you apply to the analysis of markets – a vision defined by concepts of "opportunity" and "choice."

VO: We need not think of "government" or "governance" as something provided by states alone. Families, voluntary associations, villages, and other forms of human association all involve some form of self-government. Rather than looking only to states, we need to give much more attention to building the kinds of basic institutional structures that enable people to find ways of relating constructively to one another and of resolving problems in their daily lives. Which, in addition, also connect to more encompassing communities and patterns of interaction. People can rely on self-help in arranging their institutions, rather than depending upon "the elite decision makers of government." By relying upon principles of self-governance to apply to diverse units of government in fashioning a highly federalized and decentralized system, people can begin to alter, in a significant way, the price that applies to the supply of institutional arrangements in self-governing societies.

When an individual within a local economy can help to provide the infrastructure of communal services – develop public thoroughfares, provide for the security of persons and property in a local community, arrange effective sanitation facilities, fire services, and healthful water supplies, etc., while at the same time extending the range of his or her own entrepreneurial opportunities to reach out to larger economic horizons – he or she can create indigenous patterns of economic and political development. In such circumstances, each person can learn how both to serve his or her own interests and, at the same time, to serve others in their communities. Democratic societies cannot be fashioned without such roots of self-governance. Nor can democracies survive in military struggles for power, whether within nation-states or between nation-states. For this reason, the basic architecture of modern societies must, as Tocqueville has argued, draw upon a science of association to fashion rules of social interaction that apply from the level of the village to the level of the nation-state and beyond.

Q: An important part of your work is dedicated to the examination of the conditions under which such communities could form institutions and organizations that reflect their own choices and the opportunities facing them.

VO: Yes, I've dedicated a large part of my work to understanding the conditions affecting the way human beings relate to one another and those that generate a functional social order. Some of these conditions, and consequently my work, refer to very concrete institutional structures. For instance, the viability of market relationships depends upon the availability of public or quasi-public goods and services. Most operating economies will thus be mixed economies, containing both public and private enterprises. However, the work done at the Workshop demonstrates that public services need not be provided by a central government or the state. Many streets, roads and other thoroughfares, fire protection, police services, and other such services may be arranged by local communities. These arrangements may rely on private entrepreneurs, but under terms and conditions that are communally specified.

Other, perhaps deeper, conditions for social order include shared beliefs and norms within communities about how they regard one another, what they consider to be fair, how they distinguish right from wrong, and how they see society and nature as wholes coming together to constitute a universal order. If there were no bases for trust, and no shared community of understanding about the meaning of right and wrong, then the terms of trade in exchange relationships, or the patterns of reciprocity in communal and social relationships, would become extraordinarily precarious. Such societies could not "develop." This is why it is necessary to see the role of religious institutions, for instance, as blending with and contributing to the economic, social, and political institutions in a society.

Q: In your own work you also put a special emphasis on the role of ideas . . .

VO: There are numerous ways in which ideas influence social order and institutional arrangements. Lord Bauer, for instance, makes the very interesting point that the success of the market order is challenged everywhere because it "provides no mechanism for its own survival." Success in the market, Bauer argues, "requires concentration on concrete problems of production and marketing." These problems require a devotion of time and energy that does not leave room for people to develop "sustained and perceptive interests in general issues and their analysis." They lack a clear idea of the market, its functioning, and its implications for the general institutional performance of the social system. This is much the same issue that Tocqueville raised when he expressed concern that the pursuit of wealth, in a democratic society, might come at the cost of citizenship. Individuals who pay attention only to market prices in determining their choices may soon become vulnerable to political arguments such as that "workers and peasants" could achieve greater advantage by expropriating private property and instituting a socialist society. The naïve maximizer might select the option offered by those who make the biggest promises.

Bauer's "workers and peasants" need to be aware of the benefits of a market order. They would then understand the naïveté of revolutionary rhetoric and the likelihood that radical political intervention in the market order will lead to increasing oppression and deteriorating conditions of life. Real revolutionary potential exists when people establish processes of decision making that specify the terms and conditions of government where citizens reserve to themselves fundamental authority that applies to the governance of society including the authority to set the terms and conditions of government. When people exercise the prerogatives of constitutional choice we can view people as citizens exercising, at the constitutional level, the basic prerogatives that control the other aspects of institutional choice that may be exercised by instrumentalities of government. When such conditions prevail we might think of people becoming self-governing.

Q: What could be done in order to create such conditions for self-governance?

VO: The answer to this question has many dimensions. The most basic is that people would need to know more than how to make decisions on the basis of the prices that are available in markets. They would also need to know, as Tocqueville has suggested, the science and art of association. In order to secure the advantages that come both from working together in diverse types of cooperative enterprise, and come from systems of government where no one exercises unlimited authority, and where all officials can be held to account for the proper discharge of the public trust, people need to know, to some extent, how these things work and why they are important. Each individual would then be a knowledgeable actor in a self-governing society where opportunity is a function of both organizational diversity and complexity. A Tocquevillian science of association – a body of knowledge that helps us to understand the nature of social order, and the forms of social interaction that lead to mutual advantage – is the foundation for choosing among the institutional alternatives open to us. Now, it remains to be determined whether human beings can actually use such methods of discussion, reflection, and choice to fashion the future course of human civilization. There is some basis for an affirmative response to the question posed by Alexander Hamilton in the opening paragraph of the first essay in *The Federalist Papers*: "whether societies of men are really capable or not of establishing good government from reflection and choice . . ." Now, all societies remain vulnerable to failure. Tie conditions for an open society, as expounded by Karl Popper, such as legal due process or opportunities for constitutional revision, are necessary but not sufficient for societies to achieve "good government" from reflection and choice. Some degree of institutional weakness and failure is likely in all societies. However, it seems possible that our institutions will become increasingly subject to reflection and choice as new patterns of communication and interaction spread throughout the human population. So, to answer Hamilton, as new opportunities for reflection and choice become more widespread among humankind, we need not be confined only to exigencies of accident and force.

Q: What do you consider to be the most important intellectual challenge confronting the scholars exploring the "science of association?"

VO: We create conceptual distinctions in order to think and communicate about complex orders. Language always simplifies. Yet, recourse to overly abstract simplifications such as "states" and "markets," "capitalism" and "socialism," the "modern" and the "less developed," is becoming increasingly useless. We must take care to not reify concepts and conceptual models – to treat them as though they are realities. We should avoid simple dichotomies. The conditions for public entrepreneurship require reflection and choice grounded in the requirements of liberty and justice as well as those for economic efficiency. Our goals must meet multiple standards of acceptability. The question, then, is how can we come to terms with institutional analysis and development that is pertinent to the problems of choice confronting people in different parts of the contemporary world?

Q: How do you see the current scholarly contributions inspired by or related to your vision? How vibrant is scholarly contribution to the "science of association" these days?

VO: There are emerging communities of scholars in all parts of the world who share many of the aforementioned perspectives and presuppositions. These scholars view conceptual, cultural, economic, ethical and political considerations as closely linked. The work of these scholars is variously referred to as studying "public choice," the "new institutional economics," "transaction-cost economics," "institutional analysis and development," and the "new political economy." This work is creating a fresh understanding of the options that are available to people in different parts of the world, and new tools for analysts who are trying to come to a better understanding of human potential.

One of the most important aspects of this work is the emphasis on the range of choices available for constituting ordered social relationships. The command of the sovereign is not the only way to achieve an ordered way of life. Most societies, most of the time, have relied upon some combination of command structures and consensual arrangements. If we are to create alternatives to imperial orders, we must grapple with the problem of constituting systems of government that operate with the consent of the governed. The scholars working in these areas are contributing to a better understanding of that simple, crucial and so much neglected issue.

Elinor Ostrom: rethinking governance systems and challenging disciplinary boundaries

Q: For most people, your name is associated with your well-known research on "common-pool resources": groundwater basins, irrigation systems, fisheries, grazing areas and communal forests. In the absence of special institutional arrangements for their management, these resources are in danger of being overused, overgrazed, etc. and depleted. Your research on common-pool resources has been defined by disciplinary and methodological pluralism with a very focused empirical and policy concern. This approach has become an identifying mark of the Bloomington Workshop in Political Theory and Policy Analysis, and has become a model for cutting-edge social science research. Less well known is that your work on common-pool resources is part of a broader research program that uses this distinctive approach to institutional analysis to challenge currently existing disciplinary boundaries and to advance the study of collective action and governance systems.

Elinor Ostrom: Indeed, the Workshop's research on common-pool resources is part of a broader effort to develop an empirically supported theory of self-organizing and self-governing forms of collective action. The nature of the task demands an interdisciplinary approach. A great deal of contemporary policy tends to recommend Smith's concept of market order for all private goods and Hobbes's conception of the Leviathan – now called "the sovereign State" – for all collective goods. The poverty of the oppositions between private and public, market and state, stems, to some extent, from the separation of political economy into two disciplines, political science and economics, which have developed along separate paths. While academic specialization has advantages, overspecialization has dangers. Part of the unfortunate legacy of overspecialization is this kind of sweeping policy prescription based on overly stylized ideas about the institutional possibilities.

On the one hand, when economists show that market arrangements fail, they are frequently willing to make simple recommendations that *the* State should take care of these problems without asking how incentives are generated within State bureaucracies to improve performance. The existing theory of collective action, which underlies the work of all political economists, has accentuated the presumed necessity of the State as an alternative to the Market, since the accepted theory predicts that voluntary self-organization to provide public goods or manage common-pool resources is highly unlikely. On the other hand, when political scientists and policy analysts show that over-centralized governmental units fail to perform, they sometimes recommend "privatization" without working through the logic of how to create a set of private incentives that increases performance and accountability.

My academic career has been devoted to the development of empirically grounded theories to cross the great divide between economics and the other social sciences in the conduct of comparative institutional analysis. In the 1970s and early 1980s, we conducted extensive research on how institutional arrangements affect the output, efficiency, and adaptability of urban service delivery in American metropolitan areas. Our more recent research on common-pool resources is relatively well recognized, while the theoretical dimensions of this effort are less known. My hope is, however, that the examination and analysis of common-pool resources in the field, in the experimental laboratory, and in theory, contribute to the development of an empirically valid theory of self-organization and self-governance.

Q: You mentioned the analytical and theoretical relevance of the problem of the "commons." However, doesn't the "commons" as a phenomenon have relevance that goes beyond institutional analysis?

EO: Many think the commons problem refers to self-organized governance and management of various natural resource systems by communities of the past. They endow these communities with a sort of archaic or exotic aura. Others think that they will slowly disappear – relics of a dying past, to be taken over by modern institutions. To those who doubt the viability of commons governance institutions in the modern age, let me point out that many such institutions exist and are proliferating, and not only in the area of natural resources management.

The modern corporation is itself a case in point. Since the foundational work of Ronald Coase, students of industrial organization understand that that a firm shares many aspects with other common-property institutions. A contemporary housing condominium is also a commons institution. While individual families own the apartments in a "condo," they have joint rights and duties in relationship to the buildings and the grounds of the condominium complex. Some of the most imaginative work on enhancing urban neighborhoods relates to helping tenants of public housing projects acquire joint ownership and management of these projects. This is a shift from government ownership to a common-property arrangement. The Internet is another commons that is certainly relevant to modern life. So the problem of the commons has an ongoing practical relevance.

Let me go back to the notion that the commons is a "relic." Local, self-organized institutions are a significant asset in the institutional portfolio of humankind, and need to survive into the twenty-first century. Many indigenous institutions that developed to govern and manage local common-pool resources have proven themselves capable of enabling individuals to use these resources intensively over the long run. Some have survived centuries or even millennia without destroying the delicate resource base on which individuals depend for their livelihood. International donors and nongovernmental organizations, as well as national governments and charities, have often acted, under the banner of environmental conservation, in a way that has unwittingly destroyed the very social capital – shared relationships, norms, knowledge and understanding – that has been used by resource users to sustain the productivity of natural capital over the ages. The effort to preserve biodiversity should not lead to the destruction of institutional diversity. We have yet to adequately recognize how the wide diversity of rules groups have devised through the ages work to protect the resources on which they rely. These institutions are most in jeopardy when central government officials assume that they do not exist (or are not effective) simply because the government has not put them in place.

Thus, in response to your question, my answer is straightforward: indeed the commons have an enormous relevance beyond theory. If we do not find the means to develop and enhance the capabilities to govern and manage common-pool situations effectively, the absence of such institutions in the twenty-first century will lead to fundamental social and economic problems. Commons governance institutions are by no means relics of the past. The more we learn about them over time, the more likely it is that future policy-making will build more effectively on the strengths of these forms of institutions, and avoid some of the errors of the past.

Q: In your work, you stress the danger of using models and metaphors unchecked by comparison to empirical reality. One of your major concerns about the treatment of commons and collective action problems in the literature was that the dominant models and metaphors were misleading.

EO: In general, I am not opposed to modeling and using models for policy analysis. I am opposed to the persistent reliance upon models like the "prisoners' dilemma" or the metaphor of "the tragedy of the commons," after years of empirical research in both the lab and the field has called their universal applicability into question. Many researchers drawing on these models have concluded that the participants in a commons dilemma are trapped in an inexorable process from which they cannot extract themselves. It is then inferred that external authorities are necessary to impose rules and regulations on local resource users who are otherwise incapable of saving themselves. This vision of the problem, according to which resource users are trapped in a tragedy of their own making, was consistent with early textbooks on resource economics, and with predictions derived from non-cooperative game theory for finitely repeated dilemmas. Contemporary policy analysts also share the belief that it is possible to design and impose optimal rules for the management of common-pool resources from the top down. Because common-pool resources, and their users, are viewed as relatively similar to one another, and because of the simplicity of the models, officials (assumed to be acting in the public interest) are thought to be capable of devising uniform and effective rules for an entire region. Prescriptions calling for central governments to impose uniform regulations over most natural resources are thus consistent with important bodies of theoretical work.

However, empirical research does not support the idea that a central agency could solve all resource problems for a large region with simple, top down directives. Field studies in all parts of the world have found that local groups of resource users, sometimes by themselves and sometimes with the assistance of external actors, have created a wide diversity of institutional arrangements for cooperating with common-pool resources. Field studies have also found multiple cases where resource users have failed to self-organize.

Thus, the core empirical and theoretical question is why self-organization is successfully undertaken in some cases and not in others. With better knowledge about what enhances local self-governance, it is possible to design larger-scale institutional arrangements that generate accurate information, provide open and fair conflict-resolution mechanisms, share risk, and back up efforts at local and regional levels.

Q: One important feature of your approach is the role of fieldwork and case studies in testing the models and theories you employ. The conclusion that overuse and destruction of common-pool resources is not an inescapable outcome, but that users facing a commons dilemma can voluntarily devise effective management strategies, is the result of extensive empirical evidence gathered in the field. For instance you have traveled to Nepal.

EO: The study of irrigation systems in Nepal found that irrigation systems built and governed by the farmers themselves are on average in better repair, deliver more water, and have higher agricultural productivity than those provided and managed by a government agency. Also we found greater equity of water delivery in traditional, farmer-managed systems than in more modern, agency-managed systems. Therefore, one of the questions we have studied has been: how is it possible that "primitive" irrigation systems significantly outperform systems that have been improved by the construction of modern, permanent, concrete-and-iron head-works, funded largely by donors, and constructed by professional engineering firms?

Many factors contribute to these counterintuitive results. But most of them relate to the different incentives faced by key participants in the finance, design, construction, operation, and maintenance of farmer-governed and agency-run systems. On farmer-governed irrigation systems, farmers craft their own rules, which frequently offset the perverse incentives they face in their particular physical and cultural settings. These rules may be almost invisible to outsiders, especially when they are well accepted by participants who do not even think of them as especially noteworthy. To discover this diversity of locally designed rules, to understand how the institutional arrangements work given the biophysical conditions of a resource, and the culture of the users, you have no other choice but to go there and do field work. I have also been blessed by the opportunity to work with wonderful colleagues and graduate students who have together spent many years in the field. We are now working with a network of Collaborating Research Centers in Africa, Asia, and Latin America to study the rules used in government-managed, privately-managed, and communally-managed forests and their impact on forest sustainability.

Q: The conclusions of the Bloomington research program have very significant implications for economic development policy.

EO: Academics, aid donors, international nongovernmental organizations, central governments and local citizens need to learn and relearn that no government can develop the full array of knowledge, institutions and social capital needed to govern development efficiently and sustainably. The sheer variety of cultural and biological adaptations to diverse ecological conditions is so great that I am willing to make the following assertion: any single, comprehensive set of formal laws intended to govern a large expanse of territory containing diverse ecological niches is bound to fail in many of the areas where it is applied.

Improving the abilities of those directly engaged in the particulars of their local conditions to organize themselves in deeply nested enterprises is potentially a more successful strategy for solving resource problems than attempting to implement idealized, theoretically optimal institutional arrangements. There is plenty that national government officials can do to help a self-governing society. They can provide efficient, fair, and honest court systems, effective property right systems, and large-scale infrastructure projects – such as national highways – that cannot be provided locally.

Probably one of the most telling illustrations of this issue comes from the work I just mentioned on irrigation systems. Irrigation systems are pivotal for sustainable growth in the developing world. Most efforts to develop irrigation focus on physical capital in the form of dams, aqueducts, diversion weirs and canals. The development of adequate physical capital is, of course, a necessary step in achieving enhanced benefits. But many technically advanced irrigation systems have not been sustainable. Underlying all these problems is a variety of perverse incentives and institutional failures. The initial plans for many of the major irrigation projects in developing countries focused almost exclusively on engineering designs for the physical systems and ignored organizational questions. This engineering bias leads to the neglect of proper incentives. Project engineers, for example, face strong pressures to focus on the design of physical works while ignoring social infrastructure, and to focus on larger rather than smaller projects. Few engineering schools offer any courses on property rights or institutional arrangements. So, engineers are trained to think that physical infrastructure is the "whole bag."

Farmers on large-scale projects often face perverse incentives. Because they lack control over water availability, there is a substantial temptation to refrain from contributing resources to maintenance. Moreover, when very large sums are channeled through politicians who use the process to enhance their power and wealth, project plans cannot be expected to accurately reflect conditions on the ground. When engineers assigned to operations and maintenance hold low-status positions, are underpaid, and are not dependent on the farmers of a system for budgetary support or career advancement, large government-managed systems cannot be expected to perform very well. And, one can expect major problems of corruption.

Performance is good where the incentive systems for operations and maintenance units reward engineers for drawing on local knowledge and working directly with farmers. The irrigation agency's budget is not even loosely linked to system performance when the revenue received is not linked to taxes levied on the value of crop yield, or the amount of water taken. Where fees are imposed in name only, and do not represent an important source of revenue to the units operating and maintaining systems, and where hiring, retention, and promotion of employees are in no way connected with the performance of a public facility, nothing offsets the dependency of the community on insulated officials. Thus, while some improvements in the operation of irrigation systems can come from building better physical structures, the key problems relate to the incentives facing officials and farmers.

Over the next several decades, the most important consideration in irrigation development will be that of institutional design – the process of developing a set of rules that participants in a process understand, agree upon, and are willing to follow, so long as they know that most other participants are also following them or face sanctions for non-compliance.

Therefore, while it is essential to understand the physical side of development projects, the emphasis should be on the institutional side. Crafting an institution is a process that must directly involve the users throughout. The term "crafting" emphasizes the artisanship required to devise institutions that both match the unique combinations of variables present in any one system and can adapt to changes in these variables over time. Involving users directly in this process increases the likelihood of institutions that are well matched to the local physical, economic, and cultural environment. Experience with organizing farmers over the last several decades has shown that simply giving individuals organizational blueprints is not enough to change the incentives and behavior of those individuals. Nor is the problem simply one of organizing farmers. The failure to achieve sustainability and the failure to organize farmers are symptoms of pervasive ignorance about how effective institutions are crafted over time and about the role donor institutions and governments should play in that process.

Q: The role proposed for central governmental officials and for donor agencies is quite different from that proposed by earlier approaches that called for the top down creation of institutions and organizations based on a single institutional blueprint.

EO: Crafting development-enhancing institutions is an ongoing process that must directly involve the users. Instead of designing a single blueprint for all places and circumstances, officials need to enhance the capability of social actors to design their own institutions. The incentives facing farmers, villagers, and officials are more important in determining long-term performance than is the engineering of the physical systems. When farmers select – and compensate – their own officials to govern and manage an irrigation system that the farmers own and operate, the incentives faced by the officials are closely aligned to the incentives of farmers in the system, while the performance of the system is linked to that of the officials. In many centralized, national government systems, no such linkage exists.

Donor agencies need to direct their efforts toward enhancing the productive capabilities of a larger proportion of the local community rather than simply trying to replace primitive infrastructures with modern, technically sophisticated ones. Showering a region with funds is a poor investment if that serves mainly to bolster political careers and builds little at the ground level. It makes more sense to invest modest levels of donor funds in local projects in which the recipients are willing to invest some of their own resources. If the level of external funding becomes very large without being strongly tied to a responsibility for repayment over time, local efforts at participation may be directed more at rent seeking than at productive investment activities.

Q: It is noteworthy that the ability to overcome local collective action problems and build functional institutions requires an internal capacity of communities to mobilize, organize and cooperate.

EO: That is why the Workshop puts special emphasis on the concept of "public entrepreneurship." Entrepreneurship is not limited to the private sector. When there is an environment that enhances their capacities to organize, mobilize resources and invest in public facilities, local public entrepreneurs can develop a wide variety of efficiency-enhancing solutions to local collective-action problems. In some cases, donors can encourage national governments to reduce restrictions on the ability of individuals to form local associations, to establish a common treasury, and to undertake a wide variety of local community projects. Encouraging such groups to form associations of associations enhances their ability to learn from each other about what works, and to monitor their own members.

Investing in short-term projects to enhance citizen participation has, however, frequently failed in the past. Solving collective-action problems is a costly and time-consuming process. If it is to succeed, it requires a parallel effort to create solid and functional institutions at the national level. Many of the so-called participation programs initiated by donors, NGOs and national governments involve little more than calling meetings, with little extension of real responsibility. Just attending meetings is boring and costly and not worth it.

Q: It seems that your research has two distinctive implications for policy. On the one hand, an upbeat one: people can overcome collective action problems in very creative ways without needing a Leviathan. On the other hand, a cautious one: self-governance is not an easy process and there is no guaranteed universal blueprint for achieving it.

EO: It is now obvious that the search for rules that will improve institutions and government is not as straightforward as many scholars – some of them not at all utopian or naïve – were once inclined to believe. For instance, there is an incredibly large combination of rules that could be adopted to overcome the commons dilemmas in different ecological and social settings. Because multiple rules affect each of the many components of a particular setting, conducting such a complete analysis would involve more time and resources than many policy analysts have assumed in the past. Instead of assuming that designing effective governance systems is a relatively simple analytical task that can be undertaken by a team of objective analysts sitting in the national capital, or at an international headquarters, it is important that we understand policy design to require experimentation with combinations of large numbers of component parts.

When we change policy – when we add a rule, change a rule, or adopt some new set of rules – we are in effect running an experiment based on more or less informed expectations about the likely outcome. It is important to recognize that the complexity of the ever-changing biological and socio-economic environment, combined with the complexity of institutional rules, makes it fairly likely that any proposed change of rules will fail.

The need to experiment and the chance that we're going to make mistakes alerts us to the positive side of redundancy and multiple, parallel jurisdictions. In any design process that involves a substantial probability of error, using redundant teams of designers has been shown as one way of reducing the costs of big mistakes. If there are multiple jurisdictions with considerable autonomy at the local level, policy makers can experiment more or less simultaneously within their separate jurisdictions. It is potentially feasible for a central government to undertake pilot programs in order to experiment with various options. However, when central governments do this, they usually intend to identify the set of rules that works best for a single, large, diverse jurisdiction, which misses the point.

Q: This discussion of experiments within social units or decision arenas is an excellent way to introduce two other key notions of the Bloomington research program: "polycentricity" and "complex adaptive systems."

EO: Many scholars consider the very concept of organization to be closely tied to the presence of a central director who designed a system to operate in a particular way. Consequently, many self-organized governance systems are invisible to them. In contrast to forms of organization that result from central direction, most self-organized groups are better viewed as complex adaptive systems. Complex adaptive systems are composed of a large number of active elements whose rich patterns of interaction produce emergent properties that are not easy to predict by analyzing the separate parts of a system. One can see them as consisting of rules and interacting agents that adapt by changing the rules dynamically on the basis of experience. Complex adaptive systems differ from the kind of simple non-adaptive physical systems that have been the focus of much scientific effort. Unfortunately, the relatively straightforward physical sciences have been the model for many aspects of contemporary social science, even though contemporary physics and biology are starting to address similar problems of complex systems. Thus, social scientists have yet to develop many of the concepts needed to understand the adaptability of systems. No general theory of complex adaptive systems yet exists to provide a coherent explanation for processes shared by all such systems.

Many of the capabilities of complex adaptive systems are retained in a polycentric public enterprise system. By "polycentric" I mean a system where citizens are able to organize not just one but multiple governing authorities, as well as private arrangements, at different scales. Each unit may exercise considerable independence to make and enforce rules within a circumscribed scope of authority for a specified geographical area. In a polycentric system, some units are general-purpose governments, whereas others may be highly specialized. Self-organized resource governance systems, in such a system, may be special districts, private associations, or parts of a local government. These are nested in several levels of general-purpose governments that also provide civil equity as well as criminal courts.

Polycentric systems are themselves complex adaptive systems without one dominating central authority. Thus, no guarantee exists that such systems will find combinations of rules at diverse levels that are optimal for any particular environment. In fact, one should expect that all governance systems would be operating at less than optimal levels, given the immense difficulty of fine-tuning any complex, multi-tiered system. But because polycentric systems have overlapping units, information about what has worked well in one setting can be transmitted to other units. And when small systems fail, there are larger systems to call upon – and vice versa.

Q: A concern with "failure," "error" and "vulnerability" appears to play a major role in the approach developed by the Bloomington School. Vincent Ostrom wrote an entire book on the vulnerability of democratic societies, while your own work has given special attention to the vulnerability of "social-biophysical systems."

EO: Given the complexity of rule systems, and the complexity of the biophysical world that we are trying to regulate, all efforts to devise effective governance systems face a nontrivial probability of error. When you have a system that is vulnerable to disruption by external shocks – for example, a hurricane, or a military invasion – the probability of error increases substantially. Polycentric governance systems are frequently criticized for being too complex, redundant and lacking a central direction when viewed from a static, simple-systems perspective. They have considerable strengths when viewed from a dynamic, complex-systems perspective, particularly one that is concerned with the vulnerability of governance systems to external shocks.

The strength of polycentric governance systems is that each of the subunits has considerable autonomy to experiment with diverse rules for a particular type of resource system and with different response capabilities to external shock. In experimenting with rule combinations within the smaller-scale units of a polycentric system, citizens and officials have access to local knowledge, obtain rapid feedback from their own policy changes, and can learn from the experience of other parallel units. Instead of being a major detriment to system performance, redundancy builds in considerable capabilities.

If only one government exists for a large geographic area, failure of that unit to respond adequately to external threats may mean a major disaster for the entire system. If there are multiple governance units, organized at different levels for the same geographic region, a failure of one or more of these units to respond to external threats may lead to small-scale disasters. But these may be offset by the successful reaction of other units in the system. Policy analysts can learn a lot from the important role that redundancy plays in the design of robust physical systems as well as by a serious study of the human immune system and its capacity to cope with external threats by the presence of a large number of seemingly redundant systems that are ready to combine and recombine in order to fight off the threat of various types of infections. Redundancy is a means of keeping systems running in the presence of external shocks or internal malfunctions.

In an earlier era, policy analysts simply criticized polycentric systems as being grossly inefficient due to excessive levels of redundancy. These criticisms were made on the basis of static theories of optimal management and not on the basis of empirical research. Simply listing the number of governments in a region was seen by some scholars as sufficient proof of inefficient governance. In both the United States and Western Europe, massive consolidation campaigns were waged during the past century to eliminate so-called "overlapping, redundant units of government," which were, however, vigorously defended by the populations they served.

Serious empirical research has now shown that polycentric systems tend to generate higher levels of output at similar or lower costs than monocentric systems governing similar ecological, urban and social systems. Empirical studies of the vulnerability of differently linked social-biophysical systems are highly likely to demonstrate that governance systems composed of multiple units at multiple scales of organizations are less vulnerable to many types of external shocks than centralized systems. Studying the vulnerability of governance systems thus provides an important opportunity to build a better theory of governance based on the recognition that no social-biophysical system is a static system, and that in order to cope with external shocks one needs robust systems that possess considerable redundancy in their capacities to respond and learn from one another.

Q: Considering the analytical challenges posed by the study of polycentricity and complex adaptive systems, it seems that an interdisciplinary approach is not just one option among other, but unavoidable. In your own work, it looks like your interdisciplinary efforts went well beyond the social sciences.

EO: In a sense, your observation is correct. For instance, in the case of the CPR work published in *Governing the Commons,* I combined the strategy used by many scholars associated with the "new institutionalism" with the strategy used by biologists for conducting empirical work. The institutionalist strategy is based on the assumption that individuals try to solve problems as effectively as they can and also try to ascertain what factors help or hinder them in these efforts. When the problems under observation involve a lack of predictability, information, or trust, as well as high levels of complexity and transactional difficulties, then the efforts to explain must take these problems overtly into account rather than assuming them away.

The biologists' scientific strategy involves identifying for the simplest possible organism in which the process under investigation occurs in a clarified, or even exaggerated, form. The organism is not chosen because it is representative of all organisms. Rather, the organism is chosen because particular processes can be studied more effectively using this organism than using another. These cases are in no sense a "random" sample of cases. Rather, these are cases that provide clear information about the processes involved.

My "organism" for much of my work has been a particular type of human situation – the common-pool resource situation. Colleagues and I have studied this situation using game theory and agent-based models, in the experimental laboratory, in single case studies, in small-N, comparative studies, and in large-N statistical studies. We have deployed multiple methodologies in order to develop a series of reasoned conjectures about how it is possible that some individuals organize themselves to govern and manage common-pool resources while others do not. We hope that these conjectures contribute to the development of an empirically valid general theory of self-organization and self-governance.

However, this discussion about interdisciplinary and general theory shouldn't be misleading. In my view, there are important specific differences between social sciences and the natural sciences. Complex adaptive systems involve learning. The role of knowledge, conditional action, and anticipation are fundamental. In this respect I might say that the work that we have done at the Workshop is deeply rooted in the central tradition of human and social studies. There is no better testimony for that than the questions that structure our work: how can fallible human beings achieve and sustain self-governing entities and self-governing ways of life? How can individuals influence the rules that structure their lives? Similar questions were asked by Aristotle and other foundational social and political philosophers. These were the concerns of Madison, Hamilton and Tocqueville. Today these central questions unite political scientists, economists, geographers, sociologists, psychologists, anthropologists, and historians who study the effect of diverse rules on human behavior in various institutional contexts, countries or at different geographic scales.

Moreover, one of our greatest priorities at the Workshop has been to ensure that our research contributes to the education of future citizens, entrepreneurs in the public and private spheres, and officials at all levels of government. We have a distinct obligation to participate in this educational process as well as to engage in the research enterprise so that we build a cumulative knowledge base that may be used to sustain democratic life. Self-governing, democratic systems are always fragile enterprises. Future citizens need to understand that they participate in the constitution and reconstitution of rule-governed polities. And they need to learn the "art and science of association." If we fail in this, all our investigations and theoretical efforts are useless.

Bibliography

Advisory Commission on Intergovernmental Relations (1966), *Metropolitan America: Challenge to Federalism*, Washington, DC.

Agrawal, A. (1999), *Greener Pastures: Politics, Markets, and Community among a Migrant Pastoral People*, Durham, NC: Duke University Press.

Albert, H. (1977), *Kritlsche Vernunft und menschliche Praxis*, Stuttgart: Philipp Reclam.

Alchian, A., and Demsetz, H. (1972), "Production, Information Costs, and Economic Organizations", *American Economic Review*, vol. 62, December, pp. 777–795.

Aligica, P. D. (2006), "Institutional and Stakeholder Mapping: Frameworks for Policy Analysis and Institutional Change", *Public Organization Review*, vol. 6, no. 1, March, pp. 79–90.

Allen, B. (2005), *Tocqueville, Covenant, and the Democratic Revolution: Harmonizing Earth with Heaven*, Lanham, MD: Lexington Books.

Alt, J. E., Levi, M., and Ostrom, E., eds. (1999), *Competition & Cooperation: Conversations with Nobelists about Economics and Political Science*, New York: Russell Sage Foundation.

Anderson, W., and Weidner, E. W. (1950), *American City Government*, New York: Henry Holt.

Bauer, P. (1981), *Equality, the Third World, and Economic Delusion*, Cambridge, MA: Harvard University Press.

Becker, G. (1976), *The Economic Approach to Human Behavior*, Chicago: University of Chicago Press.

—— (1975), *Human Capital: A Theoretical and Empirical Analysis*, 2nd edn, New York: Columbia University Press for the National Bureau of Economic Research.

—— ([1957]1971), *The Economics of Discrimination*, 2nd edn, Chicago: University of Chicago Press.

Benson, B. (1990), *The Enterprise of Law*, San Francisco, CA: Pacific Research Institute for Public Policy.

Bernstein, L. (1992), "Opting Out of the Legal System: Extralegal Contractual Relations in the Diamond Industry", *Journal of Legal Studies*, vol. 21, January, pp. 145–153.

Bish, R. (1971), *The Public Economy of Metropolitan Areas*, Chicago: Markham Press.

Boettke, P. (1994), "Virginia Political Economy: A View from Vienna", reprinted in *The Market Process: Essays in Contemporary Austrian Economics*, Aldershot, UK and Brookfield, USA: Edward Elgar Publishing.

—— (1990), "Interpretive Reasoning and the Study of Social Life", *Methodus: Bulletin of the International Network for Economic Method*, vol. 2, no. 2, December, pp. 35–45.

Buchanan, J. (1991), *The Economics and Ethics of Constitutional Order*, Ann Arbor: University of Michigan Press.

—— (1979), *What Should Economists Do?*, Indianapolis, IN: Liberty Press.

—— (1975), *The Limits of Liberty: Between Anarchy and Leviathan*, Chicago: University of Chicago Press.

Buchanan, J. and Tullock, G. (1962), T*he Calculus of Consent: The Logical Foundations of Constitutional Democracy*, Ann Arbor: University of Michigan Press.

Carlyle, T. (1984), *Carlyle Reader: Selections from the Writings of Thomas Carlyle*, Cambridge and New York: Cambridge University Press.

Coase, R. H. (1988), *The Firm, the Market, and the Law*, Chicago: University of Chicago Press.

Coleman, J. (1990), *Foundations of Social Theory*, Cambridge, MA: Belknap Press of Harvard University Press.

—— (1988), "Social Capital in the Creation of Human Capital", *American Journal of Sociology*, vol. 94 (supplement), pp. 95–120.

Committee for Economic Development (1970), *Reshaping Government in Metropolitan Areas*, New York.

Crawford, Sue E. S., and Ostrom, E. (1995), "A Grammar of Institutions", *American Political Science Review*, vol. 89, no. 3, pp. 582–600.

Dewey, J. (1938), *Logic: The Theory of Inquiry*, New York: Henry Holt.

Dolsak, N., and Ostrom, E. (2003), *The Commons in the New Millennium*, Cambridge, MA: MIT Press.

Ellickson, R. (1991), *Order Without Law*, Cambridge, MA: Harvard University Press.

Etzioni, A. (1988), *The Moral Dimension: Toward a New Economics*, New York: The Free Press.

Frieden, B. J. (1966), *Challenge to Federalism*, Advisory Commission on Intergovernmental Relations, Washington, DC: Metropolitan America.

Friedman, D. (1973), *The Machinery of Freedom*, New York: Harper & Row.

Friesema, H. P. (1966), "The Metropolis and the Maze of Local Government", *Urban Affairs Quarterly*, vol. 2, December, pp. 68–90.

Garn, H. A., Fox, M. J., Springer, M., and Taylor, J. B. (1976), *Models for Indicator Development: A Framework for Policy Analysis*, Washington, DC: Urban Institute.

Greer, S. (1961), "Dilemmas of Action Research on the Metropolitan Problem", in *Community Political Systems*, ed. Morris Janowitz, Glencoe, IL: Free Press.

Gibson, C., Andersson, K., Ostrom, E., and Shivakumar, S. (2005), *The Samaritan's Dilemma: The Political Economy of Development Aid*, Oxford: Oxford University Press.

Godwin, W. ([1973] 1985), *An Enquiry Concerning Political Justice*, Harmondsworth: Penguin.

Granovetter, M. (1985), "Economic Action and Social Structure: The Problem of Embeddedness", *American Journal of Sociology*, vol. 91, no. 3, November, pp. 481–510.

Greif, A. (1989), "Reputation and Coalitions in Medieval Trade", *Journal of Economic History*, vol. 49, no. 4, pp. 857–882.

Hamilton, A., Jay, J., and Madison, J. (n.d.), *The Federalist*, ed. Edward M. Earle, New York: Modern Library. First published in 1788.

Hawley, A. H., and Zimmer, B. C. (1970), *The Metropolitan Community: Its People and Government*, Beverly Hills, CA: Sage.

Hayek, F. A. (1979), *Law, Legislation and Liberty, volume 3*, Chicago: University of Chicago Press.

—— (1973), *Law, Legislation and Liberty, volume 1*, Chicago: University of Chicago Press.

—— (1945), "The Use of Knowledge in Society", American *Economic Review*, vol. 35, September, pp. 519–530.

Herzberg, R. (1992), "An Analytic Choice Approach to Concurrent Majorities: The Relevance of John C. Calhoun's Theory for Institutional Design", *The Journal of Politics*, vol. 54, no. 1, February, pp. 54–81.

Herzberg, R. (2005), "Commentary on Richard Wagner's 'Self-Governance, Polycentrism, and Federalism: Recurring Themes in Vincent Ostrom's Scholarly Oeuvre' ", *Journal on Economic Behavior & Organization*, vol. 57, no. 2, pp. 189–197.

Hess, C., and Ostrom E. (2006), "A Framework for Analysing the Microbiological Commons", *International Social Science Journal*, vol. 188, June, pp. 335–349.

Hirschman, A. O. (1970), *Exit, Voice, and Loyalty: Responses to Decline in Firms, Organizations, and States*, Cambridge, MA: Harvard University Press.

Hobbes, T. (1960), *Leviathan, or the Matter, Forme and Power of a Commonwealth Ecclesiasticall and Civil*, ed. Michael Oakeshott, Oxford: Basil Blackwell. First published in 1651.

Institute for Local Self Government (1970), *Special Districts or Special Dynasties? Democracy Diminished*, Berkeley, CA: Institute for Local Self Government.

Kaminski, A. (1989), "Coercion, Corruption, and Reform: State and Society in the Soviet-type Socialist Regime", *Journal of Theoretical Politics*, vol. 1, no.1, January, pp. 77–102.

Kaufmann, Franz-Xaver, ed. (1991), *The Public Sector-Challenge for Coordination and Learning*, Berlin and New York: Walter de Gruyter.

Kaufmann, F.-X., Giandomenico, M. and Ostrom V., eds. (1986), *Guidance, Control, and Evaluation in the Public Sector*, Berlin and New York: Walter de Gruyter.

Kiser, L. L. (1984), "Toward an Institutional Theory of Citizen Coproduction", *Urban Affairs Quarterly*, vol. 19, no. 4, June, pp. 485–510.

Kiser, L. L., and Ostrom, E. (1982), "The Three Worlds of Action: A Metatheoretical Synthesis of Institutional Approaches", in *Strategies of Political Inquiry*, ed. Elinor Ostrom, Beverly Hills, CA: Sage, pp. 179–222.

Kiser, L. L., and Percy, S. (1980), "The Concept of Coproduction and Its Prospects for Public Service Delivery", Working Paper No. W80–6, Workshop in Political Theory and Policy Analysis Bloomington, IN: Indiana University.

Kuhnert, S. (2001), "An Evolutionary Theory of Collective Action: Schumpeterian Entrepreneurship for the Common Good", *Constitutional Political Economy*, vol. 12, March, pp. 13–29.

Lachmann, L. M. (1978), *Capital and Its Structure*, Kansas City: Sheed Andrews and McMeel.

Landa, J. (1995), *Thust, Ethnicity and Identity*, Ann Arbor, MI: University of Michigan Press.

Lineberry, R. L. (1970), "Reforming Metropolitan Governance: Requiem or Reality", *The Georgetown Law Journal*, 58, vol. March/May, pp. 675–718.

Machlup, F. (1962), *The Production and Distribution of Knowledge in the United States*, Princeton, NJ: Princeton University Press.

McGinnis, M. D. (2000), *Polycentric Games and Institutions: Readings from the Workshop in Political Theory and Policy Analysis*, Ann Arbor: University of Michigan Press.

—— (1999a), *Polycentric Governance and Development: Readings from the Workshop in Political Theory and Policy Analysis*, Ann Arbor: University of Michigan Press.

—— (1999b), *Polycentricity and Local Public Economies: Readings from the Workshop in Political Theory and Policy Analysis*. University of Michigan Press.

McGinnis, M., and Ostrom E. (1996), "Design Principles for Local and Global Commons", in *The International Political Economy and International Institutions*, Volume II, ed. O. R. Young, Cheltenham, UK: Edward Elgar, pp. 465–493.

Mitchell, W.C. (1988) "Virginia, Rochester, and Bloomington: Twenty-Five Years of Public Choice and Political Science", *Public Choice*, vol. 56, no. 2, pp. 101–119.

North, D. C. (2005), *Understanding the Process of Economic Change*, Princeton, NJ: Princeton University Press.

—— (1990), *Institutions, Institutional Change and Economic Performance*, Cambridge: Cambridge University Press.

Nozick, R. (1974), *Anarchy, State and Utopia*, New York: Basic Books.

Oakerson, R. J. (1999), *Governing Local Public Economies: Creating the Civic Metropolis*, San Francisco, CA: ICS Press.

Oakerson, R. J., and Parks, R. B., (1988), "Citizen Voice and Public Entrepreneurship: The Organizational Dynamic of a Complex Metropolitan County", *Publius: The Journal of Federalism*, vol. 18, no. 4, pp. 91–112.

O'Driscoll G., and Rizzo M. (1985), *The Economics of Time and Ignorance*, Oxford and New York: Basil Blackwell.

Olson, M. (1965), *The Logic of Collective Action: Public Goods and the Theory of Groups*, Cambridge, MA: Harvard University Press.

Ostrom, E. (2005), *Understanding Institutional Diversity*, Princeton, NJ: Princeton University Press.

—— (2000), "The Danger of Self-Evident Truth", *PS: Political Science & Politics*, vol. 31, no. 1, March, pp. 33–44.

—— (1998), "The Comparative Study of Public Economies", Presented upon acceptance of the Frank E. Seidman Distinguished Award in Political Economy, Memphis, TN: P.K. Seidman Foundation.

—— (1997), *A Behavioral Approach to the Rational Choice Theory of Collective Action*, Presidential Address, American Political Science Association, Indiana University.

—— (1996), "Crossing the Great Divide: Coproduction, Synergy, and Development", *World Development*, vol. 24, no. 6, June, pp. 1073–1087.

—— (1990), *Governing the Commons: The Evolution of Institutions for Collective Action*, Cambridge: Cambridge University Press.

—— (1986), "An Agenda for the Study of Institutions'", *Public Choice*, vol. 48, no. 1, January, pp. 3–25.

—— (1983), "A Public Choice Approach to Metropolitan Institutions: Structure, Incentives, and Performance", *Social Science Journal*, vol. 20, no. 3, July, pp. 79–96.

——, ed. (1982), "Strategies of Political Inquiry", Working Paper No. W82–16, Workshop in Political Theory and Policy Analysis, Bloomington, IN: Indiana University.

—— (1972), "Metropolitan Reform: Propositions Derived from Two Traditions", *Social Science Quarterly*, vol. 53, December, pp. 474–493.

—— (1964), "Public Entrepreneurship: A Case Study in Ground-Water Basin Management", unpublished PhD dissertation, UCLA, Los Angeles, CA.

Ostrom, E., Gardner, R., and Walker, J. (1994), *Rules, Games, and Common-Pool Resources*, Ann Arbor: University of Michigan Press.

Ostrom, V. (1999), "Memo to DPA", Workshop Archives, Workshop in Political Theory and Policy Analysis, Bloomington, IN: Indiana University.

—— (1997a), *The Meaning of Democracy and the Vulnerability of Democracies: A Response to Tocqueville's Challenge*, Ann Arbor: University of Michigan Press.

—— (1997b), "Buchanan's Opening to Constitutional Choice and Meta Levels of Analysis", Presented at the APSA meetings, Washington, DC, August 28–31.

—— (1993a), "Epistemic Choice and Public Choice", *Public Choice*, vol. 77, no. 1, September, pp. 163–176.

—— (1993b), "The Place of Languages in the Political Economy of Life in Human Societies", Working Paper No. W93–6, Workshop in Political Theory and Policy Analysis, Bloomington, IN: Indiana University.

—— (1992), "Opportunity, Diversity, and Complexity", *in Rethinking Institutional Analysis and Development: Issues, Alternatives, and Choices*, eds. Vincent Ostrom, David Feeny, and Hartmut Picht, San Francisco, CA: ICS Press.

—— (1991a), *The Meaning of American Federalism: Constituting a Self-Governing Society*, San Francisco, CA: ICS Press.

—— (1991b), "Some Ontological and Epistemological Puzzles in Policy Analysis", Working Paper No. W82–16, Workshop in Political Theory and Policy Analysis, Bloomington, IN: Indiana University.

—— (1991c), "Some Puzzles in Using Knowledge to Inform Choices about Public Affairs", Working Paper No. W91–4, Workshop in Political Theory and Policy Analysis, Bloomington, IN: Indiana University.

—— (1990a), "Problems of Cognition as a Challenge to Policy Analysts and Democratic Societies", Working Paper No. 90–5, Workshop in Political Theory and Policy Analysis, Bloomington, IN: Indiana University.

—— (1990b), "American Constitutionalism and Self-Governance" *in European and American Constitutionalism in the Eighteenth Century*, ed. M. Rozbicki, Vienna, Austria: U.S. Regional Program Office.

—— (1990c), "Problems of Cognition as a Challenge to Policy Analysts and Democratic Societies", *Journal of Theoretical Politics*, vol. 2, no. 3, pp. 243–262.

—— (1986a), "A Fallabilist's Approach to Norms and Criteria of Choice", in *Guidance, Control, and Evaluation in the Public Sector*, eds. F.-X. Kaufmann, G. Majone, and V. Ostrom, Berlin: Walter de Gruyter, pp. 229–244.

—— (1986b), "The Constitutional Level of Analysis: A Challenge" Working Paper No. 85–41, Workshop in Political Theory and Policy Analysis, Bloomington, IN: Indiana University.

—— (1984), "Why Governments Fail: An Inquiry into the Use of Instruments of Evil to do Good", in *The Theory of Public Choice – II*, eds. J. M. Buchanan and R. D. Tollison, Ann Arbor: University of Michigan Press.

—— (1982a), "The Human Condition", Workshop Archives, Workshop in Political Theory and Policy Analysis, Bloomington, IN: Indiana University.

—— (1982b), "The Problem of Deriving Further Criteria of Choice", Working Paper No. 82–20(3) Workshop in Political Theory and Policy Analysis, Bloomington, IN: Indiana University.

—— (1980), "Artisanship and Artifact", *Public Administration Review*, vol. 40, no. 4, July–August, pp. 309–317.

—— (1973a), *The Intellectual Crisis in American Public Administration*, 2nd edn, Tuscaloosa: University of Alabama Press.

—— (1973b), "Order and Change Amid Increasing Relative Ignorance", Working Paper No. W73–1, Workshop in Political Theory and Policy Analysis, Bloomington, IN: Indiana University.

—— (1972), "Polycentricity", Workshop Archives, Workshop in Political Theory and Policy Analysis, Bloomington, IN: Indiana University. Presented at Annual Meeting of the American Political Science Association, September 5–9, Washington, DC.

—— (1971), *The Political Theory of a Compound Republic: Designing the American Experiment*, 2nd edn, Lincoln: University of Nebraska Press.

Ostrom, V., and Ostrom, E. (1977), "Public Goods and Public Choices", in *Alternatives for*

Delivering Public Services. Toward Improved Performance, ed. E. S. Savas, Boulder, CO: Westview Press, pp. 7–49.

—— (1971), "Public Choice: A Different Approach to the Study of Public Administration, *Public Administration Review*, vol. 31, March/April, pp. 203–216.

—— (1965), "A Behavioral Approach to the Study of Intergovernmental Relations", *The Annals of the American Academy of Political and Social Science*, vol. 359, May, pp. 137–146.

Ostrom, V., Bish, R., and Ostrom, E. (1988), *Local Government in the United States*, San Francisco: ICS Press.

Ostrom, V., Tiebout, C. M., and Warren R. (1961), "The Organization of Government in Metropolitan Areas: A Theoretical Inquiry", *American Political Science Review*, vol. 55, December, pp. 831–842.

Parks, R. B. (1993), "Comparative Metropolitan Organization: Service Production and Governance Structures in St. Louis (MO) and Allegheny County (PA)", *Publius*, vol. 23, no. 1, Winter, pp. 19–39.

Parks, R. B., and Oakerson, R. J. (1989), "Metropolitan Organization and Governance: A Local Public Economy Approach", *Urban Affairs Quarterly*, vol. 25, no. 1, September, pp. 18–29.

Parks, R. B., Baker P., Kiser, L., Oakerson, R. J., Ostrom. E., Ostrom. V., Stephen L, Percy, S. L., and Scott, E. J. (1985), *Demand Processing and Performance in Public Service Agencies*, Tuscaloosa: University of Alabama Press.

Percy, S. L. (1984), "Citizen Participation in the Coproduction of Urban Services", *Urban Affairs Quarterly*, vol. 19, no. 4, June, pp. 431–446.

Polanyi, M. (1951), *The Logic of Liberty*, London: Routledge and Kegan Paul.

Polski, M. (2005), "The Institutional Economics of Biodiversity, Biological Materials, and Bioprospecting", *Ecological Economics*, vol. 53, no. 45, pp. 543–557.

Popper, K. R. (1964), *The Poverty of Historicism*, New York: Harper Torchbooks.

Prakash, A. (2000), *Greening the Firm: The Politics of Corporate Environmentalism*, Cambridge: Cambridge University Press.

Press, C. (1963), "The Cities within a Great City: A Decentralist Approach to Centralization," *Centennial Review*, vol. 7, winter, pp. 113–130.

Radnitzky, G., and Bartley, W. W. III, eds. (1987), *Evolutionary Epistemology, Rationality, and the Sociology of Knowledge*, La Salle, IL: Open Court.

Robbins, L. (1984), *An Essay on the Nature and Significance of Economic Science*, New York: New York University Press.

Rothbard, M. (1973), *For a New Liberty*, New York: Macmillan.

Sabetti, F. (2004), "Local Roots of Constitutionalism", *Perspectives on Political Science*, vol. 33, no. 2, Spring, pp. 70–78.

—— (2002a), *The Search for Good Government: Understanding the Paradox of Italian Democracy*, Montreal, Quebec: McGill-Queen's University Press.

—— (2002b), *Village Politics and the Mafia in Sicily*, 2nd edn, Montreal, Quebec: McGill-Queen's University Press.

Sawyer, A., and Adekeye A. and Rashid, I., eds. (2004), "Governance and Democratization", in *West Africa's Security Challenges: Building Peace in a Troubled Region*, Boulder, CO: Lynne Rienner Publishers, pp. 93–116.

Schultz, T. (1960), "Capital Formation by Education", *Journal or Political Economy* LXVIII, December, pp. 571–583.

Searle, J. (1969), *Speech Acts: An Essay In the Philosophy of Language*, New York: Cambridge University Press.

Shivakumar, S. (2005), *The Constitution of Development: Crafting Capabilities for Self-Governance*, New York: Palgrave Macmillan.

Smith, A. (1982), *The Theory of Moral Sentiments*, Indianapolis, IN: Liberty Press.

—— (1981), *The Wealth of Nations*, Indianapolis, IN: Liberty Press.

Sproule-Jones, M. (2002), *The Restoration of the Great Lakes*, Vancouver: University of British Columbia Press.

Sproule-Jones, M., Allen, B., and Sabetti, F., eds. (2008), *The Struggle to Constitute and Sustain Productive Orders: Vincent Ostrom's Quest to Understand Human Affairs*, Lanham, MD: Lexington Books.

Stigler, G. J. (1962), "The Tenable Range of Functions of Local Government", in *Private Wants and Public Needs*, ed. Edmund S. Phelps, New York: W. W. Norton, pp. 167–176.

Tiebout, C. M. (1956), "A Pure Theory of Local Expenditures", *Journal of Political Economy*, vol. 64, October, pp. 416–435.

Tocqueville, A. de ([1835] 1945), *Democracy in America*, Vols. 1 and 2, trans. H. Reeves, New York: Alfred A. Knopf.

Tullock, G. (1965), *The Politics of Bureaucracy*, Washington, DC: Public Affairs Press.

Wagner, R. (2005), "Self-Governance, Polycentrism, and Federalism: Recurring Themes in Vincent Ostrom's Scholarly Oeuvre", *Journal on Economic Behavior & Organization*, vol. 57, no. 2, pp. 189–197.

Wagner, R., and Weber, Warren E. (1975), "Competition, Monopoly, and the Organization of Government in Metropolitan Areas", *Journal of Law and Economics*, vol. 18, December, pp. 661–684.

Warren, R. (1964), "A Municipal-Services Market of Metropolitan Organization", *Journal of the American Institute of Planners*, vol. 30, August, pp. 193–204.

Weber, M. ([1922] 1978), *Economy and Society: An Outline of Interpretive Sociology*, New York: Bedminster Press.

Weingast, B. (1995), "The Economic Role of Political Institutions", *Journal of Law, Economics and Organization*, vol. 11, no. 1, pp. 1–31.

Whitaker, G. (1980), "Coproduction: Citizen Participation in Service Delivery", *Public Administration Review*, vol. 40, no. 3, pp. 240–246.

Wilson, W. (1956), *Congressional Government*, New York: Meridian Books. First published in 1885.

Zimmerman, J. F. (1970), "Metropolitan Reform in the U.S.: An Overview", *Public Administration Review*, vol. 30, September/October, pp. 531–543.

Index